ENDORSEMENTS

Never before in history has there been such an interest in end-time prophecy. What we see unfolding before our eyes here in America every day is staggering. There is no doubt these are the last days! So how do we understand what God is doing? What signposts should we be looking for? In Joseph Z's latest book, you'll find keys to understanding the times we are living in, what you need to pray for, and what you need to prepare for.

Eschatology can be quite depressing, and many authors leave you wanting to dig a hole and prep for the worst. While Joseph does not pull any punches, he does leave the reader with encouraging words for where we go from here. Grab your highlighter and crack open this book!

Gene Bailey
FlashPoint

If you're hungry to understand the mysteries of the end times and God's prophetic plan for the ages, this book is a must-read! *The Prophetic Endgame* is filled with revelation, biblical insight, and practical wisdom for believers who want to discern the times and walk in victory. You'll be inspired and equipped for what's ahead!

Sid Roth
Host, *It's Supernatural*

Out of 31,102 verses in Scripture, over 8,300 contain prophecy. That's 27% of God's Word devoted to revealing what is to come. Yet according to Lifeway Research, only 24% of evangelical pastors discuss end-times prophecy with their congregations with any regularity. Think about that. The Church is largely silent on more than a quarter of the Bible. And yet, Pew Research found that 4 out of 10 Americans, including people with no religious affiliation, believe we are living in the end times right now. The hunger is there.

The discernment is not. People are sensing the shaking, but too few shepherds are showing them where to look in Scripture.

This is exactly why *The Prophetic Endgame* is needed right now. Joseph Z has done what too few voices in the Body of Christ are willing to do. He has taken Bible prophecy, from eternity past to eternity future, and made it accessible, scripturally anchored, and impossible to ignore. I was honored that Brother Joseph chose to include a portion of my own writing on the last trump within these pages, and I can tell you firsthand that this man handles the prophetic Word with both reverence and precision. This is not sensationalized date-setting. This is not newspaper theology. This is a Spirit-filled, biblically rigorous work that equips the saints to understand the times and know what the Church ought to do.

From the fall of Lucifer to the rise of the Antichrist, from the restraining force of the *Ekklesia* to the Millennial Reign of Jesus, Joseph Z connects the dots so that you can understand the hour we're living in and what God has called you to do. If you've been waiting for a comprehensive, faith-building guide through the prophetic landscape of Scripture, you are holding it in your hands. Read it. Study it. Share it. The King is coming, and His people should not be caught unaware.

Alan DiDio
Host, *Revival Nation*
Pastor, Revival Nation Church

Joseph Z carries a genuine burden for revival and reformation in this generation. Through this book, he is calling everyday Christians to arise with faith, courage, and holy responsibility to make a lasting impact in our world. While I may view the end times through a different theological lens, I believe this message will encourage you to contend for God's purposes in your sphere of influence and beyond.

Dr. Ché Ahn
Senior Leader, Harvest Rock Church, Pasadena, CA
President, Harvest International Ministry
International Chancellor, Wagner University

The Prophetic Endgame, by Joseph Z, is a fascinating read that explores the revelatory significance of the past, the state of today's world in reference to God's divine timeline, and the accelerated activity to come. Piecing together biblical prophecy and today's occurrences, Joseph Z skillfully paints a clear picture of chaotic times, ultimately making way for a new and redeemed creation.

David Diga Hernandez
Evangelist

Joseph Z. is one of our favorites at Daystar Television. His prophetic voice has proven true time after time. That's why I'm excited about his book *The Prophetic Endgame.* Joseph believes that God desires for us to know His word and His plan for eternity. *The Prophetic Endgame* is sure to unveil those secrets not yet revealed and provide hope, authority, and purpose.

Joni Lamb
Daystar Television Network

Joseph Z brings much-needed accuracy, enthusiasm, and passion for understanding God's Word to a world that is starving for meaning and an authentic understanding for who God truly is. In his sermons, podcasts, and books, Joseph Z unapologetically shares the Gospel in a compelling way that is hard to find!

Clay Clark
2007 Oklahoma U.S. SBA Entrepreneur of the Year,
Founder, The ReAwaken America Tour,
Host, *ThrivetimeShow.com Podcast,*
Bestselling Author and Co-Founder of five children

In an era when prophetic conversations are often polarizing, *The Prophetic Endgame* invites the reader into something deeper than speculation. It invites engagement.

I have come to know Joseph Z as a humble, submissive, servant-hearted prophetic voice who carries genuine reverence for Scripture and a sincere desire to serve the Body of Christ. That posture matters, particularly when navigating themes as weighty and controversial as eschatology.

While end-times prophecy must always be prayerfully weighed and discerned, there are revelations in this book that are thoughtful, provocative, and worthy of careful consideration. Joseph Z does not write to sensationalize fear, but to awaken discernment, stir responsibility, ignite faith, and point readers back to God's redemptive purposes across history, the present age, and the age to come.

The Prophetic Endgame challenges readers to think biblically, engage spiritually, and live purposefully. It prompts reflection, conversation, and deeper searching of the Scriptures, and for that reason, it holds value for those who are serious about understanding the times while keeping their hearts in pursuit of the One who orchestrates it all.

Patricia King
Minister, Author, Media Host
Patriciaking.com

Joseph Z is one of the most seasoned and trusted prophetic voices in the world today—and what makes him even more impactful is his heart. He loves Jesus. He loves people. And he refuses to let believers stay trapped in confusion, fear, or deception.

The Prophetic Endgame is more than a timely word—it's Scripture-rich, theologically deep, and incredibly empowering. Joseph tackles big theological topics (including the pre-Adamic age and the origins of spiritual conflict) for all the right reasons: to reveal who God is, expose the works of darkness, and equip the Church to stand with clarity and authority in the days ahead.

These are epic days—and you were born for them. If you're ready to get anchored, equipped, and empowered, I highly recommend this timely, bold, and necessary book.

Robert Hotchkin
Founder, Robert Hotchkin Ministries
roberthotchkin.com

Prophet Z's book, *The Prophetic Endgame*, is both a source of encouragement and divine revelation for every believer. With clarity and prophetic insight, he takes readers from the foundation of God's eternal plan all the way through the realities of the end times, helping us see what's ahead through the lens of biblical truth. This book doesn't create fear—it builds faith. It equips, strengthens, and prepares the Church to navigate these last days with confidence and spiritual authority. I believe the revelation shared in these pages will awaken believers to the power we carry as blood-bought sons and daughters of God—to influence culture, impact nations, and walk boldly in God's purposes. This is a timely and important message for the Body of Christ.

Pastor Brian Gibson
Lead Pastor, His Church
Gibson Ministries

This is not a book for the passive. It's for the awakened. It's for those who refuse to drift through history half-asleep while prophecy unfolds in real time. I have had the gift of knowing Joseph Z for many years and have seen firsthand his deep love for Jesus and his unwavering commitment to the Church. This book was forged out of that love—not written for hype, but born from prayer, conviction, and a burden to strengthen believers. Joseph doesn't speculate. He equips. He doesn't alarm. He anchors.

Read this book like someone hungry for clarity and transformation—and you will not be disappointed.

Dr. Malachi A. O'Brien
Ultra Runner
Author of *Time To Rise*

Joseph Z is a trusted "times and seasons" prophetic voice who connects you with Heaven's unfolding agenda as revealed in the Scriptures. Get ready for many *Ah-ha* moments, not because you are receiving some new revelation.

But rather, because you are revisiting Scripture holistically, in context, and seeing where the end of the age fits within the grand scope of redemptive history, particularly the age we are presently living in. Jesus is coming back, and history is moving toward His *glorious appearing*. This timely book will equip a company of biblically informed and victorious believers to discern the signs of the times—and know what to *do*.

Larry Sparks, MDiv.
Founder, Sparks Ministries
Bestselling Author of *Pentecostal Fire*
Vice President of Publisher, Nori Media Group

Joseph and I became epic friends many years ago and have maintained our friendship by sharing a mutual respect for each other, even with differing and sometimes opposing views on the interpretation of the Book of Revelation, the timing of the Rapture, and other eschatological teachings.

I have always admired Joseph's commitment to the Word of God, his influence with and direct leadings of the Holy Spirit, and his passionate heart of love for Jesus and His Church!

Joseph and I are in full agreement on some striking themes in his new book, such as "the eternal plan of God through the ages," the truth that we are currently living in "the last of the Last Days," and others.

He shares some deep insights in this book that will both challenge you and instruct you. I was very touched by his full account of the martyrdom of Polycarp. What a triumphant end that continues to inspire!

I was also especially blessed by Joseph's unique insights and thoughts on eternity and what it may look like to reign with the LORD—forever!

And, like I shared, although we come from two different schools of interpretation on how to study the Book of Revelation and the timing of events yet to unfold, I LOVE two of his powerful ending phrases, "Keep Watching!" and "Keep Discerning!" to which, if I may, I would like to add, "and Keep Listening!" Thank you, Joseph, for a unique and timely book.

Rev. Carl Wesley Anderson
Equipping Evangelist, Author, and Documentary Filmmaker
with episodes based on 2 books, *Revelation's Battle Plans: Your Marching Orders from Today to the Last Day* and
Love Speaks: 21 Ways to Recognize God's Multi-Faceted Voice

Reading *The Prophetic Endgame* is like flying at 30,000 feet in an F-18 with a God's-eye view of history—from Genesis to Revelation, from the Garden to eternity. Joseph Z doesn't just explain prophecy… he equips you with it. No hype. No fear-mongering. Just solid, Bible-based clarity that lands deep in your spirit.

Here's what I love: Joseph doesn't use end-times teaching to scare you (or sell water filters or whatever). He uses it to wake you up, wake me up, wake the Church up. (After all, we need a little awakening from time to time…and now just happens to be one of those times.)

Plus, this isn't a book about hiding in bunkers—it's about what we Marines love best, WINNING.

So if you've ever been confused by Revelation, overwhelmed by headlines, or just wondering what in the world is going on—this book is your map. It's bold. It's biblical. And it's surprisingly hope filled. Keep your Bible in one hand and this book in the other… and don't be shocked if you find yourself braver by the last page than you were on the first.

Ed Rush
Top Gun Fighter Pilot
Bestselling Author

In a time when confusion is everywhere, Joseph Z points readers back to the one place that never changes—the Word of God—and sets the conversation about the future in a clear, Christ-centered frame. *The Prophetic*

Endgame invites believers to think deeply, discern wisely, and live courageously as we anticipate the fulfillment of God's promises. You'll be strengthened by Joseph's biblical sweep, urgency, and unwavering confidence that Jesus is Lord over history and the age to come.

Steve Ram
Business Owner, Investor,
Independent Journalist,
SteveRamNews.com

We are living at the end of the last days. However, it is not a time of doom and gloom for believers. It is a time of victory—a time where we advance and "occupy until He comes." In *The Prophetic Endgame,* Joseph Z shares scriptural insights that will help you understand the current times and make a difference in this age. Read the book, ponder its insights, apply its wisdom, and take your place in the endgame.

Kerrick Butler
Pastor, Faith Christian Center
Mableton, Georgia

Joseph Z opens Scripture in a way that makes prophecy come alive. In *The Prophetic Endgame*, he shows that the events unfolding around us are not random—they are markers, warnings, and signs that it is later than we think. This book isn't just about the end times—it unveils God's plan from the very beginning, His ultimate victory over evil, and the hope we carry as His people. It equips believers to stay rooted in God's Word, sharpen discernment, and walk confidently in the authority Christ has already given them. We are the Revelation generation, called to awaken in this hour, and this message is essential for the Church. I can't recommend it highly enough.

Mondo De La Vega
Host of *The Mondo Show*
Author of *My Crazy Life: The Moments That Brought a Gangster to Grace*

This book is timely, bold, and deeply relevant. It offers a clear and compelling understanding of biblical eschatology and prepares the reader for the days ahead. It will challenge you, awaken you, and stir your hunger for truth!

Matt Cruz
Evangelist
www.mattcruzministries.com

I've been teaching on eschatology for years, and I've seen how easily prophecy teaching can either breed fear or drift into speculation. Joseph Z avoids both traps in *The Prophetic Endgame.*

What impressed me most was how he refuses to separate end-times prophecy from the rest of Scripture. He traces God's plan from creation through the dispensations, showing how each age ends with a dramatic transition. By the time you reach the Tribulation and Armageddon, you understand why these events are necessary.

Joseph also addresses the Church's role right now. He doesn't let believers retreat into passivity while waiting for the Rapture. Instead, he calls us to occupy and engage. That balance between understanding what's coming and living with purpose today is rare in eschatology books.

Larry Ragland
Pastor, Solid Rock Church (Birmingham, AL)
Host, *The Big Picture Podcast*
Author of *The Final Flood* and *I See Greatness In You*

What a phenomenal and exciting book! This is the all-encompassing story of the world. The way Joseph brings together the understanding of the big picture of humanity and existence is magnificent. I believe every Christian should read this book. It is our origin story—the prequel, the sequel, and the present dispensation we're living in.

This book ties it all together. I especially appreciate how Joseph presents both the Old Earth and Young Earth views from a biblical perspective, helping us understand that it is okay to live with questions we may not have answers to until we see God face to face. Scripture reminds us of this clearly—especially in the prophetic—for now we know in part.

Joseph is not just a very articulate teacher and writer, but a powerful, accurate, and Bible-grounded prophet. He is my dear friend, and he is the real deal. I'm very excited for this new book to get into the hands of many people.

Ben Díaz
Author of *Radical Healing*
Senior Pastor, Vida Church, Mesa, Arizona

The past, the now, and the end with the future all in one amazing book. This must be one of the most awesome books I've read, giving the reader revelation, understanding, wisdom, and HOPE!

Joseph's ability to share a solid Scriptural foundation of insight and answers to many questions people have probably had, for untold generations, about God, the whys, how we fit, and what the real future holds is absolutely outstanding. *The Prophetic Endgame* will cause people to develop a deeper love and respect for how the Lord works prophetically with individuals and Nations. It definitely solidifies the work of the prophets, prophecy, and God speaking through His prophets to assist each one in their walk with our Heavenly Father, our Lord Jesus Christ, and the Holy Spirit of Truth.

It explains where we are now and what to expect, so we can be properly prepared for the new times and seasons unfolding. This book is meant to be studied, not just read. It's like going to a year of prophetic Bible school! I loved it and gained tremendous revelation. I highly recommend it to everyone, especially parents, as a way to train their children for their destiny and future.

Enjoy this awesome journey into seeing the spirit realm more clearly as God unfolds our real future.

Ginger Ziegler
GingerZieglerMinistries.com
Teacher, Pastor, Author

Joseph Z's *The Prophetic Endgame* is a compelling and insightful journey through biblical prophecy and the destiny of humanity. With clarity and passion, my friend of nearly 35 years, Joseph Z unpacks complex end-times themes, offering hope, practical wisdom, and a call to cultural impact for believers today. I highly recommend it for anyone seeking a faith-filled, scripturally grounded perspective on the last days and beyond.

Joshua Ercoli
Founder of Souled Out International

I have done ministry with Joseph Z for 25 years. To see where he started and where God has taken him is incredible and a testament of God's favor on someone's life. Joseph has never given up, and God has continued to promote him. He is a true prophet of God with revelation knowledge. Joseph Z's *The Prophetic Endgame* will show you where we are headed by looking at how we started. The way he breaks down scripture will take you on a journey and provoke your thoughts. Some people are afraid of end times teaching, but *The Prophetic Endgame* will give you peace in a crazy world. To be informed is to be prepared. Joseph Z is one of the best Bible teachers and a gift to the body.

Ryan Edberg
Ryan Edberg Ministries
Kingdom Movement

The Prophetic Endgame is a weighty and timely message that invites the reader to look beyond the chaos of the present age and align with God's eternal plan. By investing in thorough theological study, Joseph Z grounds prophetic insight firmly in Scripture. Then, with great clarity, he addresses the spiritual forces shaping our world today, equipping believers to discern the times without fear or speculation. *The Prophetic Endgame* challenges the Church to walk with discernment, courage, and spiritual authority—living as a force for cultural change and victory in a pivotal hour.

Kyle Loffelmacher
Publisher, Harrison House

THE PROPHETIC ENDGAME

HARRISON HOUSE AND DESTINY IMAGE BOOKS BY JOSEPH Z

The Prophetic Endgame: The Book of Revelation, the Return of Jesus, and the Battle for Eternity

The Prophetic Endgame Study Manual

Servants of Fire: Secrets of the Unseen War & Angels Fighting for You

Breaking Hell's Economy: Your Guide to Last-Days Supernatural Provision

Breaking Hell's Economy Study Manual

Jesus and the Kingmakers

The Origin of the Cosmic Battle

Punishing the Darkness: Spiritual Warfare That Works

Punishing the Darkness Study Manual

Demystifying the Prophetic: Understanding the Voice of God for the Coming Days of Fire

Demystifying the Prophetic Study Manual

The Secret to the Life of John: A Revelation for a Supernaturally Long-Lasting Life

The Spirit of Elijah: Expose the Truth. Embrace God's Power. Break the Antichrist Spirit.

The Spirit of Elijah Study Manual

A Prophet's Reward: Partnering with the Prophetic for Your Faith, Favor, and Financial Miracles

Weaponizing Your Faith: Supernaturally Equipped to Receive Your Breakthrough

THE PROPHETIC ENDGAME

THE BOOK OF REVELATION, THE RETURN OF JESUS, AND THE BATTLE FOR ETERNITY

JOSEPH Z

All emphasis within Scripture quotations is the author's own.

Published by Harrison House Publishers
Shippensburg, PA 17257

ISBN 13 TP: 978-1-6675-0633-3
ISBN 13 eBook: 978-1-6675-0634-0

For Worldwide Distribution, Printed in the U.S.A.
1 2 3 4 5 6 7 8 / 30 29 28 27 26

DEDICATION

I want to dedicate this book to Rick Renner. Eschatology, with its unique vantage points and insights, has fascinated me for most of my Christian walk of faith. My love for the last things accelerated immensely when, many years ago, I read Rick's captivating work, *A Light in Darkness,* volumes I and II. As with all his books, he brought to life a masterful presentation in those volumes, which made the early Church and the Seven Churches come alive to me in technicolor. Even more, it was a catalyst of the Holy Spirit, causing me to lean into the book of Revelation and all the apocalyptic scriptures with prophetic expectation of what is to come at the end of the age.

Since that time, my wife, Heather, and I have had the privilege of accompanying Rick to the Seven Churches of Revelation, and amazingly, to what we believe is the site of Noah's Ark in the mountains of Ararat. Every journey with Rick has been life-altering thanks to his on-site commentary. Rick is a prolific author, excellent Greek teacher, and wordsmith. When describing anything, his vocabulary is much like a painter's brush detailing a clear image to behold.

That is why I am dedicating this book to Rick Renner, a man of God very similar to the apostle Paul in his service to the Lord. Who has not only greatly influenced countless people around the world with his daily teaching, churches, global television networks, and written works, but has also made a forever impact on my walk with the Lord. He has also been a tremendous influence on me to be a writer. Rick is someone I talk to in one way or another nearly every day. He often asks me, "Did you read your Bible today?" He and his wife, Denise, along with their amazing family, have truly become family to us.

To Rick Renner, Sir, thank you for all you have done to serve the Lord and the body of Christ globally. Your teaching and example have made a mark on my life that will last for eternity. I don't think you will ever realize how much you mean to me and the inspiration you have been in my life to write and do ministry to the very highest and best unto the Lord. You consistently challenge me to be better in every way. My life has been tremendously impacted by who you are and your obedience to Jesus.

I honor you for carrying the heart of a true father. You are truly a spiritual father to me. This book is a direct result of your influence and life's work.

Joseph Z

ACKNOWLEDGMENTS

Each book I write is a unique project with a special message. When a book project arrives at its destination, the presence of those who worked alongside me during its conception and completion is so valuable to me, as they greatly enhanced the process. Without each of the tremendous people I am surrounded by, the message of a book like this would not reach its greatest potential. Therefore, let me mention some people who helped make this book possible.

First and always, my amazing wife, Heather, my biggest supporter and greatest friend. You stand by me in everything, daily broadcasts, filming schedules, extensive travel, and of course, the hours of time it takes to write a book. Thank you, I love you, and I don't know what I would do without you.

Followed by our adult children and grandbaby. Alison and her awesome husband, Jeremy, now with our grandbaby, Sophia! Baby girl, one day you will read this and know that Papa believes in you and Jesus has His mighty hand on your life. The world has yet to see all you will accomplish for God Almighty.

Our amazing son, Daniel, you are such a friend and companion to us in this journey. Your creativity and daily assistance are invaluable. You are a tremendous man of God, and we have many more adventures to come!

Heather, Alison, Jeremy, Sophia, and Daniel, you are my best friends; God must surely love me to have placed each of you into my life. Thank you for your constant support while writing this book and the many daily projects you assisted me with. I love each one of you very much.

Mary Ercoli, what can I say? After nearly two decades, you are one of the hardest-working people I know. Your prophetic insights and prayers have been such a blessing to us over the years. This project certainly would not be what it is without your commitment and discipline to see it through. Your assistance in fact-checking my source material, asking probing doctrinal questions, and even debating me on issues for accuracy, while digging into historical archives, is astonishing. You and Josh have been such a support in one way or another through it all, and we are so grateful. Thank you for your diligence and belief in this project. I am sincerely honored to work with you. Now onto the next one!

Barb Wiles. Thank you for being a part of our editing team. You are such a blessing on each and every written project we do!

Every day during this process, several people make everything work:

Holly Eide, Heather and I both don't know what we would do without you. Thank you for your time and leadership to our staff and team. From day one, we have seen growth and monumental advancements that are a direct result of your executive structure. What you bring daily to this ministry and all its wonderful people is nothing short of supernatural and amazing. You are a gift. Thank you!

Arielle Carver, the schedule whisperer and HR powerhouse. Thank you for your discernment and for being part of this ministry. You carry a gift of wisdom and a refreshing organizational structure that gets actual results. You and Brandon have made a major impact and played an integral role in this ministry and in our lives, bringing so much through your service, insights, and being great friends. Thank you for everything!

Elijah and Anya Bulgin, there are not enough words to describe how much value you both bring daily. Your work ethic is so far above and beyond, and you do the daily work of an entire media department. Thank you for traveling the world with us over the past few years and for creating daily programs and LIVE broadcasts for our viewers. Good things come from Russia! It is an honor to have such a dedicated couple as part of this assignment. We believe in you both and can only thank you for dedicating yourself to becoming who God has called you both to be as we build content, travel the nations, and get the message out to so many daily. Thank you!

Eric Miller, you work every day with clarity and diligence to see the daily TV programs go from filming to airing, as well as our daily LIVE broadcasts. Your hard work is making a massive difference. Thank you. It is a thrill getting to work with you every day!

Julia Miller, not only do you handle a tremendous amount of logistical scenarios every day, but you also pray. Your prayers mean so much to Heather and me. They are effective and powerful. You are a tremendous blessing to everyone in this ministry.

To so many who work as unto the Lord, Cody, your sincerity and hard work are so admirable. Thank you! Joanna, thank you for the many reports and daily updates. You bring so much joy to this staff and team. Jed, you are a blessing, and thank you for being such a wonderful presence to our prayer ministers and call team.

To all my staff and team, thank you for being amazing people and believers. Thank you for representing Jesus to our partners, followers, and friends through this ministry. From the office to the call team, I have the greatest staff and team in the world!

Our dear partners, you mean the world to us. We pray daily and thank God for you. Our constant prayer is to gain wisdom and discernment about how to pray for you and see the Lord's blessing manifest in your life. Thank you for your faithfulness and support. This could not be accomplished without you. We love you!

CONTENTS

SPECIAL MESSAGE

Joseph Z has delivered a bold and deeply needed work for this hour. *The Prophetic Endgame* is not a speculative book designed to stir fear or chase headlines. It is a sober, scripturally anchored road map that helps the Church understand where we are, how we got here, and where God is taking history.

What sets this book apart is its scope and clarity. Joseph does not shy away from the hard questions. He walks the reader from the beginning of creation to the final renewal of all things, carefully connecting biblical foundations, prophetic timelines, and spiritual realities with what believers are witnessing right now. He treats Scripture with reverence while addressing complex topics like creation, Lucifer's rebellion, national judgment, global systems, and the coming Kingdom of Christ with precision and balance.

This book does something many fail to do. It strengthens faith instead of weakening it. It equips believers instead of confusing them. It reminds the Church that we are not victims of history but participants in God's redemptive plan. The emphasis on the authority of the believer, the restraining role of the Church, and our responsibility in cultural and spiritual engagement is especially timely.

Joseph Z calls the Church to maturity, discernment, and courage without drifting into sensationalism or compromise. *The Prophetic Endgame* will challenge seasoned believers and awaken those who sense that something far bigger is unfolding in our generation.

I wholeheartedly recommend this book to pastors, leaders, and believers who want a clear-eyed, biblically faithful understanding of the times we are living in and the hope that lies ahead. This is a book for those who refuse to be passive and are ready to stand with confidence, authority, and unwavering trust in Jesus Christ.

Pastor Todd Coconato

Todd Coconato Ministries

Todd Coconato Show

Firepower

www.PastorTodd.org

FOREWORD

In your hands is the pinnacle of Joseph Z's literary work thus far. This masterpiece not only dazzles with its content but also beautifully illustrates Joseph's evolution as a writer. This book captures your attention and holds it unswervingly from cover to cover.

Delving into the mysteries of the end times, Joseph provocatively questions, "Are we in the final days as foretold in the book of Revelation?" "Where is all this leading?" "What lies at the ultimate conclusion?"

And with deft skill, Joseph weaves a narrative that reminds us of the crucial role of prophecy, illuminating the idea that to truly understand the future, we often need to revisit *origins*, as our destiny is often written in the echoes of the past.

Joseph expresses that there exists a realm of divine insights that God has chosen to keep exclusive, a realm known as the "secret things." These secrets belong solely to Him, and they remain elusive until, if ever, He decides to unveil them. But there is yet another mystical chamber that is full of "concealed things," which the Lord offers to those who earnestly seek Him, and these treasures are within reach, but only through a diligent quest.

This journey of discovery is navigated by delving into the Bible with the Holy Spirit as your Guide—and through earnest study and the insights garnered from the scholarly endeavors of others, the layers of mystery will begin to peel away. In this dance between divine hiddenness and human pursuit, God unveils secrets and concealed truths to those who earnestly seek with open hearts and minds.

In this captivating volume, Joseph embarks on an extraordinary exploration of ancient history, reaching back to epochs predating the conventional timeline of human understanding. He ventures into the cosmic revolt led by Lucifer and events that transpired even before the familiar narrative of

Genesis. Along this journey, Joseph meticulously examines the Luciferian flood that coincided with Lucifer's dramatic expulsion from the heavens, and wades into the depths of debates about the earth's true antiquity.

Readers will be enthralled by the array of theories Joseph presents, each thought inviting them to ponder the authenticity of these primordial incidents. For those ready to expand their horizons and entertain the provocative ideas within this book, it promises to illuminate age-old mysteries and provide possible answers to enduring questions about our universe's distant past. Joseph delves into the Bible accounts of angels who descended to cohabit with women, resulting in the birth of giants, and he probes the underlying motives for such shadowy occurrences. But what I particularly admire is Joseph's honest and methodical approach to laying out the various arguments about these antediluvian events, ultimately entrusting readers with the power to discern which narratives resonate as truths.

Connecting past events to the present, Joseph compellingly argues that a malevolent force is currently at work among the global elites, who are crafting strategies that they believe will ultimately elevate the rebellious fallen angel to God's throne. Joseph also unveils a sinister agenda aimed at subjugating humanity entirely under Satan's sway, with the ultimate objective to pave the way for the Antichrist to seize power on earth. Yet Joseph astutely notes that despite this nefarious plan for evil to triumph, it will be thwarted in a climactic moment when Jesus Himself descends from the heavens, obliterating the Antichrist with the mere breath of His mouth.

But also in this skillful narrative, Joseph masterfully delves into the annals of history to depict the genesis of evil that began with Lucifer's rebellion. Joseph expertly portrays Lucifer in his pre-fallen splendor, describing his breathtaking adornment and the insidious germ of error that took root within him. Transformed into the tormented figure of Satan, Lucifer has perennially sought to dethrone God with twisted ambitions to overshadow the divine realm. Yet with profound insight, Joseph assures us of Christ's ultimate triumph over Satan, dismantling his nefarious schemes with victorious power and grace.

But before the momentous return of Christ, who will banish evil with His arrival at the close of a seven-year Tribulation, the world is destined for an age of unparalleled chaos. This epoch will witness cataclysmic devastation, an earth-shattering quake of such magnitude that every metropolis will be leveled, and islands will be swallowed by the ocean's depths. From the heavens, colossal hailstones, each weighing hundreds of pounds, will descend with relentless fury, penetrating everything in their path. Unleashed upon the world will be horrors untold—including plagues of incomprehensible scope and demonic legions, perhaps even in tangible form—that will ravage the land with no hope of respite. These prophetic events are vividly depicted in the mysterious book of Revelation, expertly unraveled by Joseph in the riveting book you hold in your hands.

In the very end of times, a moment of breathtaking glory will arrive when Jesus triumphantly returns to the earth once again for His Second Coming. He will vanquish all foes arrayed against both Himself and His Church, consigning them to eternal judgment. The Lord will then build His earthly dominion from Jerusalem, a seat of sovereignty from which His rule will spread across the globe. An era of unparalleled serenity will dawn with no illness nor conflict, ushering in a millennium of peace. His Kingdom will transcend earthly limitations, for He will reign as the supreme King of kings and Lord of lords. Yet astonishingly, this Kingdom is but the precursor to an even greater reality. From this sacred ground will rise the ultimate empire, stretching endlessly into eternity, where we will dwell alongside Him forever.

But as good as the sweeping historical perspective Josephs provides is—bridging epochs and prophecies past and future to our current world—his true brilliance lies in his analysis of present-day events unfolding within the grand tapestry of divine prophecy. In an age that feels saturated with chaos and bewilderment, many are left questioning the trajectory of our world. But in this book, Joseph offers insightful and compelling answers that will encourage and equip every Christian with the wisdom to stand resiliently against the pervasive shadows of moral upheaval.

This work by Joseph Z leaves no doubt that God has not forsaken those who pursue righteousness, and it promises that His justice will ultimately extinguish the machinations of those aligned with wickedness. Although the Babylonian systems of this world seem robust, Joseph assures us they are impermanent, destined to crumble before the triumphant emergence of God's Kingdom. Joseph elucidates the essential role of the Church in the Great Commission to usher in this Kingdom, revealing our individual and collective mandates within this holy cosmic narrative. In doing so, Joseph crafts a road map for believers everywhere to push back the darkness and assume their rightful place in this divine saga.

I could spill endless words about this extraordinary book, but let me simply say that it's a journey you must undertake for yourself to the very last page. Prepare to arm yourself with pen, paper, and Bible, because this book will ignite a relentless desire to delve deeper into the divine mysteries contained in its pages. I believe that the Holy Spirit, who is the Spirit of revelation, will reveal the secrets and hidden treasures of God's grand design for you in such a way that you will uncover your unique role within it.

Throughout the years, I've penned countless endorsements and forewords for many books, none of which has captivated me as profoundly as this one. This book dares me to stretch my thoughts, elevate my spiritual senses, and invite the Holy Spirit to broaden my horizons—and I'm convinced it will do the same for you. So, dear reader, dive headlong into the pages before you with an open heart and a curious mind—and prepare yourself for an exhilarating journey into the prophetic endgame we find ourselves navigating at this very time.

Rick Renner

Minister, Author, Broadcaster

Moscow, Russia

FOREWORD

Joseph Z is not only a dear friend of mine, but he is also one of the clearest and most courageous prophetic voices God has raised up for this hour. In *The Prophetic Endgame*, Joseph brings biblical depth, historical insight, and prophetic clarity together in a way that helps believers understand where we've been, where we are, and where we're going. Instead of stirring up fear, this book awakens faith, strengthens discernment, and anchors hope in the victory of King Jesus. If you want to understand the times without losing your footing in truth, this is a resource you can trust. I highly recommend it to anyone who wants to be prepared, grounded, and confident in the days ahead.

There has never been a time in modern history when people have been more aware that something significant is unfolding on the earth. Nations are shifting. Technology is advancing at lightning speed. Cultural pressures are rising, and many believers are asking the same question: *Where is all of this going?*

The truth is, the Bible has never been silent about the days we are living in.

Scripture gives us a prophetic map. From Genesis to Revelation, the Lord has laid out a storyline that reveals not only the beginning of creation but the ultimate conclusion of human history and the glorious future that awaits those who belong to Him. Joseph Z steps into that conversation with remarkable clarity, guiding readers through the great biblical narrative that stretches from the fall of Lucifer and the earliest ages of the earth all the way to the return of Jesus Christ and the Kingdom that will never end.

One of the things I deeply respect about Joseph is that he refuses to treat prophecy like entertainment. In a generation where sensationalism often replaces sound teaching, Joseph does the opposite. He approaches the Word of God with reverence, diligence, and a genuine desire to equip the body of Christ. That matters.

Prophecy is not meant to confuse the Church. It is meant to prepare her.

The prophetic Scriptures were never given to make believers fearful. They were given to make us ready. They remind us that history is not spinning out of control.

God is still the Author of the story. He is still the Alpha and the Omega, the Beginning and the End. And every headline in our world is ultimately moving toward a moment when Jesus Christ will step back onto the stage of human history and establish His Kingdom forever.

Joseph does something powerful in this book: he helps readers see that the end cannot be understood without first understanding the beginning. God Almighty is famous for declaring the end from the beginning. From the earliest chapters of Genesis to the final chapters of Revelation, there is a thread running through the entire Bible. It is the story of God redeeming what was lost and restoring His creation to its intended glory.

Throughout these pages, Joseph explores questions that many believers quietly wrestle with.

What really happened in the earliest days of creation? What role did Lucifer's rebellion play in shaping the world we live in today? How do ancient events connect to the rise of modern systems that oppose God? And most importantly, what does the Bible say about the days ahead?

These are not casual questions.

They are Kingdom questions.

Joseph approaches each of these with both courage and humility, grounding every discussion in the authority of Scripture. What I appreciate most about *The Prophetic Endgame* is that it does not leave the reader staring into darkness. Instead, it points us to the unstoppable victory of Jesus Christ. Yes, the Bible tells us that difficult times will come. It speaks of deception, global upheaval, and spiritual conflict, unlike anything the world has ever seen. But the final chapter of the story has already been written.

King Jesus wins. And His people reign with Him.

Joseph reminds us that believers are not powerless spectators in these last days. The Church is described in Scripture as a restraining force in the earth, standing against the rise of lawlessness until the appointed time. That means you and I are here for a reason. We are not simply waiting for the future. We are called to shape the present.

God has always raised up men and women who understand the times and know what to do. From the prophets of old to the reformers of history, the Lord has consistently given insight to those who seek Him. I believe Joseph Z is part of that prophetic company in our generation. His voice carries both urgency and hope, reminding believers that we are not abandoned in a chaotic world but positioned by God for such a time as this.

The message of this book ultimately leads to one powerful conclusion: the story of humanity is not heading toward destruction, but toward restoration. The battle may intensify. Darkness may attempt to rise. But the light of Christ will always prevail.

As you read the pages ahead, I encourage you to approach them with both curiosity and faith. Let the Scriptures speak. Let the Holy Spirit illuminate truth in your heart. And allow the prophetic promises of God to strengthen your confidence in what lies ahead.

The greatest days for the Kingdom of God are still in front of us.

The King is coming, and His Kingdom will have no end.

Pastor Troy Brewer
Troy Brewer Ministries
Lead Pastor, OpenDoor Church, Burleson, Texas

PREFACE

REVELATION IS NOT HISTORY, IT IS PROPHECY

It is worth noting that the book of Revelation is not a historical account; it is a prophecy. Revelation 1:3 says, "Blessed *is* he who reads and those who hear the words of this *prophecy,* and keep those things which are written in it; for the time *is* near." John, in Revelation 1, was influenced by three prophetic aspects.

> *Write the things which you* ***have seen****, and the things* ***which are****, and the things which* ***will take place after this****.*
>
> —Revelation 1:19

1. Things you *have seen*—a reference to the vision of Jesus Christ in Revelation 1.
2. The things *which are*—a reference to the letters to be written to the seven churches present in John's time.
3. The events that *will take place after this*—the future as prophetically shown in Revelation 4–22.

THE KING IS COMING WITH HIS ETERNAL KINGDOM

When entering the book of Revelation, the primary focus is to understand that the kingdom without end is approaching. Jesus, the warrior King, will arrive on the scene to take authority over all the kingdoms of this earth. As we move toward this time, we are being plunged into what is known as the last of the last days. Matthew 24 prophetically describes what we can expect and what we will walk through by faith. Faith that occupies is the kind of faith God has provided for each member of the *Ekklesia,* the Church, with Jesus as its Cornerstone.

> *And you will hear of wars and rumors of wars. See that you are not troubled; for all these things must come to pass, but the end is not yet.* [7] *For nation will rise against nation, and kingdom against kingdom. And there will be famines, pestilences, and earthquakes in various places.* [8] *All these are the beginning of sorrows.*
>
> —Matthew 24:6-8

When the end times begin, there will be a change once again in the ages. The Church will be removed, and the world will return to an Old Testament relationship with God Almighty. Jesus will have come for His Church; we will be in heaven at the Marriage Supper of the Lamb; and the earth will not have the same privileges it had while the believing Church was present.

John the Revelator was admonished to write the prophetic things he had seen, the things which are (or were current to his time), and what will take place in the future. Each vantage point is prophecy: what was, what is, and what is to come. Historically, John saw many things about Jesus and experienced them in his own time. It is what is to come that both John and we who are watching for the return of the Lord must discern and study. As they watch, the radiant believers anticipate the Lord's return, and throughout the book of Revelation, there are stunning predictions about the future.

Many would say that Revelation is an allegory and a work of symbolism. Although it does indeed have those elements woven throughout, Revelation also clearly prophesies events that will occur at the very end, which have not yet come to pass. In Section Three, we will address these major issues. As you venture into the pages ahead, keep in mind that we are looking at prophecy and will ultimately arrive at a glimpse of our eternal future with Jesus, and what a thrill it is to think about!

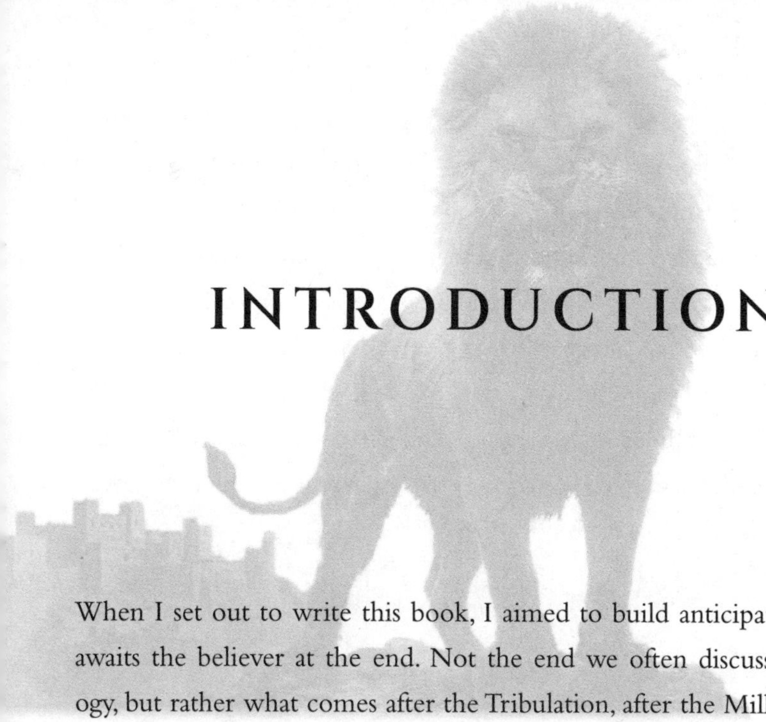

INTRODUCTION

When I set out to write this book, I aimed to build anticipation for what awaits the believer at the end. Not the end we often discuss in eschatology, but rather what comes after the Tribulation, after the Millennial Reign of Jesus, and following the Great White Throne Judgment. Eternity's future captivates my heart at times, as I realize we are in a long-term epoch with God Almighty, one He chose to endure on our behalf. All of it for a purpose not fully known to us through the Scripture, which lit a spark in me as I pondered what God Almighty, the Maker of heaven and earth, might have planned for us after the end. Knowing that God, in His infinite wisdom, chose to keep certain things concealed in the Old Testament era yet revealed them in the New Testament era, such as the Church, a concept not in the Old Covenant but announced at the precipice of the New Covenant by Jesus to Peter, I wonder what He might be concealing about eternity future at this time. That is a secret and a mystery, but a wonderful concept to ponder nonetheless.

GOD REVEALS HIS SECRET TO HIS SERVANTS THE PROPHETS

> *Surely the Lord God does nothing, unless He reveals His secret to His servants the prophets.*
>
> —Amos 3:7

True to the operation of God and His method of revealing His secret to His servants, the prophets, we see that this is exactly what is taking place in the book of Revelation. Jesus showed John His secret of what God would do in the future, and by unveiling the plan to John, God was working in accordance with Amos 3:7. Notice that it says He (God) reveals His secret. His plan for a matter, not necessarily every exact detail, but rather His secret, or what He plans for the future. Proverbs 25:2 says, "It is the glory of God to conceal a matter, but the glory of kings is to search out a matter." God desires that the concealed matters be searched out; even greater is when He reveals His secret of what is to come to prophets.

> *It is the glory of God to conceal a matter, but the glory of kings is to search out a matter.*
>
> —Proverbs 25:2

Concealed matters differ from God's secrets, as they are to be searched out; why? Because God wants to be pursued. Secrets are with the Lord, and only He can unveil them to whom He chooses. According to Amos 3:7, prophets are those to whom He reveals His secrets in advance before He accomplishes them. Deuteronomy 29:29 says, "The secret things belong to the LORD our God, but those things which are revealed belong to us and to our children forever, that we may do all the words of this law." A caveat regarding the secret and concealed things is that the New Testament believer has a relationship with the Holy Spirit, who also provides access to the secret of the Lord. Psalm 25:14 states, "The secret of the LORD is with those who fear Him, and He will show them His covenant." New Testament believers who are baptized with the Holy Spirit have revelatory access to all the mysteries of God; I believe this is why it is parallel with being shown His covenant. As born-again believers, we are fully loaded with all things that pertain to life and godliness in Christ Jesus. This means that, as we renew our minds by reading the Scripture and getting to know the Lord through the Holy Spirit, His Covenant secrets will be with us. However, *God will reveal His secret as He wishes to whom He wishes*, as was the case with John the Revelator.

THE SECRET REVEALED TO JOHN

John was shown the Revelation of Jesus concerning what was, what is, and what is to come. As New Testament believers, we should take the book of Revelation seriously when considering what lies ahead.

Events rising from the four corners of the earth are merely an extension of ancient mischief that transpired at the beginning of the universe and led to our present-day world. In this current age, we are constantly faced with life and death, truth versus lies, clarity opposed by chaos, and global powers that will stop at nothing to achieve all-out domination of society. This clash of kingdoms in the natural realm and the unseen realm is only gaining momentum before our eyes. God has called His people to be a shining light in the darkness, offering the culture a narrow path as a remedy to this plight. It is, of course, the Way, the Truth, and the Life—Jesus Christ. To understand the end of a matter, it sometimes requires grasping the beginning; another way of saying it is that the future can be discovered by examining the past.

Along the way, we will consider questions a believer might have. Are we living in the end times as described in the book of Revelation? Where is this all headed? What is the ultimate end? In this journey, we will examine the beginning, the controversies surrounding it, and the final destination, and then go beyond. From Lucifer's fall to Adam's occupancy in the garden, through the Old Testament narrative, we see God's will for humanity colliding with the dark forces within each age.

LUCIFER'S ENDGAME STARTED AT THE BEGINNING

Is it possible the earth is far older than many have suspected? Or is the 6,000-year theory the reality of it all? We are going to explore that in depth.

We will look at the true rebellion of Lucifer and why Luciferians may be the driving force behind the global elites who are attempting to develop mechanisms that, in their view, would lead to the eventual placement of that mutinous fallen angel on God's throne. Their endgame is for Lucifer to win and for all of humanity to come completely under his domain. They are operating more in the spirit of Antichrist, which will follow a path to the actual Antichrist coming into power upon the earth. We will also examine the current-day Church and its role in the church-government conversation.

Ultimately, the book of Revelation is filled with stunning prophetic insights pointing to a glorious future, but along the way will come the Great Tribulation and what that entails for all of civilization before the complete and total triumph of Jesus.

THE WORD BECAME FLESH SHOWS THE EXTREMES GOD WENT TO FOR JESUS TO STAND ON EARTH

In light of God's ultimate plan, we see His will and desire in the story of Adam and Eve. Throughout the ages, a theme unfolds: God wants His family with Him and has gone to great lengths to make that a reality. Consider what was required for Him to see Jesus manifest in the womb of a virgin. Four thousand years of prophetic declarations had to be released into the world through prophets, psalmists, and kings who uttered the inspired will of God under the unction of the Holy Spirit, until, after many centuries, those prophetic words came to fruition: The Word became flesh.

God could not simply create the Last Adam (Jesus Christ) right after the fall of the original Adam, who fell into original sin. Rather, God Almighty had to work within the framework He had empowered Adam with to take dominion over the earth, be fruitful and multiply, and name every creature. This dominion was tragically given over to Satan through Adam's agreement with that deceptive serpent. God could have wiped out all of creation and started over! Why didn't He? The answer is found in God's desire for eternity with His children, and forever with His children is what He has always had in His heart.

I believe that God so loved the world that He was unwilling to lose what He loved, which led to His infinite strategy to defeat the devil at his own game. We know God is far superior to the fallen angel, and in a match, there isn't even a comparison; however, in a legal technicality, the devil gained authority over humanity through Adam's disobedience to the One True Living God. This necessitated God's working within the rules He Himself had set. God did not break His word to Adam by taking back dominion over the earth, even though Adam came under the devil's dominion. God would not be outdone, and like a master chess player, God Almighty intentionally wove the plan of redemption into the fabric of the world. Because God would not violate His own Word, He chose to take the long road of beating darkness at their own game. In this book, we will look at the endgame of nations and ultimately where we will arrive at the end of the age, then go beyond.

It is the pinnacle of hope to know that our Great God loves to conceal Himself so that we may draw out His concealed truth. He delights in being sought after by His people, who desire to know Him more. That was the foundation of this writing. As a result of searching the Scripture about what awaits us after the end, it became clear that, to better grasp where we are heading for eternity, we would need to examine the beginning and potentially what might have been taking place in eternity past.

You will discover that detailed information from the Word of God is woven throughout every page of this work, and it is my prayer that it will strengthen your faith and set a course in your heart to uncover God's concealed things in His Word.

May you find hope as you read through each page and discover God's grand plan for humanity, made available only through the Lord and Savior, Jesus Christ.

> *Wisdom is the principal thing; therefore get wisdom....*
>
> —Proverbs 4:7

In all your getting, may you gain understanding of what was, and is, and is to come.

Joseph Z

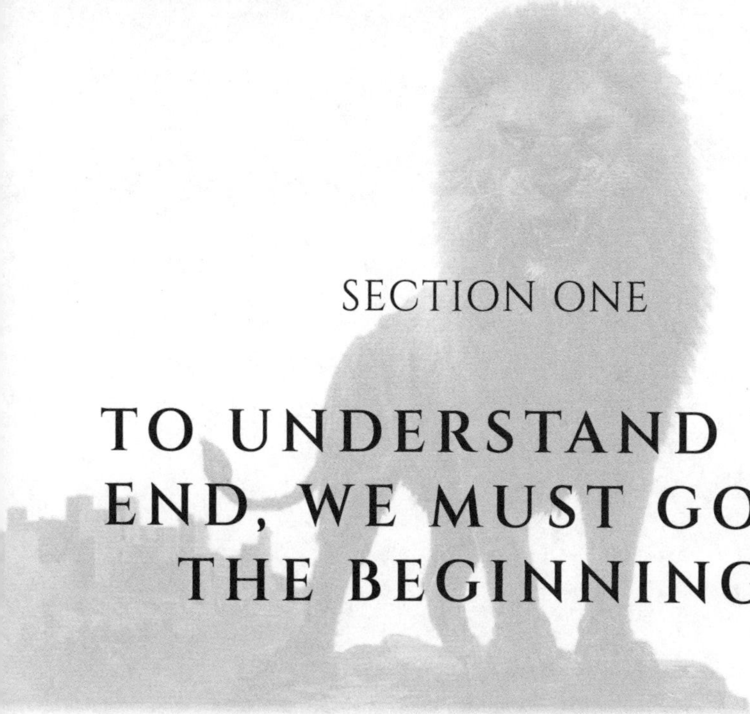

SECTION ONE

TO UNDERSTAND THE END, WE MUST GO TO THE BEGINNING...

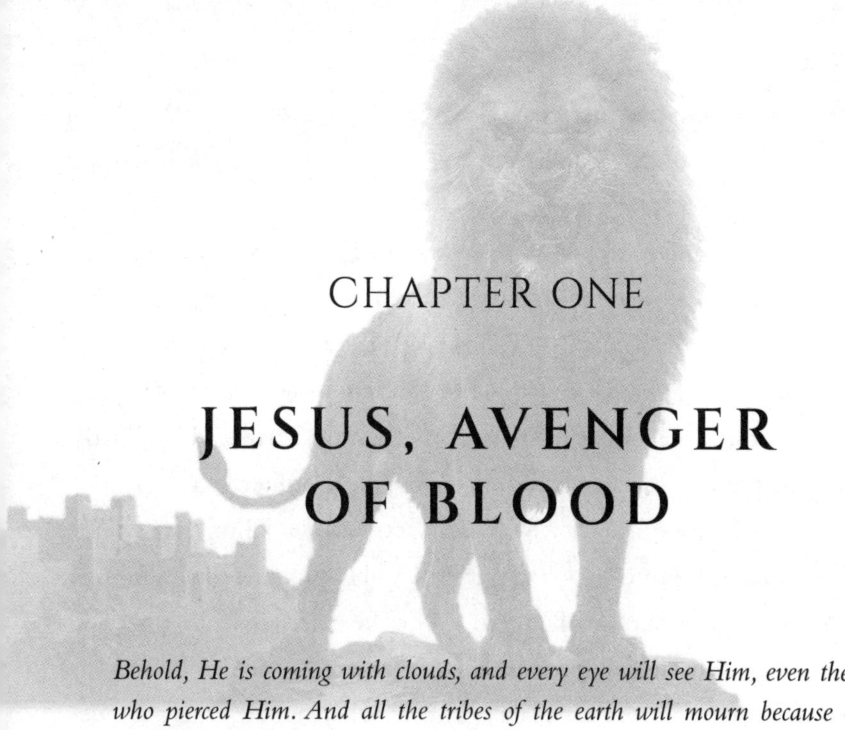

CHAPTER ONE

JESUS, AVENGER OF BLOOD

Behold, He is coming with clouds, and every eye will see Him, even they who pierced Him. And all the tribes of the earth will mourn because of Him. Even so, Amen. 8 *"I am the Alpha and the Omega, the Beginning and the End," says the Lord, "who is and who was and who is to come, the Almighty."*

—Revelation 1:7-8

Imagine the worldwide alarm and panic at the second advent of Jesus, bursting through the atmosphere for the entire earth to witness? At the end of the Tribulation, following worldwide decimation, society will have experienced a global earthquake so violent that every major city will be razed, including all islands that will fall beneath the sea. The world will have endured what the Bible calls *Wormwood*, the result of a fiery mountain passing through the atmosphere and colliding with earth, causing mass toxicity in the oceans and destroying much of the world's ecosystems. During the Tribulation, hailstones will fall from the sky, weighing several hundred pounds, and penetrate all structures in their path. Unspeakable plagues and demonic hordes, possibly appearing in physical form, will be unleashed upon the earth, offering no reprieve.

The earth, as we know it, will largely be terraformed into a wasteland of ash and ruin. Wrath will be the palpable encounter for all who reject the

One True Living God in those days. Horrors we cannot comprehend will encompass the face of the earth as fierce waves cascade across the landscape. Just as one judgment seems to reach its fullness, another will immediately begin. Exhaustion and crisis will be the norm for all who dwell on the earth, without reprieve. Following these events, a vast military presence will gather at the very end of the Great Tribulation. In those fateful moments, as the arrogant, unrepentant, and God-hating horde accumulates to make war, Jesus will break through the clouds to arrive at the Battle of Armageddon, marking the conclusion of one age and the beginning of another.

During this transitional cataclysm, every eye will see Him; they will be awestruck, gazing at Him, grappling with the suspension of belief. An image of earthshaking proportions will unfold before the entire global audience. In that moment, all the tribes of the earth will mourn because of Him. They will grieve as they confront the reality of what is happening; their own ideologies and religious beliefs will be blatantly proven false, forcing those who would not receive Jesus to remain on the earth and finally acknowledge that Jesus is indeed the Way, the Truth, and the Life, and that no one comes to the Father except through Him—yet they rejected Him.

In this time of prophetic fulfillment, every living person will experience the same revelatory epiphany: Jesus is truly the Son of God, and He has returned as He promised. For some, this will bring horror; for others, sorrow and anger. The wicked—those who hate God and the notion of Jesus as Lord—will respond with intense shock and rage.

THE FIERCE WRATH OF THE LAMB

> *And the kings of the earth, the great men, the rich men, the commanders, the mighty men, every slave and every free man, hid themselves in the caves and in the rocks of the mountains,* [16] *and said to the mountains and rocks, "Fall on us and hide us from the face of Him who sits on the throne and from the wrath of the Lamb!"*
>
> —Revelation 6:15-16

Jesus will not return in the same way He left. When He appears, splitting the eastern sky and announcing His arrival on earth, the great final rightsizing will begin. A societal earthquake will strike the international population as He descends, as He promised, with His persona locked in for fierce battle. All that has happened since the beginning of the world, from the fall of humanity to the rise of the Antichrist, will be dealt with by the King. Yes, Jesus is coming, and wrath will be unleashed like a consuming fire.

So fierce will be the wrath of the Lamb that those subject to the horrors accompanying His wrath will try to hide in caves, possibly in underground fortresses hidden in the mountains. Even then, they will plead with the rocks and mountains to fall on them to shield them from the face of Him who sits on the throne. God will reveal Himself to these evil doers as the wrath of His Son is poured out on the world. No one can see God's face and live; the wicked dwelling on the earth at this time will experience God's face and the wrath of Jesus in full force. Exodus 33:20 says, "But He said, 'You cannot see My face; for no man shall see Me, and live.'"

EVERY EYE WILL SEE HIM

> *Behold, He is coming with clouds, and every eye will see Him, even they who pierced Him. And all the tribes of the earth will mourn because of Him. Even so, Amen.*
>
> —Revelation 1:7

Let's consider the phrase, "Every eye shall see Him." It refers to a personal, firsthand observation, not an arbitrary experience. It will be a firsthand eyewitness account through mass, empirical recognition. We could say they will see Him with their own eyes. For every eye to see Him at the same time will either be a supernatural act of God, allowing all humanity to witness it, or a technological advancement that integrates with humanity, allowing all to behold this universal event virtually. Regardless of how every person sees Him, it will be total. No one will escape the Second Coming of Jesus!

PROPHETIC SCRIPTURES SHOWING THE WHOLE WORLD WILL BE IMPACTED BY JESUS' RETURN

> *I was watching in the night visions, and behold, One like the Son of Man, coming with the clouds of heaven! He came to the Ancient of Days, and they brought Him near before Him.* [14] *Then to Him was given dominion and glory and a kingdom, that all peoples, nations, and languages should serve Him. His dominion is an everlasting dominion, which shall not pass away, and His kingdom the one which shall not be destroyed.*
>
> —Daniel 7:13-14

> *Then the sign of the Son of Man will appear in heaven, and then all the tribes of the earth will mourn, and they will see the Son of Man coming on the clouds of heaven with power and great glory.*
>
> —Matthew 24:30

> *Jesus said to him, "It is as you said. Nevertheless, I say to you, hereafter you will see the Son of Man sitting at the right hand of the Power, and coming on the clouds of heaven."*
>
> —Matthew 26:64

> *And I will pour on the house of David and on the inhabitants of Jerusalem the Spirit of grace and supplication; then they will look on Me whom they pierced. Yes, they will mourn for Him as one mourns for his only son, and grieve for Him as one grieves for a firstborn.* [11] *In that day there shall be a great mourning in Jerusalem, like the mourning at Hadad Rimmon in the plain of Megiddo.*
>
> —Zechariah 12:10-11

THE BATTLE OF EDOM

> *Who is this who comes from Edom, with* ***dyed garments*** *from Bozrah, this One who is glorious in His apparel, traveling in the greatness of His strength? — "I who speak in righteousness, mighty to save."* [2] ***Why is Your apparel red****, and* ***Your garments like one who treads in the winepress?*** [3] ***"I have trodden the winepress alone****, and from the peoples no one was with Me. For I have trodden them in My anger, and trampled them in My fury;* ***their blood is sprinkled upon My garments****, and I have stained all My robes.* [4] *For the day of vengeance is in My heart, and the year of My redeemed has come.* [5] *I looked, but there was no one to help, and I wondered that there was no one to uphold; therefore My own arm brought salvation for Me; and My own fury, it sustained Me.* [6] *I have trodden down the peoples in My anger, made them drunk in My fury, and brought down their strength to the earth."*
>
> —Isaiah 63:1-6

A fascinating caveat in Isaiah 63:1-6 offers an intriguing perspective on the electrifying time of the Lord's second advent, leading some to believe that Jesus may not come directly to the Battle of Armageddon. He may instead stop first to slaughter the oppressors of His people, surrounded in Bozrah, the capital of Edom, in response to the cry of His Jewish people calling for Him at His return. There are differing points of view on the exact location this refers to. Still, some have believed the location to be Petra in Jordan, where Jewish believers will be hiding for sanctuary away from the Antichrist and his evil minions, who are pursuing them and attempting to destroy them. It is a picture of terrain like Helm's Deep in *The Lord of the Rings: The Two Towers*. When the evil orc army breaches the walls and surrounds the people hiding within for safety, just as they are about to be destroyed, in the very last moment, Gandalf arrives with an army riding down and slaughters the evil orc army. In the case of Jesus, He does not fight alongside an army—He kills them alone and by Himself.

According to Isaiah 63:5, "Therefore My own arm brought salvation for Me; and My own fury, it sustained Me," we see that Jesus first arrives to rescue those trying to hold off the wicked assault. He alone fights and singlehandedly slaughters all their murderous oppressors who torment His people. Jesus unleashes His fury against these enemies not by the sword of His mouth but by His own arm and fury. This leaves our Lord drenched in the blood of those He annihilates, suggesting a catastrophic bloodbath unlike anything seen before. This battle will differ from His use of the sword of His mouth at Armageddon. It will be a physical battle, pitting Jesus against an army of hell-powered villains who have sworn allegiance to the Antichrist. While the specifics remain unclear, one thing is certain: this will be a violent encounter.

AVENGER OF BLOOD

> *When He avenges blood, He remembers them; He does not forget the cry of the humble.*
>
> —Psalm 9:12

It is possible that the historical title "avenger of blood" evolved from the family obligation to seek blood revenge when a clan member was slain. Such a process, while typical of tribal society, is extremely disruptive to maintaining order within an organized state. As a result, the "avenger of blood" may have been appointed by the government to serve both the needs of the family and the state by apprehending the accused and then carrying out the sentence if the verdict was murder. In the case of Jesus, He is avenging His people.[1]

> *Then the Lord spoke to Moses, saying, [10] "Speak to the children of Israel, and say to them: 'When you cross the Jordan into the land of Canaan, [11] then you shall appoint cities to be cities of refuge for you, that the manslayer*

who kills any person accidentally may flee there. [12] *They shall be cities of refuge for you from the avenger, that the manslayer may not die until he stands before the congregation in judgment.* [13] *And of the cities which you give, you shall have six cities of refuge.* [14] *You shall appoint three cities on this side of the Jordan, and three cities you shall appoint in the land of Canaan, which will be cities of refuge.* [15] *These six cities shall be for refuge for the children of Israel, for the stranger, and for the sojourner among them, that anyone who kills a person accidentally may flee there.* [16] *But if he strikes him with an iron implement, so that he dies, he is a murderer; the murderer shall surely be put to death.* [17] *And if he strikes him with a stone in the hand, by which one could die, and he does die, he is a murderer; the murderer shall surely be put to death.* [18] *Or if he strikes him with a wooden hand weapon, by which one could die, and he does die, he is a murderer; the murderer shall surely be put to death.* [19] ***The avenger of blood himself shall put the murderer to death****; when he meets him, he shall put him to death.* [20] *If he pushes him out of hatred or, while lying in wait, hurls something at him so that he dies,* [21] *or in enmity he strikes him with his hand so that he dies, the one who struck him shall surely be put to death. He is a murderer.* ***The avenger of blood shall put the murderer to death when he meets him****.* [22] *However, if he pushes him suddenly without enmity, or throws anything at him without lying in wait,* [23] *or uses a stone, by which a man could die, throwing it at him without seeing him, so that he dies, while he was not his enemy or seeking his harm,* [24] *then the congregation shall judge between the manslayer and the avenger of blood according to these judgments.* [25] *So the congregation shall deliver the manslayer from the hand of the avenger of blood, and the congregation shall return him to the city of refuge where he had fled, and he shall remain there until the death of the high priest who was anointed with the holy oil.* [26] *But if the manslayer at any time goes outside the limits of the city of refuge where he fled,* [27] ***and the avenger of blood finds him outside the limits of his city of refuge, and the avenger of blood kills the manslayer, he shall not be guilty of blood****,* [28] *because he should have remained in his city of refuge until the death of* *the high priest. But after the death of the high priest the manslayer may return to the land of his possession.* [29] *And these things shall be a statute of judgment to you throughout your generations in all your dwellings.* [30] *Whoever kills a person, the murderer shall be put to death on the testimony of witnesses; but one witness is not sufficient testimony against a person for the death penalty.* [31] *Moreover you shall take no ransom for the life of a murderer who is guilty of death, but he shall surely be put to death.* [32] *And you shall take no ransom for him who has fled to his city of refuge, that he may return to dwell in the land before the death of the priest.* [33] *So you shall not pollute the land where you are; for blood defiles the land, and no atonement can be made for the land, for the blood that is shed on it, except by the blood of him who shed it.* [34] *Therefore do not defile the land which you inhabit, in the midst of which I dwell; for I the Lord dwell among the children of Israel.'"*

—Numbers 35:9-34

When Jesus arrives at the battle of Edom in Isaiah 63, He displays the characteristics of an avenger of blood, as seen in Numbers 35.

ROBE DIPPED IN BLOOD

The connection is drawn from the image in Revelation 19:13, which portrays Jesus wearing a robe dipped in blood. This blood is not His own but that of His defeated enemies as He descends into the Battle at Armageddon.

He was ***clothed with a robe dipped in blood****, and His name is called The Word of God.* [14] *And the armies in heaven, clothed in fine linen, white and clean, followed Him on white horses.*

—Revelation 19:13-14

With dyed garments - That is, with garments dyed in blood. The word rendered here 'dyed' (חָמוּץ châmûts), is derived from חמץ *châmats,* to be sharp and pungent, and is usually applied to

> anything that is sharp or sour. It is applied to color that is bright or dazzling, in the same manner as the Greeks use the phrase χρῶμα ὀξύ chrōma oxu - a sharp color - applied to purple or scarlet. Thus, the phrase πορφύραι ὀξύταται porphurai oxutatai means a brilliant, bright purple (*see* Bochart, Hieroz. i. 2. 7). It is applied to the military cloak which was worn by a warrior, and may denote here either that it was originally dyed of a scarlet color, or more probably that it was made red by the blood that had been sprinkled on it. Thus in Rev 19:13, the Son of God is represented as clothed in a similar manner: 'And he was clothed with a vesture dipped in blood.' In Isa 63:3, the answer of Yahweh to the inquiry why his raiment was red, shows that the color was to be attributed to blood.
>
> —Albert Barnes Commentary on Isaiah[2]

Why would Jesus get off mission as He is heading to Armageddon? I want to address this by asking you to consider another example that may shed light on the idea of Jesus altering His trajectory for His people. In the instance we are about to look at as a parallel, Jesus was on a mission after He gave up His life on the cross, descended, took captivity captive, and led them into heaven after He defeated death, hell, and the grave.

FAITH CAN INTERRUPT GOD

Consider that faith can interrupt heaven's goal. Once again, we recognize that Jesus gave up His Spirit on the cross, died, and descended to take the captives captive. He went to Abraham's bosom, also known as Paradise. From there, He led them out and began the victorious procession, which I imagine was like a parade to heaven. Psalm 24 tells us the story.

> *Lift up your heads, O ye gates; and be ye lift up, ye everlasting doors; and the King of glory shall come in.* [8] *Who is this King of glory? The* LORD

strong and mighty, the L*ORD mighty in battle.* 9 *Lift up your heads, O ye*
gates; even lift them up, ye everlasting doors; and the King of glory shall
come in. 10 *Who is this King of glory? The* L*ORD of hosts, he is the King*
of glory. Selah.

—Psalm 24:7-10 KJV

The volley of declarations regarding Jesus went back and forth. Following Jesus was not only for angels but also for those in Abraham's bosom; they followed as well. This was after Jesus made an open display of the powers of darkness and took the keys of death, hell, and the grave!

MARY INTERRUPTED JESUS' PARADE

But Mary stood without at the sepulchre weeping: and as she wept, she
stooped down, and looked into the sepulchre, 12 *and seeth two angels in*
white sitting, the one at the head, and the other at the feet, where the body
of Jesus had lain. 13 *And they say unto her, Woman, why weepest thou?*
She saith unto them, Because they have taken away my Lord, and I know
not where they have laid him. 14 *And when she had thus said, she turned*
herself back, and saw Jesus standing, and knew not that it was Jesus. 15
Jesus saith unto her, Woman, why weepest thou? whom seekest thou? She,
supposing him to be the gardener, saith unto him, Sir, if thou have borne
him hence, tell me where thou hast laid him, and I will take him away. 16
Jesus saith unto her, Mary. She turned herself, and saith unto him, Rab-
boni; which is to say, Master. 17 ***Jesus saith unto her, Touch me not; for I***
am not yet ascended to my Father*: but go to my brethren, and say unto*
them, I ascend unto my Father, and your Father; and to my God, and your
God. 18 *Mary Magdalene came and told the disciples that she had seen the*
Lord, and that he had spoken these things unto her.

—John 20:11-18 KJV

Something fascinating happened during this spectacle. A woman found herself searching for the body of her Lord at the garden tomb. As she did, she saw someone she assumed was the gardener. "Please tell me where you laid Him." Finally, this individual said to her, "Mary." "Rabboni!" she responded. Why bring this story up? Well, Jesus was in the middle of the largest celebration in all of history up to that time. He was leading the parade to heaven! Suddenly, He must have had to stop everything. Someone who loved Him was pulling on Him. Mary desired to see Him so intensely that she interrupted His party by her longing faith. She pulled Him out of the realm of the Spirit and into the natural. How do we know? Because Jesus said, "Do not cling to me, for I haven't ascended to My Father." Wow! This proves she interrupted His planned ascension. A vital understanding can be gained through this—when we do things in faith that line up with God's Word, like taking Him at His promise, there is something special that happens.

Much like the story of Mary, there are moments we can stretch our faith based on His Word. Through this, tremendous things can happen.[3]

In the case of Edom and Bozrah, it is possible that Jesus was once again on His way, leading another procession of saints and angels toward earth. The people, pressed by their enemies, called upon Him during His descent, and He made a detour for them. We can only speculate, but one thing we do know is that the battle of Edom will be a powerful display of Jesus and His fierce actions in defense of His people.

THE END OF AN AGE

At the end of each age, there is a cataclysmic bang before the next one begins. In the Church Age, it will end when Jesus returns; He will defeat all His enemies and the enemies of His Church. He will cast them all into eternal judgment. However, before this happens, there is a fascinating time when the Lord will establish His earthly kingdom here on earth, from Jerusalem, and from there He will reign over the entire world.

There will be no sickness, no war; there will be peace on earth for 1,000 years, and this kingdom will know no end. Jesus will reign as King of kings and Lord of lords from this place, but even that is not the final kingdom; it will be the staging ground for the ultimate kingdom. His last kingdom will extend far into eternity, and we will be with Him forever!

This opening chapter is a snapshot of what we can expect at the return of Jesus. In the next chapter, to better understand the ultimate end and eternity future, we will journey to the beginning. Eternity past.

CHAPTER TWO

ANCIENT EARTH AND LUCIFER'S FLOOD

Understanding the end of the age must be predicated on the beginning of the world. We know Jesus will return at the end and restore everything; however, much remains to be accomplished between that imminent moment and the time leading up to it. I want to examine the beginning of the world from two perspectives: Old Earth Theory and Young Earth Theory. Regardless of the conclusions one might reach, we can discover the plan God has had for man all along, as well as the nefarious plot by darkness to prevent humanity's highest purpose. As we look into eternity past and consider the two main views on Earth's age, remember that we have been engaged in a cosmic war since the very beginning of creation.

Personally, it has been fascinating and revelatory to grasp the ancient world that was, as the narratives repeat themselves.

THERE IS NOTHING NEW UNDER THE SUN!

That which has been is what will be, that which is done is what will be done, and there is nothing new under the sun. 10 *Is there anything of which it may be said, "See, this is new"? It has already been in ancient times before us.* [11] *There is no remembrance of former things, nor will there be any remembrance of things that are to come by those who will come after.*

—Ecclesiastes 1:9-11

It is remarkable that scripture clearly states that there is nothing new under the sun, and that this has been true since ancient times. If you allow the magnitude of that statement to settle in your mind, it has profound ramifications.

Could it be that all the civilization we see today is only a repeat of times long forgotten by humanity? Could it be that there is far more hidden and lost to antiquity than we can fathom? Well, according to Ecclesiastes 1:10, that is indeed the case.

NO REMEMBRANCE OF THE FORMER THINGS

There is no remembrance of former things, nor will there be any remembrance of things that are to come….

—Ecclesiastes 1:11

Startling is the only word I can use to describe the statement that *there is no remembrance of the former things*. When you couple this with that whole passage in Ecclesiastes, we can take away the understanding that there have been many things in ancient times we will likely never know about until we are in the eternity future with the Lord. Yet we can consider what is said through clues and insights gleaned from glimpses through the keyholes of Scripture and ancient writings.

THE SECRET THINGS BELONG TO THE LORD—CONCEALED THINGS ARE MEANT TO BE SEARCHED OUT

The secret things belong to the Lord our God, but those things which are revealed belong to us and to our children forever, that we may do all the words of this law.

—Deuteronomy 29:29

God has chosen to keep a category of knowledge and insights to Himself; they are called the "secret things." Secret things are His; no one will discover them unless the Lord chooses to reveal them. There is another category hidden with the Lord, but He offers it to those who seek Him in this matter; this category is marked as "concealed things."

> *It is the glory of God to conceal a matter, but the glory of kings is to search out a matter.*
>
> —Proverbs 25:2

God has designated certain things as accessible for extraction. Studying and understanding the Word of God and knowing who He truly is through it will reveal these things. A process of revelation unfolds through the study of Scripture and the power of the Holy Spirit. Still, no revelation or understanding can ever contradict the counsel of the Word of God. It is our plumb line, our standard and canon by which we measure our entire life and understanding. An important scripture on the subject that I often recite to myself and others when speaking or writing is 1 Corinthians 4:6 NIV, which says, "...to not go beyond what is written."

Crucial is the conviction that we who grapple with anything involving speculation or insights that rest on so little data as to not add to what is actually written. There is safety in this discipline and in life. Having said this, we can delve into what is written and areas of conjecture; we state it as such. What is thrilling is the treasure hunting to discover what the Lord would like us to bring to light as we search the rich depths of Scripture and His heart in it all. Now, let us begin looking at a time long before us—the creation of the world.

OLD EARTH OR YOUNG EARTH?

Much ink has been spilled on the debate over whether the earth is old or young. Is the earth millions or even billions of years old? Or is it only six thousand years old? Let's explore the arguments for each. The Old Earth and

Young Earth viewpoints are not issues of salvation, nor are they considered heresy. The information presented in this chapter aims to help you understand the different perspectives on both scenarios. Ultimately, it is up to you to seek guidance and conduct your own research to make an informed decision about what you believe.

OLD EARTH CREATIONISM

Old Earth Creationism is the idea that God created the universe and everything in it over a long period of time. Old Earth creationists place the creation event at approximately 13.7 billion years ago, thus being more in line with "mainstream" science, at least on this point.[1] In Genesis 1–2, during the creation account, the Bible lists what was created each day over the course of six days, and God rested on the seventh day. The word "day" in these verses, in Hebrew, is *yom,* and is defined as *a day (as the warm hours), whether literal (from sunrise to sunset, or from one sunset to the next), or figurative (a space of time defined by an associated term).*[2]

> ***A thousand years** in your sight are like a **day** that has just gone by, or like a watch in the night.*
>
> —Psalm 90:4 NIV

> *But do not forget this one thing, dear friends: With the Lord a **day** is like a **thousand years**, and a **thousand years** are like a **day**.*
>
> —2 Peter 3:8 NIV

Old Earth creationists use Psalm 90:4 and 2 Peter 3:8 to say that the word "day" in the creation scenario represents a thousand years. When Genesis 1–2 describes the different days and states that creation took place over six days, some speculate that the creation story occurred over thousands or possibly billions of years rather than in six days.

This thought process has some inconsistencies. For example, if this process for the word "day" were applied to other scriptures, then Jesus would have been in the grave for 2,000 years. This is indeed a vital argument. Yet this does not dismiss the point; it simply means we must look at the context in which and how it is being used.

THE GAP THEORY

> *In the beginning God created the heavens and the earth.* [2] *Now the earth was formless and empty, darkness was over the surface of the deep, and the Spirit of God was hovering over the waters.*
>
> —Genesis 1:1-2 NIV

There is a term called "Gap Theory" that has been controversial in the Christian community, yet it has staggering ramifications. This theory is based on Genesis 1:1-2. It's a viewpoint that holds that a long time elapsed between Genesis 1:1 and Genesis 1:2. During this period, God created a fully functional earth, filled with animals, including dinosaurs. Genesis 1:2 says, "Now the earth was formless and empty…." The theory suggests that a cataclysmic event occurred, destroying the previous earth and leaving it as the "formless and empty" earth. This event could have been the fall of Lucifer, now Satan, to earth.

LUCIFER'S ROLE

> *You were in Eden, the garden of God; every precious stone adorned you: carnelian, chrysolite and emerald, topaz, onyx and jasper, lapis lazuli, turquoise and beryl. Your settings and mountings were made of gold; on the day you were created they were prepared.* [14] ***You were anointed as a guardian cherub****, for so I ordained you. You were on the holy mount of God; you walked among the fiery stones.*
>
> —Ezekiel 28:13-14 NIV

Many Christian scholars and traditions interpret Ezekiel 28:13-14 as referring to Lucifer. Verse 14 shows that he was anointed and ordained as a guardian cherub. Looking at Genesis 3, when Satan tempts Eve to eat the forbidden fruit, it's evident that at this point, Lucifer had already fallen and was full of rage and hate toward the new human race. The timeframe in Genesis indicates that the fall of Lucifer occurred between Genesis 1:1 and 1:2.

Before his fall, Lucifer was the highest-ranking cherub, governing the earth in harmony with God. The exact length of time Lucifer remained in this position before he fell into sin is unknown. According to Ezekiel 28:14, Lucifer walked on *the holy mount of God* and among *the fiery stones*. Some suggest the holy mount of God refers to Mount Hermon. This is the same mountain on which the fallen angels descended before taking an oath to marry human wives (*see* the extra-biblical texts Enoch 6 and 7). Another idea is that the mountain of God represents a place of divine presence and authority. This is often associated with the heavenly realm, where God's throne is believed to be located.

When discussing "fiery stones," some argue that they could be planets or even an early primal world in the process of formation, characterized by volcanic activity and molten rock across the entire planet; however, I believe that when referring to "fiery stones," it symbolizes Lucifer's role in governing a thriving and resource-rich civilization under divine law.

LUCIFER WAS COVERED IN PRECIOUS STONES

Lucifer was adorned with every precious stone: carnelian, chrysolite and emerald, topaz, onyx and jasper, lapis lazuli, turquoise and beryl. His settings and mountings were made of gold. Ezekiel 28:12 says that Lucifer was "the seal of perfection, full of wisdom and perfect in beauty." To say he was bedazzled is an understatement. Some believe that his body was adorned with musical instruments.

This notion comes from Ezekiel 28:13 in the King James Version, which says, "...the workmanship of *thy tabrets and of thy pipes* was prepared in thee in the day that thou wast created."

- Tabrets are small drums, similar to tambourines, that were common in ancient times.

- Pipes refer to wind instruments, such as flutes or pipes, and are used by blowing air through them to create a sound.

It can't be said with certainty that his body bore instruments, yet the image can be inferred from these scriptures.

LUCIFER, THE WORSHIP LEADER IN HEAVEN

Another idea that is often discussed but not mentioned in Scripture is that Lucifer, before his fall, was the worship leader in heaven. This thought is drawn from Ezekiel 28:13 and other scriptures, demonstrating that angels continually worship God. It could be said that, since Lucifer held a high-ranking position and was adorned with beauty and wisdom, his potential as a worship leader could have helped him persuade one-third of heaven to leave their assigned places and rebel against the One True Living God. (*See* Revelation 12:3-9.)

THE REBELLION AND FALL

> *You were **blameless** in your ways from the day you were created till **wickedness** was found in you.*
> *16 Through your widespread trade you were filled with **violence** and you sinned. So I drove you in disgrace from the mount of God, and I expelled you, guardian cherub, from among the fiery stones.*
> *17 Your heart became **proud** on account of your beauty, and you **corrupted** your wisdom because of your splendor. So I threw you to the earth; I made a spectacle of you before kings.*
> *18 By your **many sins** and **dishonest trade** you have desecrated your sanctuaries....*
>
> —Ezekiel 28:15-18 NIV

Ezekiel 28:15-18 employs key words to describe Lucifer before his fall and then afterward. Verse 15 begins by stating that he was *blameless* in all he did. "The term 'blameless' refers to a state of moral integrity and uprightness, where an individual is free from guilt or fault in the eyes of God and man."[3]

The next set of words describes the opposite of blameless. Verse 15 continues and says, "till *wickedness* was found in you." Another commentary describes wickedness as follows: "Wickedness goes way past being naughty or mischievous; it means a quality of true evil."[4]

TRUE EVIL AND VIOLENCE

Verse 16 says he was full of *violence*, which led him to sin. The definition of "violence" from Merriam-Webster is *the use of physical force so as to injure, abuse, damage, or destroy.*[5] Continuing in verse 17, Lucifer became *proud* because of his beauty. To be "proud" is to *feel pleased about something good that you possess or have done.*[6] Lucifer loved himself so much.

He was proud of his gems, tabrets, and pipes. He loved looking at himself, and this brought forth a very ugly pride, which brought corruption to his wisdom. The KJV Dictionary Definition of "corrupt" means *to change from a sound to a putrid or putrescent state.*[7] Lucifer became so full of pride that it corrupted his wisdom. According to this definition, his wisdom became putrid and putrescent. That's strong.

LUCIFER HAD A LOVE OF MONEY AND WAS FILLED WITH GREED

Verse 18 continues by saying, "By your *many sins* and *dishonest trade* you have desecrated your sanctuaries." When someone is consumed by evil, violence, hate, and pride, corruption inevitably follows. The fruit of these brings forth many sins, and it comes out in the way someone lives. In Lucifer's case, he operated in dishonest trade. In his position, he exploited his role and abused it.

WHEN AND WHERE WAS LUCIFER INVOLVED IN DISHONEST TRADE BEFORE HIS FALL?

A question should come to mind for anyone reading this: When did Lucifer have control over trade? The context here refers to a time before Lucifer was cast out or fell. This strongly suggests a time before Adam and supports the idea of an old earth.

GREED WAS AN ISSUE THAT MADE LUCIFER WANT TO BE LIKE GOD HIMSELF!

> *How you are fallen from heaven, O Lucifer, son of the morning! How you are cut down to the ground, you who weakened the nations!* [13] *For you have said in your heart: "I will ascend into heaven, I will exalt my throne above the stars of God; I will also sit on the mount of the congregation on the farthest sides of the north;* [14] *I will ascend above the heights of the clouds, I will be like the Most High."* [15] *Yet you shall be brought down to Sheol, to the lowest depths of the Pit.*
>
> —Isaiah 14:12-15

Once Lucifer was filled with corruption and iniquity was found in him, he concluded that he wanted to be like God. As seen in Isaiah 14:13, Lucifer said in his heart, "I will ascend into heaven, I will exalt my throne above the stars of God; ...[14] ...I will be like the Most High." He was so self-absorbed and filled with greed that he truly believed he could be like God.

This indicates that self-centeredness can blur the distinction between truth and falsehood. There was absolutely no way he could ever be like God; yet he still believed it and transgressed.

Once Lucifer had violated his position and sin was found in him, God stepped in and removed him from his place of guardianship and his assigned roles. Isaiah 14:15, "Yet you shall be brought down to Sheol, to the lowest depth of the Pit," leads me to believe that the moment Lucifer sinned, hell was created. This is likely why the creation of hell was a reaction to Lucifer's action.

THE HORRIFIC FATE OF SATAN

> *...So I made a fire come out from you, and it consumed you, and I reduced you to ashes on the ground in the sight of all who were watching.*
>
> —Ezekiel 28:18 NIV

Ezekiel 28:18 reveals the action that God immediately took once Lucifer, now Satan, rebelled and was full of sin. Like previously stated, hell was created, and Satan was cast out of heaven. After this, one-third of the angels in heaven joined him. They believed a lie over the truth, and their judgment is imprisonment for their sin (*see* 2 Peter 2:4).

> *And He said to them, "I saw Satan fall like lightning from heaven."*
>
> —Luke 10:18

We know that Jesus was there when Satan was thrown out of heaven. In Luke 10:18, Jesus tells His disciples that He saw *Satan fall like lightning.* Jesus' saying this echoes the ancient overthrow of Satan. Imagine the sight of him being cast out. According to Jesus' description of him as falling like lightning, this could have resembled a meteor or a falling star. Isaiah 14:12 NIV describes Satan as the "morning star," so it is highly possible that he fell at the speed of lightning and looked like a falling star.

A FIRE CAME FROM WITHIN LUCIFER, WHICH LIKELY BURNED AWAY HIS GLORY

> *Those who see you will gaze at you, and consider you, saying: "Is this the man who made the earth tremble, who shook kingdoms, [17] who made the world as a wilderness and destroyed its cities, who did not open the house of his prisoners?" [18] All the kings of the nations, all of them, sleep in glory, everyone in his own house; [19]* ***But you are cast out of your grave like an abominable branch, like the garment of those who are slain, thrust through with a sword, who go down to the stones of the pit, like a***

> ***corpse trodden underfoot.*** [20] *You will not be joined with them in burial, because you have destroyed your land and slain your people. The brood of evildoers shall never be named.*
>
> —Isaiah 14:16-20

> *All the nations who knew you are appalled at you; you have come to a horrible end and will be no more.*
>
> —Ezekiel 28:19 NIV

When considering the large picture, Satan has a judgment awaiting him that everyone will see, revealing his true nature. Alternatively, it may be that the ancient world saw him for who he was—stripped of glory and fallen like ashes after a fire erupted from within him, burning away his original state.

Considering the term "Lucifer" and the image of fire rising from within him is a striking picture. This fire, which manifested internally, represents judgment, as fire often does throughout Scripture. As I read this passage, I believe the fire that rose from within Lucifer was God's judgment on his actions and against his glory. Let me explain. The fire that arose was consuming, affecting his person and stripping him of his glorious visage. In simpler terms, the fire burned away Lucifer's glory, reducing him to what these people were commenting on. His appearance was shocking in comparison to his actions. They were expecting to see a mighty, horrifying, warlike being arrayed in tremendous power and presence. All who gazed upon Lucifer, now demoted by fire, were astonished at what he was not!

COMMENTS OF THOSE WHO SEE HIM IN HIS DEMOTED STATE

> *...Is this the man who made the earth tremble, who shook kingdoms,* [17] *who made the world as a wilderness and destroyed its cities, who did not open the house of his prisoners?*
>
> —Isaiah 14:16-17

These verses reveal that the eyes of those viewing Satan's demise will be surprised at his presence, emphasizing "Is this really the one?" Could it be that his appearance is far different from his grand and extravagant jeweled body at the beginning of time? According to Isaiah 14:19, he will be treated like an *abominable branch*, a *garment of those who are slain, thrust through with a sword*, and like *a corpse trodden underfoot*. All of these describe a pitiful and possibly disturbing appearance. It's safe to say that the image of the devil will be one of disgust and revelation. Revelation of the fact that he truly is nothing and is a defeated foe.

Again, a point must be considered: according to Isaiah 14:17, when it says the devil made the world a wilderness and destroyed its cities, this may well point to a time from eternity past—a reference to the world that was—an old earth.

FINAL DESTINATION–THE LAKE OF FIRE

> *The devil, who deceived them, was cast into the lake of fire and brimstone where the beast and the false prophet are. And they will be tormented day and night forever and ever.*
>
> —Revelation 20:10

The devil's final judgment will be the eternal torment in the lake of fire. When he is thrown into eternity's punishment, he will never be able to tempt, harm, or threaten anyone ever again! When the evil that came into his heart to become as God happened, the verdict was made, hell was created, and his future fate was set in place.

EARTH AFTER ANCIENT JUDGMENT AND DESTRUCTION

> *Now the earth **was** formless and empty, darkness was over the surface of the deep, and the Spirit of God was hovering over the waters.*
>
> —Genesis 1:2 NIV

After the fall of Satan and his being cast out of heaven, many suggest that God destroyed the pre-Adamic earth. According to Genesis 1:2, *the earth was formless and empty.* The word "was" is the Hebrew word *hayah,* which means *to be, become, come to pass, exist, or happen.*

This same word is used in Exodus 9:24, which says, "So there *was* hail, and fire mingled with the hail, so very heavy that there *was* none like it in all the land of Egypt since it *became* a nation." Notice the italicized words. Three times in this verse, *hayah* is used. Twice for the word "was" and once for the word "became."

Another example using the same Hebrew word comes from Genesis 19:26: "But his wife looked back behind him, and she became a pillar of salt." Lot's wife "became" a pillar of salt. This is the same word Finis Dake interprets the word "was," used in Genesis 1:2, as the word "became." Because of this, Dake holds that the previous earth *became* formless and empty.[8] Thus, considerable proof of a world before the creation of the new earth.

GEOLOGICAL TIME SCALE AND EARTH'S AGE

When examining the timeline in relation to the gap theory, it is essential to consider geologists' views on the age of the earth. We can't say for certain how old the earth is; however, I believe it is relevant to outline the process by which geologists test and make decisions from their perspective. The following is a process known as Radiometric Age Dating.

RADIOMETRIC AGE DATING

> Radiometric dating calculates an age in years for geologic materials by measuring the presence of a short-life radioactive element, e.g., carbon-14, or a long-life radioactive element plus its decay product, e.g., potassium-14/argon-40. The term applies to all methods of age determination based on nuclear decay of naturally occurring radioactive isotopes.
>
> —Bates and Jackson (1984)

> To determine the ages in years of earth materials and the timing of geologic events such as exhumation and subduction, geologists utilize the process of radiometric decay. Geologists use these dates to further define the boundaries of the geologic periods shown on the geologic time scale. Radiometric decay occurs when the nucleus of a radioactive atom spontaneously transforms into an atomic nucleus of a different, more stable ***isotope***. This transformation happens via the emission of particles such as electrons (known as beta decay) and alpha particles.[9]

DATING FOSSILS

Through radiometric dating, they have found fossils ranging from 10,000 years old to nearly 4 billion years old. The oldest fossils found to date are the stromatolites. The Invertebrate Paleontology Collection features a stromatolite, which is approximately 3.4 billion years old. They believe this fossil represents some of the earliest life on the planet.[10]

GEOLOGIC TIME SCALE

Another method that is used to determine the age of the earth is the Geologic Time Scale. "The Geologic Time Scale or Geological Time Scale (GTS) is a representation of time based on rock record of earth. It is a system of chronological dating that uses chronostratigraphy (the process of relating strata to time) and geochronology (a scientific branch of geology that aims to determine the age of rocks). The time scale has been developed through the study of rock layers and the observation of their relationships, and identifying features such as lithologies, paleomagnetic properties, and fossils."[11]

Due to these processes, geologists and some scientists estimate that the earth is approximately 4.5 billion years old.[12] There are certainly arguments that challenge modern science and the way it determines the age of these objects. Yet, what if science and the Bible aligned on these issues? It would be astonishing and bring clarity to many issues that, at times, seem problematic regarding Scripture and the age of the earth.

PRE-ADAMIC ERA

Not only do some conclude that dinosaurs roamed the earth during the gap theory timeframe, but some also believe in a pre-Adamic era. The pre-Adamic era is a theological concept referring to the period preceding the biblical account of Adam. This theory proposes that intelligent creatures, or people, existed before Adam.

REPLENISH THE EARTH OR BUILD IT UP AGAIN

> *And God blessed them, and God said unto them, Be fruitful, and multiply, and* ***replenish*** *the earth, and subdue it: and have dominion over the fish of the sea, and over the fowl of the air, and over every living thing that moveth upon the earth.*
>
> —Genesis 1:28 KJV

Genesis 1:28 is used to argue the point of a pre-Adamic race. According to Genesis 1:28 in the King James Version, the Lord told Adam and Eve to "replenish" the earth. The word "replenish" means *to fill or build up again.*[13] The keyword is "again."

They take this understanding and say if they are filling up again, then there were people or beings before Adam and Eve. This is a strong argument; however, we will further discuss this verse when we examine the Young Earth Theory.

KALAMBO STRUCTURE

There is a theory about a previous civilization that predates conventional views of human history, which might be supported by an ancient artifact recently discovered. One of the oldest wooden structures is the Kalambo structure. Scientists have determined that this structure is at least 476,000 years old and predates Homo sapiens (humans). Excavations at Kalambo

Falls in 1950s and 1960s recovered wooden artifacts of possible hominin origin (members of the taxonomic tribe that includes modern humans and extinct species). The discovery was considered unusual because wood does not usually survive for so long. The structure consists of two interlocking wooden logs of large-fruited bushwillow connected by a notch securing one perpendicular to the other. The structure probably would have been part of a wooden platform used as a walkway, to keep food or firewood dry, or perhaps as a base on which to build a dwelling. The discovery could indicate that the hominins who lived at Kalambo Falls may have had a settled lifestyle, which could challenge the prevailing view that Stone Age hominins had a nomadic lifestyle.[14]

GOBEKLI TEPE

Another example of a possible society that existed before Genesis 1:2 is Göbekli Tepe. Göbekli Tepe is the megalithic settlement perched on a mountain ridge in Upper Mesopotamia, what is now southeastern Turkey. The Neolithic site, which translates to "belly hill" in Turkish, is two times older than Stonehenge and contains a series of elaborate circular enclosures constructed of massive T-shaped limestone columns. Many of the pillars feature intricate carvings of abstract symbols and wild animals, including lions, foxes, gazelles, and birds. This discovery not only challenged what we thought we knew about ancient human civilizations but also revealed that hunter-gatherers were more than simply nomadic people. In fact, they were innovative enough to use advanced architectural techniques, such as using geometric patterns to mastermind and execute the construction.[15]

The Kalambo structure and Göbekli Tepe are two examples of ancient structures. Based on the scientific and geological methods used to determine the age and possible origin of such structures from antiquity, the theory of an Old Earth seems plausible. However, this is based on the evidence from these tests and not on the Bible. It is certainly interesting and prompts one to wonder what else may await discovery.

THE FLOOD OF LUCIFER

According to the gap theory, a fully developed world was destroyed due to Satan's rebellion, and a flood must have been the source of destruction. Some believe the pre-Adamic world was flooded, which is why the world was left "without form, and void; and darkness was on the face of the deep" (*see* Genesis 1:2). According to this idea, this would answer the question, "What happened to the dinosaurs?" The term "Lucifer's flood" refers to this phenomenon, which differs from the flood during the time of Noah. According to some, the following is believed to be true:

> Noah's flood is taught to have been a localized and somewhat tame affair, since all the sedimentary rocks and fossils found on the earth today are the result of Lucifer's flood. Proponents of the gap theory, therefore, teach that the sedimentary rocks and fossils are the result of a universal, cataclysmic flood, not mentioned anywhere in the Bible, rather than the global flood of Noah's day to which three whole chapters of Genesis are devoted.
>
> Furthermore, the only universal cataclysmic flood referred to in the New Testament is Noah's flood. Jesus referred to it in Matthew 24:37-39, and Peter referred to it in 2 Peter 3:5-7. But no reference to the so-called Lucifer's flood is found anywhere in the New Testament.[16]

FINIS DAKE'S INSIGHT ON LUCIFER'S FLOOD

I wanted to include Finis Dake's thoughts on the Luciferian flood and Noah's flood. Before his words, I included the scriptures he references:

> *How you are fallen from heaven, O Lucifer, son of the morning! How you are cut down to the ground, you who weakened the nations!* [13] *For you have said in your heart: I will ascend into heaven, I will exalt my throne above the stars of God; I will also sit on the mount of the congregation*

on the farthest sides of the north; 14 *I will ascend above the heights of the clouds, I will be like the Most High.*

—Isaiah 14:12-14

For thus says the Lord, who created the heavens, who is God, who formed the earth and made it, who has established it, who did not create it in vain, who formed it to be inhabited: "I am the Lord, and there is no other."

—Isaiah 45:18

I beheld the earth, and indeed it was without form, and void; and the heavens, they had no light. 24 *I beheld the mountains, and indeed they trembled, and all the hills moved back and forth.* 25 *I beheld, and indeed there was no man, and all the birds of the heavens had fled.* 26 *I beheld, and indeed the fruitful land was a wilderness, and all its cities were broken down at the presence of the Lord, by His fierce anger.*

—Jeremiah 4:23-26

Moreover the word of the Lord came to me, saying, 12 *"Son of man, take up a lamentation for the king of Tyre, and say to him, 'Thus says the Lord God: "You were the seal of perfection, full of wisdom and perfect in beauty.* 13 *You were in Eden, the garden of God; every precious stone was your covering: the sardius, topaz, and diamond, beryl, onyx, and jasper, sapphire, turquoise, and emerald with gold. The workmanship of your timbrels and pipes was prepared for you on the day you were created.* 14 *You were the anointed cherub who covers; I established you; you were on the holy mountain of God; you walked back and forth in the midst of fiery stones.* 15 *You were perfect in your ways from the day you were created, till iniquity was found in you.* 16 *By the abundance of your trading you became filled with violence within, and you sinned; therefore I cast you as a profane thing out of the mountain of God; and I destroyed you, O covering cherub, from the midst of the fiery stones.* 17 *Your heart was lifted up because of your beauty; you corrupted your wisdom for the sake of your splendor; I cast you to the ground, I laid you before kings, that they might gaze at you."'"*

—Ezekiel 28:11-17

For this they willfully forget: that by the word of God the heavens
were of old, and the earth standing out of water and in the water, 6 by
which the world that then existed perished, being flooded with water.
7 But the heavens and the earth which are now preserved by the same
word, are reserved for fire until the day of judgment and perdition of
ungodly men.

—2 Peter 3:5-7

The earth was without form, and void; and darkness was on the face of the deep. And the Spirit of God was hovering over the face of the waters.

—Genesis 1:2

You who laid the foundations of the earth, so that it should not be moved
forever, 6 You covered it with the deep as with a garment; the waters stood
above the mountains. 7 At Your rebuke they fled; at the voice of Your
thunder they hastened away. 8 They went up over the mountains; they
went down into the valleys, to the place which You founded for them. 9
You have set a boundary that they may not pass over, that they may not
return to cover the earth.

—Psalm 104:5-9

For an unknown period, there was an original social system on this earth ruled by Lucifer as proved in (Isaiah 14:12-14; 45:18; Jeremiah 4:23-26; Ezekiel 28:11-17; 2 Peter 3:5-7). Along with this original social system there were land animals, birds, fish, and other creatures created, and they were destroyed in the flood of Genesis 1:2, Psalm 104:5-9; 2 Peter 3:5-7. It is to this period that all fossils and remains of animals belong, as well as geological formations of the earth.

Between these original creations of God, "In the beginning' and the creations of the six days, is revealed the rule of Lucifer on the earth for an unknown period, his rebellion against God, the Earth's first sinful career, the defeat of Lucifer by God, and the overthrow of his kingdom by the first recorded flood on the earth in Genesis 1:2. Lucifer was the first ruler on the earth and he already had his period of earth rule and his fall by the time of Adam.

...Noah's flood, which occurred much later, did not completely destroy the earth, shake mountains, turn them upside down, turned off the stars and the sun so that there was no light. God had already created the Heavens, they were in existence as well as the earth only their lights were withheld from shining on the earth thus causing darkness Genesis 1:2. There was no darkness during Noah's flood? There were men and animals on the earth before Noah's flood, and Noah and his family and the animals survived the flood and were on the earth after it?

That the earth ONLY was (became) without form and void (Hebrew ***tohu vabobu,*** literally waste and ruin or desolate and empty), as in Genesis 1:2. That there were mountains of earth that were shaken and turned upside down by the earthquake so severe, which no doubt caused the remains of animals to be deposited in the very depths of the earth beneath many layers of solid rock, such as are now been found. Noah's flood never buried animals hundreds of meters beneath solid rock.

...The earth was turned upside down, a process which caused all the present formations of the earth. The flood remained on the earth for an unknown period of time, and then God in six days restored the earth to a habitable state and made Adam and Eve and his creation to carry out the original plan of God concerning the earth (Genesis 1:3-2:25).

There were two floods which destroyed the earth! The first destroyed it completely, the second not. Noah, his family and animals were not destroyed. Also the light, sun moon and stars remained shining upon the earth.

God did destroy the earth and flood it as Scripture plainly shows, there was Lucifer's flood, and Noah's flood. Noah's flood was worldwide because the only people left were Noah and his family who were on the ark with him. The purpose of Noah's flood was to destroy all mankind including the giants.

There are definite contrasts between the flood of Lucifer Genesis 1:2, and the flood of Noah. The two floods are completely different floods and occurred at different times. The first, Lucifers flood is the flood of the earth "That then was." Noah's flood was on the earth "That now is."[17]

LUCIFER'S FLOOD DESTROYED EARTH, LEAVING IT WITHOUT FORM AND VOID. NOTHING WAS LEFT—ONLY DARKNESS!

The difference between Lucifer's flood and Noah's flood is how the earth was left in the wake of each.

- After Lucifer's flood, the earth was left *without form and void*. Nothing was there, only *darkness*. The Lord had to create everything for the world to function fully again.
- The scenario was different after Noah's flood. The water receded, and the earth was ready for Noah and his family to repopulate the world.

Old Earth creationism and the gap theory can be studied in greater depth. I have included a few points to illustrate how they arrived at these understandings. Please do your own research and let the scriptures guide you through these theories.

In the following chapter, I will expound on the topic of the Young Earth.

CHAPTER THREE

YOUNG EARTH CREATIONIST THEORY

In the beginning God created the heavens and the earth.

—Genesis 1:1

Young Earth creationism (YEC) is the belief that God directly created the universe in six literal days and that the earth is relatively young.[1] They believe the age of earth is between 6,000 and 10,000 years. Young Earth creationists interpret Genesis 1 as a timeline of Earth's creation. In Genesis 1, God created the heavens and the earth, along with everything in them, in six days.

> *Now the earth was formless and empty, darkness was over the surface of*
> *the deep, and the Spirit of God was hovering over the waters.* 3 *And God*
> *said, "Let there be light," and there was light.* 4 *God saw that the light*
> *was good, and he separated the light from the darkness.* 5 *God called the*
> *light "day," and the darkness he called "night." And there was evening,*
> *and there was morning—the first day.* 6 *And God said, "Let there be a*
> *vault between the waters to separate water from water."* 7 *So God made*
> *the vault and separated the water under the vault from the water above*
> *it. And it was so.* 8 *God called the vault "sky." And there was evening,*
> *and there was morning—the second day.* 9 *And God said, "Let the water*

under the sky be gathered to one place, and let dry ground appear." And it was so. [10] God called the dry ground "land," and the gathered waters he called "seas." And God saw that it was good. [11] Then God said, "Let the land produce vegetation: seed-bearing plants and trees on the land that bear fruit with seed in it, according to their various kinds." And it was so. [12] The land produced vegetation: plants bearing seed according to their kinds and trees bearing fruit with seed in it according to their kinds. And God saw that it was good. [13] And there was evening, and there was morning—the third day. [14] And God said, "Let there be lights in the vault of the sky to separate the day from the night, and let them serve as signs to mark sacred times, and days and years, [15] and let them be lights in the vault of the sky to give light on the earth." And it was so. [16] God made two great lights—the greater light to govern the day and the lesser light to govern the night. He also made the stars. [17] God set them in the vault of the sky to give light on the earth, [18] to govern the day and the night, and to separate light from darkness. And God saw that it was good. [19] And there was evening, and there was morning—the fourth day. [20] And God said, "Let the water teem with living creatures, and let birds fly above the earth across the vault of the sky." [21] So God created the great creatures of the sea and every living thing with which the water teems and that moves about in it, according to their kinds, and every winged bird according to its kind. And God saw that it was good. [22] God blessed them and said, "Be fruitful and increase in number and fill the water in the seas, and let the birds increase on the earth." [23] And there was evening, and there was morning—the fifth day. [24] And God said, "Let the land produce living creatures according to their kinds: the livestock, the creatures that move along the ground, and the wild animals, each according to its kind." And it was so. [25] God made the wild animals according to their kinds, the livestock according to their kinds, and all the creatures that move along the ground according to their kinds. And God saw that it was good. [26] Then God said, "Let us make mankind in our image, in our likeness, so that they may rule over the fish in the sea and the birds in the sky, over the livestock and all the wild animals, and over all the creatures that move along the ground." [27] *So God created mankind in his own image, in the image of God he created them; male and female he created them.* [28] *God blessed them and said to them, "Be fruitful and increase in number; fill the earth and subdue it. Rule over the fish in the sea and the birds in the sky and over every living creature that moves on the ground."* [29] *Then God said, "I give you every seed-bearing plant on the face of the whole earth and every tree that has fruit with seed in it. They will be yours for food.* [30] *And to all the beasts of the earth and all the birds in the sky and all the creatures that move along the ground—everything that has the breath of life in it—I give every green plant for food." And it was so.* [31] *God saw all that he had made, and it was very good. And there was evening, and there was morning—the sixth day.*

—Genesis 1:2-31 NIV

A LITERAL 24-HOUR DAY

Young Earth creationists interpret a day as a literal 24-hour period. Throughout Genesis 1, God created specific things each day for six consecutive days. On the seventh day, He rested. The word "day" in these verses is the same Hebrew word *yom*, and it means *day (24-hour period) as defined by evening and morning* in Genesis 1.[2]

REPLENISH THE EARTH

And God blessed them, and God said unto them, Be fruitful, and multiply, and ***replenish*** *the earth, and subdue it: and have dominion over the fish of the sea, and over the fowl of the air, and over every living thing that moveth upon the earth.*

—Genesis 1:28 KJV

> *Then God blessed them, and God said to them, "Be fruitful and multiply;* ***fill*** *the earth and subdue it; have dominion over the fish of the sea, over the birds of the air, and over every living thing that moves on the earth."*
>
> —Genesis 1:28

As mentioned in a previous chapter, Genesis 1:28 is used by Old Earth creationists to argue that it proves the existence of a pre-Adamic society. The word "fill" is the Hebrew word *mâlê',* and it means *to fill* or *to be full.* "The English translators of the King James Version knew the word means 'to fill.' They chose 'replenish' because, in 17th-century Elizabethan English, 'replenish' meant 'to fill' (similar to how in modern English the word 'replete' doesn't mean to 'abound again,' it simply means 'abundant' or 'abounding'). Language is not static, but dynamic. Words change meaning over time. Today, 'replenish' means 'to fill again.' It didn't mean the same thing in 17th-century England. Nearly all modern translations translate *mâlê'* as simply 'fill' in the passage in question (Genesis 1:28)."[3]

Based on this information, Young Earth creationists argue that human life began with Adam and Eve and that there was no pre-Adamic race before them.

GENEALOGIES

The genealogies in Genesis 5–11, Matthew 1, and Luke 3 are used to estimate the age of the earth. By summing the ages of the individuals listed in these chapters, from Adam to Jesus, the timeframe is approximately 4,000 years. From the birth of Jesus to the present, the period spans slightly more than 2,000 years. This is how YECs conclude that the earth is roughly 6,000 years old.

LUCIFER'S FALL

According to the 6,000-year-old timeline, the fall of Lucifer occurred sometime on the sixth day of creation, before God created Adam and Eve. According to the 24-hour timeframe, from the moment the last animal was created until God breathed into Adam, there are a few hours left in that day when Lucifer fell.

> *Then God saw everything that He had made, and indeed it was very good. So the evening and the morning were the sixth day.*
>
> —Genesis 1:31

Another possible theory is that Lucifer rebelled after the sixth day of creation, when God saw that everything was good, and before he tempted Eve in the Garden of Eden in Genesis 3. The timeframe for this idea is unknown and speculative at best. Some suggest it could have been as little as a couple of hours or as long as 30 years; this range is based on the assumption that Adam was around 30 years old when Cain was born. This idea appears in non-canonical texts, such as the book of Jubilees. It is also suggested that Adam and Eve did not have their first child until after they were banished from the garden. The fall of Lucifer would have occurred within that time.

LUCIFER AS THE SERPENT

> *Now* ***the serpent was more cunning*** *than any beast of the field which the Lord God had made. And he said to the woman, "Has God indeed said, 'You shall not eat of every tree of the garden'?"* [2] *And the woman said to the serpent, "We may eat the fruit of the trees of the garden;* [3] *but of the fruit of the tree which is in the midst of the garden, God has said, 'You shall not eat it, nor shall you touch it, lest you die.' "* [4] *Then the serpent said to the woman, "You will not surely die.* [5] *For God knows that in the day you eat of it your eyes will be opened, and you will be like God, knowing good and evil."*
>
> —Genesis 3:1-5

Genesis 3:1 describes the serpent as the most cunning beast of the field. The word "cunning" means *clever, in the sense of trickery. A cunning plan might involve setting traps for the innocent and pure at heart to fall into.*[4] Before the serpent tempted Eve, there was no sin in the world, only innocence. The serpent was called cunning because it was already possessed by Satan himself. The fact that the serpent spoke with Eve indicates that Satan was controlling it, because animals cannot speak. Another example in scripture of an animal speaking is the story of Balaam's donkey. In this situation, the Lord opened the mouth of the donkey in order to confront Balaam for his ignorance (*see* Numbers 22:22-38). It's evident that the serpent's mouth was controlled by something.

DID THE ANIMALS SPEAK?

> *And on that day was closed the mouth of all beasts, and of cattle, and of birds, and of whatever walks, and of whatever moves, so that they could no longer speak: for they had all spoken one with another with one lip and with one tongue.*[5]
>
> —Book of Jubilees 3:28

There is a theory that all the animals in the garden could speak. According to the extra-biblical book of Jubilees 3:28, all the animals in the garden were able to speak before Adam and Eve were banished. Another idea that supports this is that Eve wasn't surprised when the serpent spoke to her. Could it be that all the animals spoke?

Eve wasn't startled or disturbed; instead, she conversed with it. This is an interesting and thought-provoking argument. Even with this in mind, Satan would have still been controlling what the serpent said because, as previously stated, up to this point, there was no sin. Only Lucifer would have been the one to have iniquity in him. Also, when referencing a book outside the Bible, I do not place it here as an authority but a point of consideration. The Bible is the final authority, and books such as *Jubilees* or *Enoch* are interesting and should be treated as commentary rather than as authoritative.

WHAT ABOUT THE AGE OF FOSSILS?

> *Also for Adam and his wife the LORD God made tunics of skin, and clothed them.*
>
> —Genesis 3:21

> *Therefore, just as through one man sin entered the world, and death through sin, and thus death spread to all men, because all sinned.*
>
> —Romans 5:12

Young Earth Creationism holds that fossils appeared after Noah's flood. Genesis 3:21 shows that the first animal death was at God's hand, when He made clothes from animal skins. This death symbolizes the first sacrifice for sins.

Romans 5:12 is often cited to show that there was no death before Adam and Eve sinned. Just as sin entered through one man, so did death. This verse can be applied to all living things. Fossils represent death. When the fossil timeline is applied to these two scriptures, the oldest fossil would be younger than the assumed age of the earth, which YECs estimate at 6,000-10,000 years. They also conclude that Noah's flood caused the formation of most fossils, leaving them buried in sedimentary rock layers.

FALLEN ANGELS AND THE CORRUPTION

> *Now it came to pass, when men began to multiply on the face of the earth, and daughters were born to them, 2 that the sons of God saw the daughters of men, that they were beautiful; and they took wives for themselves of all whom they chose.*
>
> —Genesis 6:1-2

When looking at the flood in Genesis, it's wise to examine why the flood was sent. The book of Enoch shares a narrative similar to that of Genesis 6. Although the book of Enoch is not canonical, it is a pseudepigraphical work. This means it's a collection of ancient Jewish religious writings. Yet it is helpful to consider this commentary.

> *And it came to pass when the children of men had multiplied that in those days were born unto 2 them beautiful and comely daughters. And*

> *the angels, the children of heaven, saw and lusted after them, and said to one another: 'Come, let us choose us wives from among the children of men [3] and beget us children.' And Semjaza, who was their leader, said unto them: 'I fear ye will not [4] indeed agree to do this deed, and I alone shall have to pay the penalty of a great sin.' And they all answered him and said: 'Let us all swear an oath, and all bind ourselves by mutual imprecations [5] not to abandon this plan but to do this thing.' Then sware they all together and bound themselves [6] by mutual imprecations upon it. And they were in all two hundred; who descended in the days of Jared on the summit of Mount Hermon, and they called it Mount Hermon, because they had sworn [7] and bound themselves by mutual imprecations upon it.*
>
> —1 Enoch 6:1-7

> *And all the others together with them took unto themselves wives, and each chose for himself one, and they began to go in unto them and to defile themselves with them, and they taught them charms [2] and enchantments, and the cutting of roots, and made them acquainted with plants. And they [3] became pregnant, and they bare great giants, whose height was three thousand ells: Who consumed [4] all the acquisitions of men. And when men could no longer sustain them, the giants turned against [5] them and devoured mankind. And they began to sin against birds, and beasts, and reptiles, and [6] fish, and to devour one another's flesh, and drink the blood. Then the earth laid accusation against the lawless ones.*[6]
>
> —1 Enoch 7:1-6

WATCHERS AND NEPHILIM

When comparing the story in Genesis 6 to 1 Enoch 6–7, the book of Enoch provides more information about the angels, also known as the Watchers, who took the women as wives and created giants. The giants, known as

Nephilim, were described as each being three thousand ells tall. That would be approximately 4,500 feet tall!

Two hundred angels left their assigned positions. They sought to corrupt the original "seed." They were on a mission to take the pure things God had created and make their own race and kind of created beings. Thus, the Nephilim were created. These creatures devoured everything that men produced. It is said that the people couldn't keep up with the giants' appetites. First Enoch 7:4-6 says that they turned against men and began to eat them. They also took the animals and drank their blood.

> *And it came to pass when the children of men began to multiply on the face of the earth and daughters were born unto them, that the angels of God saw them on a certain year of this jubilee, that they were beautiful to look upon; and they took themselves wives of all whom they chose, and they bare unto them sons and they were giants.* 2 *And lawlessness increased on the earth and all flesh corrupted its way, alike men and cattle and beasts and birds and everything that walks on the earth -all of them corrupted their ways and their orders, and they began to devour each other, and lawlessness increased on the earth and every imagination of the thoughts of all men (was) thus evil continually.*[7]
>
> —Book of Jubilees 5:1-2

Another pseudepigraphical work we already referenced is the book of Jubilees, also known as the "Lesser Genesis," "Little Genesis," or "The Testament of Moses." These writings include the story of the angels of God taking beautiful women as wives. It then says *that lawlessness increased on the earth and that all flesh corrupted its way*. This corruption affected both humankind and animals. Not only were the offspring of the angels tainted, but the animals were as well.

The "corruption" mentioned in the book of Jubilees 5:2 is similar to 1 Enoch 7:5-6, which says, "And they began to sin against birds, and beasts, and reptiles, and fish, and to devour one another's flesh, and drink the blood.

Then the earth laid accusation against the lawless ones." Some believe that these giants committed bestiality, which brought forth corrupted flesh among animals. This is what "sin against" could represent. Another form of taking the pure things that God created and mutating them into monstrous beings.

DEFILEMENT BY WITCHCRAFT

> *And all the others together with them took unto themselves wives, and each chose for himself one, and they began to go in unto them and to defile themselves with them, and they taught them charms* [2] *and enchantments, and the cutting of roots, and made them acquainted with plants.*
>
> —1 Enoch 7:1-2

Not only did these fallen angels commit vile atrocities, but they also taught women witchcraft. This defiled the original plan God set forth. Lucifer is not an originator but a thief and a perverter of anything pure. These evil companions took what the Lord had established and taught women forbidden knowledge, specifically about natural elements. This opened the door to the practice of witchcraft, sorcery, and illicit manipulation of both the natural and spiritual worlds.

Charms and *enchantments* were part of a body of secret knowledge believed to be practiced in witchcraft, including the introduction of magic, spells, and occult practices used to manipulate others through spiritual or psychological means.

The cutting of roots acquainted with plants refers to the use of plants and roots for forbidden purposes, such as potion-making and pharmacology. They created concoctions, love potions, aversions, and dangerous drugs, including hallucinogens. They taught how to make poison to cause physical harm or death to the recipient, and they taught mystical practices that used substances to induce an altered state to connect with evil spirits or perform magic.

This knowledge, along with other "technologies" such as metallurgy and cosmetics, exposed humanity to spiritual deception, idolatry, and moral corruption. These led the world into deep impiety and violence, furthering their plan to destroy the God-ordained purpose of bringing Jesus onto the scene. This rebellious horde of angels sought something unnatural and created a perversion of all that is natural, holy, and pure.

DESTRUCTION BY THE FLOOD OF NOAH

> *Then the Lord saw that the wickedness of man was great in the earth, and that every intent of the thoughts of his heart was only evil continually.* [6] *And the Lord was sorry that He had made man on the earth, and He was grieved in His heart.* [7] *So the Lord said, "I will destroy man whom I have created from the face of the earth, both man and beast, creeping thing and birds of the air, for I am sorry that I have made them."*
>
> —Genesis 6:5-7

After the angels, also known as the "sons of God," procreated with women, violated the animals, and introduced witchcraft, God sent destruction. As Genesis 6:5-7 reveals, man was full of sin. In fact, it says, "The thoughts of his heart was only evil continually."

God had examined each man's heart and found it continually evil. First Samuel 16:7 says, "But the Lord said to Samuel, 'Do not look at his appearance or at his physical stature, because I have refused him. For the Lord does not see as a man sees; for man looks at the outward appearance, but the Lord looks at the heart.'" The Lord had looked over the face of the whole earth to find someone who was not only pure in heart but also pure in his DNA. Remember, the angels desired to corrupt the seed, thus altering the original DNA.

The book of Jubilees continues the narrative about the angels and their offspring. It's an interesting extra-biblical read. I have included the entire section from the book of Jubilees 5.

And it came to pass when the children of men began to multiply on the face of the earth and daughters were born unto them, that the angels of God saw them on a certain year of this jubilee, that they were beautiful to look upon; and they took themselves wives of all whom they chose, and they bare unto them sons and they were giants. [2] *And lawlessness increased on the earth and all flesh corrupted its way, alike men and cattle and beasts and birds and everything that walks on the earth -all of them corrupted their ways and their orders, and they began to devour each other, and lawlessness increased on the earth and every imagination of the thoughts of all men (was) thus evil continually.* [3] *And God looked upon the earth, and behold it was corrupt, and all flesh had corrupted its orders, and all that were upon the earth had wrought all manner of evil before His eyes.* [4] *And He said that He would destroy man and all flesh upon the face of the earth which He had created.* [5] *But Noah found grace before the eyes of the Lord.* [6] *And against the angels whom He had sent upon the earth, He was exceedingly wroth, and He gave commandment to root them out of all their dominion, and He bade us to bind them in the depths of the earth, and behold they are bound in the midst of them, and are (kept) separate.* [7] *And against their sons went forth a command from before His face that they should be smitten with the sword, and be removed from under heaven.* [8] *And He said 'My spirit shall not always abide on man; for they also are flesh and their days shall be one hundred and twenty years'.*

[9] *And He sent His sword into their midst that each should slay his neighbour, and they began to slay each other till they all fell by the sword and were destroyed from the earth.* [10] *And their fathers were witnesses (of their destruction), and after this they were bound in the depths of the earth for ever, until the day of the great condemnation, when judgment is executed on all those who have corrupted their ways and their works before the Lord.* [11] *And He destroyed all from their places, and there was not left one of them whom He judged not according to all their wickedness.* [12] *And he made for all his works a new and righteous nature, so*

that they should not sin in their whole nature for ever, but should be all righteous each in his kind alway. [13] *And the judgment of all is ordained and written on the heavenly tablets in righteousness -even (the judgment of) all who depart from the path which is ordained for them to walk in; and if they walk not therein, judgment is written down for every creature and for every kind.*

[14] *And there is nothing in heaven or on earth, or in light or in darkness, or in Sheol or in the depth, or in the place of darkness (which is not judged); and all their judgments are ordained and written and engraved.*
[15] *In regard to all He will judge, the great according to his greatness, and the small according to his smallness, and each according to his way.*
[16] *And He is not one who will regard the person (of any), nor is He one who will receive gifts, if He says that He will execute judgment on each: if one gave everything that is on the earth, He will not regard the gifts or the person (of any), nor accept anything at his hands, for He is a righteous judge.*

[17] *[And of the children of Israel it has been written and ordained: If they turn to him in righteousness He will forgive all their transgressions and pardon all their sins.* [18] *It is written and ordained that He will show mercy to all who turn from all their guilt once each year.]* [19] *And as for all those who corrupted their ways and their thoughts before the flood, no man's person was accepted save that of Noah alone; for his person was accepted in behalf of his sons, whom (God) saved from the waters of the flood on his account; for his heart was righteous in all his ways, according as it was commanded regarding him, and he had not departed from aught that was ordained for him.* [20] *And the Lord said that he would destroy everything which was upon the earth, both men and cattle, and* [21] *beasts, and fowls of the air, and that which moveth on the earth. And He commanded Noah to make him an ark, that he might save himself from the waters of the flood.* [22] *And Noah made the ark in all respects as He commanded him, in the twenty-seventh jubilee of years, in the fifth week in the fifth year (on the new moon of*

the first month). [1307 A.M.] [23] *And he entered in the sixth (year) thereof, [1308 A.M.] in the second month, on the new moon of the second month, till the sixteenth; and he entered, and all that we brought to him, into the ark, and the Lord closed it from without on the seventeenth evening.*

[24] *And the Lord opened seven flood-gates of heaven, and the mouths of the fountains of the great deep, seven mouths in number.* [25] *And the flood-gates began to pour down water from the heaven forty days and forty nights, and the fountains of the deep also sent up waters, until the whole world was full of water.* [26] *And the waters increased upon the earth: Fifteen cubits did the waters rise above all the high mountains, and the ark was lift up above the earth, and it moved upon the face of the waters.* [27] *And the water prevailed on the face of the earth five months -one hundred and fifty days.* [28] *And the ark went and rested on the top of Lubar, one of the mountains of Ararat.* [29] *And (on the new moon) in the fourth month the fountains of the great deep were closed and the flood-gates of heaven were restrained; and on the new moon of the seventh month all the mouths of the abysses of the earth were opened, and the water began to descend into the deep below.*

[30] *And on the new moon of the tenth month the tops of the mountains were seen, and on the new moon of the first month the earth became visible.* [31] *And the waters disappeared from above the earth in the fifth week in the seventh year [1309 A.M.] thereof, and on the seventeenth day in the second month the earth was dry.* [32] *And on the twenty-seventh thereof he opened the ark, and sent forth from it beasts, and cattle, and birds, and every moving thing.*[8]

—Book of Jubilees 5:1-32

As previously mentioned, the book of Jubilees is not part of the biblical canon. However, it is a fascinating ancient text that can be valuable for study, much like an old commentary. It offers additional insight into the fallen angels, their eternal punishment, the destruction of their offspring, and the flood of Noah.

NOAH PLEASED GOD BY HAVING PURE BLOOD AND UNTAINTED DNA

> *The earth also was corrupt before God, and the earth was filled with violence. [12] So God looked upon the earth, and indeed it was corrupt; for all flesh had corrupted their way on the earth. [13] And God said to Noah, "The end of all flesh has come before Me, for the earth is filled with violence through them; and behold, I will destroy them with the earth."*
>
> —Genesis 6:11-13

God looked to and fro. He scanned the whole earth, seeking flesh that was not corrupted. That's when He found Noah and his family. Genesis 6:9 states, "...Noah was a just man, perfect in his generations. Noah walked with God." It is safe to say that the truth behind these verses is that Noah and his family were the only ones whose bloodline or DNA was untainted. For God to bring forth Jesus, He had to take drastic measures and destroy the earth and all forms of corruption against humanity. This is why He sent the Flood.

HOW WERE THERE NEPHILIM AFTER THE FLOOD?

> *There were **giants on the earth in those days, and also afterward**, when the sons of God came in to the daughters of men and they bore children to them. Those were the mighty men who were of old, men of renown.*
>
> —Genesis 6:4

> *And they gave the children of Israel a bad report of the land which they had spied out, saying, "The land through which we have gone as spies is a land that devours its inhabitants, and all the people whom we saw in it are **men of great stature**. [33] There we saw **the giants** (the descendants of Anak came from the giants); and we were like grasshoppers in our own sight, and so we were in their sight."*
>
> —Numbers 13:32-33

Many question how the Nephilim continued to live after the Flood. There are several theories about how the Nephilim reappeared.

- One theory holds that a dormant Nephilim gene was carried by one of Noah's sons' wives on the ark and was later reawakened. However, this idea contradicts the purpose of the Flood.
- Another theory comes from extra-biblical traditions, such as the Targum Pseudo-Jonathan, which suggests that giants, including King Og, survived the Flood by clinging to the ark or by being protected in a special region of the land.
- One final idea worth mentioning is that after the Flood, some of the "sons of God" again engaged in forbidden relationships with human women, producing a new generation of "Nephilim." There are other ideas on the subject, but I don't feel it necessary to list them all.

CONCLUSION

The thief does not come except to steal, and to kill, and to destroy. I have come that they may have life, and that they may have it more abundantly.

—John 10:10

Lucifer and the fallen angels have tried throughout history to corrupt and destroy all things that God created.

John 10:10 says *he comes to steal, kill, and destroy*. Thankfully, we have the Father in heaven who brings *abundant life*. The great mission began at the beginning of time, and this cosmic battle in the heavens and on earth has raged since the creation of the earth, among the young and the old.

We can take comfort in Revelation 13:8, which says, "of the Lamb slain from the foundation of the world." Jesus was the plan from the very beginning: the "Last Adam" to bring salvation to those who will call upon Him.

I hope this provides insight into the difference between Old Earth and Young Earth for your consideration. I can see both points of view and am personally inclined toward the Old Earth. However, we won't know it all until we are with the Lord.

> *Dear reader, you are the reason for the cosmic battle that has raged since the beginning of time. God has been fighting for you and making a way for you from the very beginning. My purpose in walking you through the concepts that preceded us is to provide insight into the intense war we were part of before we were born.*

There is so much more to come!

CHAPTER FOUR

CATACLYSMIC TRANSITIONS THROUGHOUT HISTORY

> *Having made known to us the mystery of His will, according to His good pleasure which He purposed in Himself,* [10] *that in* ***the dispensation of the fullness of the times*** *He might gather together in one all things in Christ, both which are in heaven and which are on earth—in Him.*
>
> —Ephesians 1:9-10

On the road to the Endgame of nations, we see a cycle of cataclysmic changes. Transition points bring the preceding age to a world-shaking end! From the beginning of recorded biblical history to the end of Revelation, at every turn, something earth-shattering occurs. This offers hope that our present evil age will eventually change, ushering us into a glorious future with the Lord at its head.

It is essential to understand these times and seasons—both what has been and what will be—as they equip the believer to live in accordance with God's plan. This understanding enables the believer to learn from antiquity, discern the present signs of the times, and keep a watchful eye toward the future.

THE FULLNESS OF TIMES

Let's look at the basic understanding of what Ephesians 1:10 refers to as, "…the dispensation of *the fullness of the times*…."

According to the *IVP Bible Background Commentary,* it was a common Jewish belief that history progressed through many stages to its climax, when everything would be brought under God's rule. Some philosophers argued that the whole universe was permeated by God and would be absorbed back into Him.

Like Jewish writers who adapted the language of such philosophers, Paul believes that history moves toward a climax of subordination to God, not absorption into Him. The Old Testament and Judaism recognized that God had a sovereign plan in history to bring it to this climax.[1] A climax that we are coming toward quickly.

SEGMENTS OF TIME AND TEMPORARY KINGDOMS ALLOTTED FOR MANKIND

> *Then comes the end, when He delivers the kingdom to God the Father, when He puts an end to all rule and all authority and power. 25 For He must reign till He has put all enemies under His feet. 26 The last enemy that will be destroyed is death. 27 For "He has put all things under His feet." But when He says "all things are put under Him," it is evident that He who put all things under Him is excepted. 28 Now when all things are made subject to Him, then the Son Himself will also be subject to Him who put all things under Him, that God may be all in all.*
>
> —1 Corinthians 15:24-28

> *And* ***the world is passing away****, and the lust of it; but he who does the will of God abides forever.*
>
> —1 John 2:17

> *Those who use the things of the world, as if not engrossed in them. For* ***this world in its present form is passing away****.*
>
> —1 Corinthians 7:31 NIV

One word that best describes the world we live in is *temporary*. Even as we see the world in its present form, it is destined to pass away. In the same manner, all the kingdoms of man that we are affected by will one day bow the knee to Jesus, and He will establish His reign on the earth from Jerusalem. He will rule with those washed in His blood who followed His call and remained loyal to Him. Many of these wicked leaders and influential figures on today's global stage have no comprehension that their time is like a vapor—here today, gone tomorrow—and that the very memory of them will someday be no more. Not so with Jesus. He is coming to establish an eternal kingdom that will endure.

THE FULLNESS OF TIMES WILL COME IN THE FINAL ERA

The fullness of the times refers to the completion of what can be referred to as probationary times throughout the history of the earth. The fullness of the times will come in the final era, when the Lord Jesus establishes His kingdom on earth and reigns throughout the last dispensation of man in the Millennium. Jesus will reign for the purpose of ridding the earth of all wicked rebellion and restoring God's complete administration over His kingdom. The restoration will reestablish His Kingdom as it was before the mutinous rebellion started.[2]

PREVIOUS AGES, OR DISPENSATIONS EACH ENDING WITH A CATACLYSMIC BANG!

1. The **Age of Innocence** ended with Adam and Eve being cast out of the garden (Genesis 1:28–3:1-19).
   a) Time Period—Creation to the Fall.

   b) Key Characteristics—Humanity in a sinless state in Eden; direct communion with God.
   c) Divine Test/Stewardship—Obey God's command not to eat from the tree of the knowledge of good and evil (Genesis 2:16-17).
   d) Human Responsibility—Fill the earth, subdue it, have dominion over creation, tend the garden (Genesis 1:28; 2:15).
   e) Failure—Disobedience by Adam and Eve, tempted by Satan (Genesis 3:1-6).
   f) Judgment/Transition—Expulsion from Eden, introduction of sin and death (Genesis 3:14-24).
2. The **Age of Conscience** ends with the flood. Nephilim? (Genesis 3:23–8:19)
   a) Time Period—The fall to the flood.
   b) Key Characteristics—Moral awareness without formal law; humanity guided by an internal sense of right and wrong; increasing wickedness.
   c) Divine Test/Stewardship—Approach God through blood sacrifices in light of conscience (Genesis 4:4); live morally.
   d) Human Responsibility—Do all known good, abstain from all known evil (Genesis 4:7).
   e) Failure—Widespread corruption and violence (Genesis 6:5, 11-12).
   f) Judgment/Transition—Global Flood; Noah's family preserved (Genesis 6–8).
3. The **Age of Human Government** ends with the Tower of Babel and the confusion of language (Genesis 8:20–11:9).
   a) Time Period—The Flood to the Tower of Babel.
   b) Key Characteristics—First post-Flood era; God institutes civil authority and capital punishment to restrain sin.
   c) Divine Test/Stewardship—Govern society justly; execute judgment for murder (Genesis 9:5-6).
   d) Human Responsibility—Multiply and replenish the earth; submit to God-delegated authority (Genesis 9:1, 7).

e) Failure—Rebellion at Babel through unified idolatry and pride (Genesis 11:1-4).

f) Judgment/Transition—Confusion of languages; scattering of nations (Genesis 11:5-9).

4. The **Age of Promise** ends with the Exodus from Egypt (Genesis 11:10–Exodus 19:4).

   a) Time Period—Abraham to Exodus.

   b) Key Characteristics—God's covenants with Abraham, Isaac, and Jacob; focus on faith and family/nation-building.

   c) Divine Test/Stewardship—Trust in God's promises without law (Genesis 12:1-3; 15:6).

   d) Human Responsibility—Walk by faith; separate from the world (Genesis 17:1; Hebrews 11:8-10).

   e) Failure—Slavery in Egypt; idolatry and unbelief (Genesis 37: Joseph sold into slavery; Exodus 1).

   f) Judgment/Transition—Bondage in Egypt; call of Moses and giving of the Law (Exodus 1–19).

5. The **Age of Law** ends with the death and resurrection of Jesus Christ (Exodus 19:5–John 19:30).

   a) Time Period—Exodus to the Cross.

   b) Key Characteristics—Mosaic Covenant; Israel as a theocracy under the Ten Commandments and ceremonial laws.

   c) Divine Test/Stewardship—Obey the full Law as a standard of holiness (Exodus 20:1-17; Deuteronomy 28).

   d) Human Responsibility—Keep the commandments; offer sacrifices for sin (Leviticus 1–7).

   e) Failure—Repeated idolatry, rebellion (e.g., golden calf, Judges cycle, exile).

   f) Judgment/Transition—Crucifixion of Christ; end of sacrificial system (Matthew 27; Hebrews 10:1-18).

6. The **Age of Grace** ends with the Rapture of the Church (John 19:31–Revelation 3:22).
   a) Time Period—Pentecost to the Rapture.
   b) Key Characteristics—The Church era; salvation by grace through faith in Christ's finished work; indwelling Holy Spirit.
   c) Divine Test/Stewardship—Believe in Christ for salvation; spread the gospel (Ephesians 2:8-9; Matthew 28:19-20).
   d) Human Responsibility—Walk in the Spirit; love God and others (Galatians 5:16; John 13:34-35).
   e) Failure—Apostasy and worldliness within the Church (2 Timothy 3:1-5; Revelation 2–3).
   f) Judgment/Transition—Rapture of the Church; transition to Tribulation (1 Thessalonians 4:16-17).
7. The **Age of Divine Government, the Millennium** ends after the 1,000-year period (Revelation 20:1-10).
   a) Time Period—Second Coming to the End of Eternity.
   b) Key Characteristics—Christ's literal 1,000-year reign on earth from Jerusalem; Satan bound; fulfillment of the Davidic Covenant.
   c) Divine Test/Stewardship—Obey the King (Christ) in a restored paradise (Isaiah 11:1-9; Revelation 20:4-6).
   d) Human Responsibility—Rule under Christ; live righteously in a theocratic kingdom (Zechariah 14:16-19).
   e) Failure—Final rebellion led by Satan after release (Revelation 20:7-9).
   f) Judgment/Transition—Great White Throne Judgment; new heaven and earth (Revelation 20:11-15; 21:1).
8. **The Last Kingdom**—Eternity Future
   a) Revelation 22:5—"There shall be no night there: They need no lamp nor light of the sun, for the Lord God gives them light. *And they shall reign forever and ever.*" This represents eternity future.

We know what the end of our dispensation will bring, according to Matthew 24.

SIGNS OF THE END OF THIS AGE

Now as He sat on the Mount of Olives, the disciples came to Him pri-
vately, saying, "Tell us, when will these things be? And what will be the
sign of Your coming, and of the end of the age?" 4 *And Jesus answered*
and said to them: "Take heed that no one deceives you. 5 *For many will*
come in My name, saying, 'I am the Christ,' and will deceive many. 6 *And*
you will hear of wars and rumors of wars. See that you are not troubled;
for all these things must come to pass, but the end is not yet. 7 *For nation*
will rise against nation, and kingdom against kingdom. And there will
be famines, pestilences, and earthquakes in various places. 8 *All these are*
the beginning of sorrows. 9 *Then they will deliver you up to tribulation*
and kill you, and you will be hated by all nations for My name's sake. 10
And then many will be offended, will betray one another, and will hate
one another. 11 *Then many false prophets will rise up and deceive many.*
12 *And because lawlessness will abound, the love of many will grow cold.*
13 *But he who endures to the end shall be saved.* 14 *And this gospel of the*
kingdom will be preached in all the world as a witness to all the nations,
and then the end will come."

—Matthew 24:3-14

LIST OF BIRTH PANGS

In Matthew 24:3-14, Jesus gives a detailed list of the birth pangs that will precede the end of the age. These are prophetic signs we are to be aware of. Once we begin to see these signs, we know that the end is near. The birth pangs are listed as follows:

1. Take heed that no one deceives you.
2. You will hear of wars and rumors of wars.
3. False christs will rise to deceive many.
4. Nation will rise against nation.

5. Kingdom against kingdom.
6. Famines.
7. Pestilences.
8. Earthquakes.
9. Tribulation against believers.
10. Hated by all nations for the name of Jesus.
11. Many offended.
12. Betraying one another.
13. Hating one another.
14. False prophets will arise to deceive many.
15. Lawlessness will abound, causing the hearts of many to grow cold.

In Matthew 24:13, Jesus exhorts that *he who endures to the end will be saved.* The gospel of the kingdom will be preached to the ends of the earth, and then the end will come.

> *And: "You, Lord, in the beginning laid the foundation of the earth, and the heavens are the work of Your hands.* [11] *They will perish, but You remain; and they will all grow old like a garment;* [12] *Like a cloak You will fold them up, and they will be changed. But You are the same, and Your years will not fail."*
>
> —Hebrews 1:10-12

The earth will eventually need to be completely redone, and it will remain in that state forever. Much like a garment that has been washed repeatedly, it will eventually wear out. This means that the earth will need to be done away with and recreated.

JESUS MADE THE WORLD, ALSO KNOWN AS AGES AND DISPENSATIONS

> *God, who at various times and in various ways spoke in time past to the fathers by the prophets,* [2] *has in these last days spoken to us by His Son,*

> *whom He has appointed heir of all things, through whom also He made the worlds.*
>
> —Hebrews 1:1-2

Hebrews 1:1-2 refers to the Voice of God speaking in various ways throughout different ages. When you read the phrase, "He made the worlds," the word "worlds" really means *ages, times,* or *dispensations*. God spoke in various ways throughout the ages, or segments of time allotted to man.

The word for "worlds" or "world" in the Greek is *aion,* meaning *age—a period of time,* whether long or short.[3]

Additional scriptures that use the word *aion*:

> *Anyone who speaks a word against the Son of Man, it will be forgiven him; but whoever speaks against the Holy Spirit, it will not be forgiven him, either in this age or in the* ***age*** *to come.*
>
> —Matthew 12:32

> *The enemy who sowed them is the devil, the harvest is the end of the* ***age****, and the reapers are the angels.*
>
> —Matthew 13:39

> *That in the* ***ages*** *to come He might show the exceeding riches of His grace in His kindness toward us in Christ Jesus.*
>
> —Ephesians 2:7

> *The mystery which has been hidden from* ***ages*** *and from generations, but now has been revealed to His saints.*
>
> —Colossians 1:26

ALL THINGS WERE MADE THROUGH JESUS

> *In which you once walked according to the course of this* ***world****, according to the prince of the power of the air, the spirit who now works in the sons of disobedience.*
>
> —Ephesians 2:2

In Ephesians 2:2, the Greek word *aion* is the word "world." I also want to note that the word "course" shows that Christ was the agent in planning the ages and in carrying out God's plan for humanity. In this sense, He is the everlasting Father (*see* Isaiah 9:6). He not only planned the ages but also all creation.

Scriptures that show that Jesus took part in creation:

> ***All things were made through Him****, and without Him nothing was made that was made.*
>
> —John 1:3

> *He is the image of the invisible God, the firstborn over all creation.* [16] ***For by Him all things were created*** *that are in heaven and that are on earth, visible and invisible, whether thrones or dominions or principalities or powers. All things were created through Him and for Him.* [17] *And He is before all things, and in Him all things consist.* [18] *And He is the head of the body, the church, who is the beginning, the firstborn from the dead, that in all things He may have the preeminence.*
>
> —Colossians 1:15-18

> *And to make all see what is the fellowship of the mystery, which from the beginning of the ages has been hidden in God* ***who created all things through Jesus Christ****.*
>
> —Ephesians 3:9

FOURTEEN BIBLICAL EXPRESSIONS RELATING TO THE LAST DAYS

In Hebrews 1:2, "has in these *last days* spoken to us by His Son, whom He has appointed heir of all things, through whom also He made the worlds," we are shown that we are in the last days and that we are being addressed by the Son of God, Jesus Christ. He is the voice to His Church in the last days. It is an end-time expression when the author of Hebrews uses the phrase "the last days."

1. **Last Days**—The period beginning with the Messiah's first coming (resurrection/ascension) and extending to His Second Coming and beyond.

> *And Jacob called his sons and said, "Gather together, that I may tell you what shall befall you in the* ***last days****."*
>
> —Genesis 49:1

> *And it shall come to pass in the* ***last days****, says God, that I will pour out of My Spirit on all flesh; your sons and your daughters shall prophesy, your young men shall see visions, your old men shall dream dreams.*
>
> —Acts 2:17

> *But know this, that in the* ***last days*** *perilous times will come.*
>
> —2 Timothy 3:1

> *Has in these* ***last days*** *spoken to us by His Son, whom He has appointed heir of all things, through whom also He made the worlds.*
>
> —Hebrews 1:2

2. **Latter Days**—Equivalent to last days, focusing on future restoration and judgment for Israel and nations. This also refers to the establishment of God's eternal kingdom.

> *When you are in distress, and all these things come upon you in the* ***latter days****, when you turn to the* LORD *your God and obey His voice.*
>
> —Deuteronomy 4:30

> *For I know that after my death you will become utterly corrupt, and turn aside from the way which I have commanded you. And evil will befall you*

*in the **latter days**, because you will do evil in the sight of the LORD, to provoke Him to anger through the work of your hands.*

—Deuteronomy 31:29

*Now it shall come to pass in the **latter days** that the mountain of the Lord's house shall be established on the top of the mountains, and shall be exalted above the hills; and all nations shall flow to it.*

—Isaiah 2:2

*But there is a God in heaven who reveals secrets, and He has made known to King Nebuchadnezzar what will be in the **latter days**. Your dream, and the visions of your head upon your bed, were these.*

—Daniel 2:28

*Now I have come to make you understand what will happen to your people in the **latter days**, for the vision refers to many days yet to come.*

—Daniel 10:14

3. **Time of the End**—The final phase of God's redemption plan, marked by increased knowledge and prophetic fulfillment.

*So he came near where I stood, and when he came I was afraid and fell on my face; but he said to me, "Understand, son of man, that the vision refers to the **time of the end**."*

—Daniel 8:17

*And some of those understanding shall fall, to refine them, purify them, and make them white, until the **time of the end**; because it is still for the appointed time.*

—Daniel 11:35

*"But you, Daniel, shut up the words, and seal the book until the **time of the end**; many shall run to and fro, and knowledge shall increase."...* [9]

> *And he said, "Go your way, Daniel, for the words are closed up and sealed till the **time of the end**."*
>
> —Daniel 12:4, 9

4. **End of Days**—The close of the current age, leading to resurrection and judgment. Jesus will return to earth to save humanity from self-destruction.

> *For I know that my Redeemer lives, and He shall stand **at last** on the earth.*
>
> —Job 19:25

> *But you, go your way till the end; for you shall rest, and will arise to your inheritance at the **end of the days**.*
>
> —Daniel 12:13

5. **Day of the Lord**—A specific period of divine intervention, wrath, and salvation beginning with the Tribulation, plagues, and cosmic signs such as a darkened sun and moon. This is God's final reckoning for humanity and the establishment of God's eternal kingdom.

> *For the **day of the Lord** of hosts shall come upon everything proud and lofty, upon everything lifted up—and it shall be brought low.*
>
> —Isaiah 2:12

> *Wail, for the **day of the Lord** is at hand! It will come as destruction from the Almighty.*
>
> —Isaiah 13:6

> *Alas for the day! For the **day of the Lord** is at hand; it shall come as destruction from the Almighty.*
>
> —Joel 1:15

> *Blow the trumpet in Zion, and sound an alarm in My holy mountain! Let all the inhabitants of the land tremble; for the **day of the Lord** is coming, for it is at hand.*
>
> —Joel 2:1

Behold, I will send you Elijah the prophet before the coming of the great and dreadful ***day of the Lord****.*

—Malachi 4:5

For you yourselves know perfectly that the ***day of the Lord*** *so comes as a thief in the night.*

—1 Thessalonians 5:2

But the ***day of the Lord*** *will come as a thief in the night, in which the heavens will pass away with a great noise, and the elements will melt with fervent heat; both the earth and the works that are in it will be burned up.*

—2 Peter 3:10

6. **That Day**—Refers to the climactic day of Christ's return and establishment of His eternal kingdom. This is frequently interpreted as a specific phase of divine intervention rather than a strict 24-hour day, ending with a New Heaven and Earth.

The lofty looks of man shall be humbled, the haughtiness of men shall be bowed down, and the Lord alone shall be exalted in ***that day****.*

—Isaiah 2:11

And in ***that day*** *seven women shall take hold of one man, saying, "We will eat our own food and wear our own apparel; only let us be called by your name, to take away our reproach."*

—Isaiah 4:1

And in ***that day*** *His feet will stand on the Mount of Olives, which faces Jerusalem on the east. And the Mount of Olives shall be split in two, from east to west, making a very large valley; half of the mountain shall move toward the north and half of it toward the south.*

—Zechariah 14:4

7. **Last Time**—The era of final revelation through Christ, contrasting with former times. This period marks the closing phase before the final judgment and restoration.

> *Who are kept by the power of God through faith for salvation ready to be revealed in the* ***last time****. …*[20] *He indeed was foreordained before the foundation of the world, but was manifest in these* ***last times*** *for you.*
>
> —1 Peter 1:5, 20

> *How they told you that there would be mockers in the* ***last time*** *who would walk according to their own ungodly lusts.*
>
> —Jude 1:18

8. **Last Hour**—An urgent warning of the approaching end, linked to apostasy. This signifies a time of heightened spiritual deception, characterized by the appearance of Antichrists, representing the climax of God's redemptive plan.

> *Little children, it is the* ***last hour****; and as you have heard that the Antichrist is coming, even now many antichrists have come, by which we know that it is the* ***last hour****.*
>
> —1 John 2:18

9. **Last Times**—The final phase of human history before entering the eternal state. This represents the last era of humanity prior to divine judgment and the creation of a new, redeemed world.

> *He indeed was foreordained before the foundation of the world, but was manifest in these* ***last times*** *for you.*
>
> —1 Peter 1:20

10. **End of the World** (Age)—The termination of the current dispensation (the Church Age), ushering in the Millennial Kingdom.

> *And in the days of these kings the God of heaven will set up a kingdom which shall never be destroyed; and the kingdom shall not be left to other people; it shall break in pieces and consume all these kingdoms, and it shall stand forever.*
>
> —Daniel 2:44

> *"Teaching them to observe all things that I have commanded you; and lo, I am with you always, even to the* ***end of the age****." Amen.*
>
> —Matthew 28:20

> *He then would have had to suffer often since the foundation of the world; but now, once at the* ***end of the ages****, He has appeared to put away sin by the sacrifice of Himself.*
>
> —Hebrews 9:26

11. **Latter Times**—A variant emphasizing the final outpouring of the Spirit and judgments. The final period before Christ's return is marked by rising apostasy, deception, and moral decay.

> *You will come up against My people Israel like a cloud, to cover the land. It will be in the* ***latter days*** *that I will bring you against My land, so that the nations may know Me, when I am hallowed in you, O Gog, before their eyes.*
>
> —Ezekiel 38:16

> *Now the Spirit expressly says that in* ***latter times*** *some will depart from the faith, giving heed to deceiving spirits and doctrines of demons.*
>
> —1 Timothy 4:1

12. **The End**—The ultimate consummation after tribulation and gospel proclamation. This marks the culmination of the current age, often called the last days or end times, which precedes the return of Jesus Christ, the final judgment, and the earth's renewal into a new divine era.

Although I heard, I did not understand. Then I said, "My lord, what shall be ***the end*** *of these things?"*

—Daniel 12:8

Now as He sat on the Mount of Olives, the disciples came to Him privately, saying, "Tell us, when will these things be? And what will be the sign of Your coming, and of ***the end*** *of the age?"...* [14] *"And this gospel of the kingdom will be preached in all the world as a witness to all the nations, and then* ***the end*** *will come."*

—Matthew 24:3, 14

13. **Time of Trouble**—The Great Tribulation period, a time of unparalleled distress. This is a time marked by unparalleled global persecution and natural disasters, just before the Second Coming of Jesus.

Alas! For that day is great, so that none is like it; and it is the ***time of Jacob's trouble****, but he shall be saved out of it.*

—Jeremiah 30:7

At that time Michael shall stand up, the great prince who stands watch over the sons of your people; and there shall be a ***time of trouble****, such as never was since there was a nation, even to that time. And at that time your people shall be delivered, every one who is found written in the book.*

—Daniel 12:1

For then there will be great tribulation, such as has not been since the beginning of the world until this time, no, nor ever shall be.

—Matthew 24:21

14. **The Day**—A brief term for the day of the Lord or final judgment, referring to a specific period at the end of the age marked by God's judgment, wrath, and justice.

*Alas for the day! For **the day** of the Lord is at hand; it shall come as destruction from the Almighty.*

—Joel 1:15

*Be silent in the presence of the Lord God; for **the day** of the Lord is at hand, for the Lord has prepared a sacrifice; He has invited His guests.*

—Zephaniah 1:7

*Behold, **the day** of the Lord is coming, and your spoil will be divided in your midst.*

—Zechariah 14:1

EIGHT BIBLICAL TRUTHS ABOUT JESUS CHRIST AS THEY RELATE TO THE LAST DAYS

Has in these last days spoken to us by His Son, whom He has appointed heir of all things, through whom also He made the worlds; [3] *who being the brightness of His glory and the express image of His person, and upholding all things by the word of His power, when He had by Himself purged our sins, sat down at the right hand of the Majesty on high.*

—Hebrews 1:2-3

1. Spokesman for God (Hebrews 1:2)
2. Appointed heir of all things (Hebrews 1:2)
3. Planner of the worlds—ages (Hebrews 1:2)
4. Brightness of God's glory (Hebrews 1:3)
5. Express or exact image of God's Person (Hebrews 1:3)
6. Upholder of all creations (Hebrews 1:3)
7. Savior of the world—purged sins (Hebrews 1:3)
8. Ascension and exaltation (Hebrews 1:3)

BELIEVERS ARE HEIRS OF ALL THINGS

> *And if children, then heirs—heirs of God* ***and joint heirs with Christ,*** *if indeed we suffer with Him, that we may also be glorified together.* [18] *For I consider that the sufferings of this present time are not worthy to be compared with the glory which shall be revealed in us.* [19] *For the earnest expectation of the creation eagerly waits for the revealing of the sons of God.*
>
> —Romans 8:17-19

As believers in Jesus, we are joint heirs with Him. What an amazing concept that our Great God would send His only Son and allow us who believe in Him to have not only everlasting life but also to share with Him everything He has attained for eternity. We certainly do not deserve this gift, not at all.

It is a testament to God's gracious and loving nature. Whenever you think about the character and nature of God Almighty, remember what He did through Jesus and what is provided for you in the greatest part of your existence—eternity future. He is so good and gracious, and our response should be: "Thank You, God, for Jesus!"

JOINT HEIRS IF INDEED WE SUFFER WITH HIM

Romans 8:17 states *that we are joint heirs with Christ if indeed we suffer with Him.* Suffering is part of the believer's walk; however, religion has hijacked the word and definition of suffering. In the believer's life, suffering is primarily found in resisting sin. The writer of Hebrews points this out.

> *For consider Him who endured such hostility from sinners against Himself, lest you become weary and discouraged in your souls.* [4] *You have not yet resisted to bloodshed, striving against sin.*
>
> —Hebrews 12:3-4

When we, as believers, walk in this present world, we face many afflictions and trials, which are part of suffering. Persecution is among them, but we must also walk in the revelation that we are delivered from so many issues because of the high price Jesus paid with His own blood.

Hebrews 12:4 says something gripping: "You have not resisted or striven against sin to the point of bloodshed." A believer's mindset must be one of aggressive resistance to sin, even to the point of bloodshed. In this passage, however, we see that the early Church's mindset was to resist sin to the point of death. Resisting sin is part of suffering, which involves denying the flesh, taking up one's cross, and following Jesus.

THE PROMISE OF AN ETERNAL INHERITANCE

> *To open their eyes, in order to turn them from darkness to light, and from the power of Satan to God, that they may receive forgiveness of sins and an* ***inheritance*** *among those who are sanctified by faith in Me.*
>
> —Acts 26:18

> *To an* ***inheritance*** *incorruptible and undefiled and that does not fade away, reserved in heaven for you,* [5] *who are kept by the power of God through faith for salvation ready to be revealed in the last time.*
>
> —1 Peter 1:4-5

We are encouraged to walk worthy of the calling with which we have been called in Jesus. Why? For several reasons, one of which is an eternal future. Knowing that Jesus is preparing an awe-inspiring role for you in the future should bring you joy and drive you to achieve what God has purposed for you, an inheritance with Jesus. Your inheritance is an eternity of reigning with Jesus, and the level of what you will do and the responsibility you will have is determined by how you steward your responsibilities here and now.

CHAPTER FIVE

GOD CORRECTS NATIONS: THE SODOM AND GOMORRAH TEMPLATE

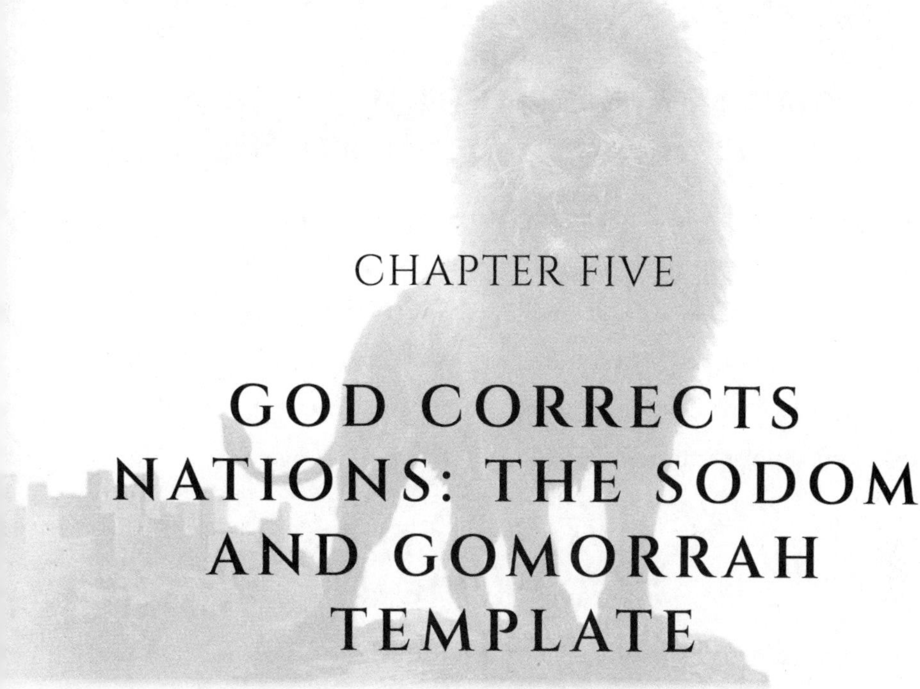

> *Why do the nations rage, and the people plot a vain thing? 2 The kings of the earth set themselves, and the rulers take counsel together, against the Lord and against His Anointed, saying, 3 "Let us break Their bonds in pieces and cast away Their cords from us." 4 He who sits in the heavens shall laugh; the Lord shall hold them in derision. 5 Then He shall speak to them in His wrath, and distress them in His deep displeasure.*
>
> —Psalm 2:1-5

As the days accumulate and we approach the very end, one thing that must be constantly at your attention is that all the nations that capitulate and align with the Antichrist kingdom will experience what I like to call the *Great Rightsizing*. God Almighty and Christ Jesus the Son will smash the kingdom of Antichrist and set the nations in order by bringing them into Christ's 1,000-year Millennial Reign. Much of what will happen during this time will be to correct the damage done to the earth by the wrath poured out upon it during the Tribulation.

GOD DEALS WITH INDIVIDUALS DIFFERENTLY FROM NATIONS

God deals with individuals differently from nations. This means that a person must be saved by repenting of their sins and following Jesus Christ completely. Nations hold a different position before the Lord. Enter the conversation of reformation. A nation's reformation not only entails widespread change that leads to God-based principles but also returns it to, or aligns it with, God's ultimate purpose for that nation.

REVIVAL PRECEDES REFORMATION

In the United States, believers are praying for a revival, and yes, we must have that. Salvation is spreading across the land at an unprecedented rate. As a result, society is being affected by a generational shift driven by the influence of many people proclaiming Jesus across every sector. After a revival takes its course, the next step is reformation. It must be recognized that reformation cannot occur without revival—it is imperative.

> *He will also go before Him in the spirit and power of Elijah, **"to turn the hearts of the fathers to the children,"** and the disobedient to the wisdom of the just, to make ready a people prepared for the Lord.*
>
> —Luke 1:17

In Luke 1:17, we see that the Spirit and power of Elijah come *to turn the hearts of the fathers to the children*, a powerful word for generational merging in the coming move of God. Also, a crucial point often overlooked is that it moves beyond that form of revival to something highly impactful on culture. Luke 1:17 goes on to say that after the hearts of the fathers are turned to the children, *the disobedient are turned to the wisdom of the just, to make ready a people prepared for the Lord.*

DISOBEDIENT TURNED TO THE WISDOM OF THE JUST

The disobedient who turns to the wisdom of the just offers insight into societal change or reformation. As the Word of God makes clear, not all humanity will experience salvation. Jesus said, "The road is narrow, and few are they who find it" (*see* Matthew 7:13-14). However, even if a nation does not see the impact of every individual accepting Jesus Christ as their Savior, it will still be affected by the reformation. How? Through the influence and authority of the land standing in a place that aligns with godly principles. As a result, those who are disobedient and follow their own hearts and way of doing things apart from the Word of God will themselves be under the influence of the just.

Revival, reformation, and the disobedient being turned to the wisdom of the just are all part of preparing the way for the Lord. Or, better said, according to verse 17, it makes ready a people prepared for the Lord. It is not a hard leap to say they are being prepared for the return of Jesus!

GOD HAS DEALT WITH NATIONS THROUGHOUT THE OLD TESTAMENT—AND HE CONTINUES THIS TODAY

Let me use the Lord's dealings with churches as a point of comparison. In Revelation, the seven churches are warned to follow the Word Jesus gives to each of them, or He will come and remove their lampstand. The disobedient church would cease to function. This does not mean that each believer would be cast away from the Lord and cease to be a believer; rather, my point is that God works in corporate settings differently than in the individual.

Israel is another strong example of this. God has made promises to that nation and to the land they are to possess. Even calling the Jewish people God's chosen people does not mean they are automatically born again. Rather, on an individual level, both Jew and Gentile are to receive Jesus Christ as their Savior, or they will not be with Him in eternity. This is why

Peter was sent to the Jews in the New Testament to preach salvation through Jesus Christ.

Additionally, this principle holds true when we consider nations: a person is not individually judged by God for what their nation has done. Rather, an individual will be judged by their personal relationship with Jesus Christ. Nations can indeed suffer the consequences of not following the Lord's system of operation and likewise experience the blessings of following God's principles.

An individual who is a believer in a disobedient nation will experience what the whole nation experiences, no different from a church in Revelation if the lampstand were removed. God wants His individual believers to follow Him regardless of whether the nation or the church to which they belong obeys Him properly.

What is crucial is that the believer knows their role in both the church they attend and serve and in the nation in which they live. We are to be salt and light, bringing the will of Almighty God to pass in every area, even if they are disobedient.

THE SODOM AND GOMORRAH TEMPLATE

When we consider judgment, even wrath on a nation, region, or the like, a compelling example is Sodom and Gomorrah. A civic region that had committed a violation against God to the point that intervention became necessary. It is a template for what happens when a nation or a people group pushes the envelope to a tipping point. Unrepentant and brazen against God to the point of an outcry from victims and those affected by the evil practiced day and night. There are extreme circumstances in which the Lord will be forced to intervene, as was the case in the Sodom and Gomorrah narrative. Upon crossing the line without remorse and harming people to the point of an outcry heard by heaven, their judgment became absolute.

ANGELIC VISITORS ON ASSIGNMENT TO DESTROY SODOM AND GOMORRAH

I will go down now and see whether they have done altogether according to the outcry against it that has come to Me; and if not, I will know.

—Genesis 18:21

For we will destroy this place, because the outcry against them has grown great before the face of the Lord, and the Lord has sent us to destroy it.

—Genesis 19:13

Angelic visitors, on their way to Sodom and Gomorrah, spoke to Abraham, saying, "We will destroy this place because the outcry against them has grown great before the face of the Lord, and the Lord has sent us to destroy it." God heard the outcries, likely from all the victims and those brutalized by these wicked towns. As a result, angels were dispatched to wipe out the villainous inhabitants of those two cities.

The judgment poured out on Sodom and Gomorrah was prompted by the cries of victims and the horrific injustice being perpetrated against the innocent. I want to present to you that, as bad as this breathtaking moment of judgment was upon Sodom and Gomorrah, and even the reality that it was burned off the face of the earth, the world has never experienced a complete outpouring of God's wrath; it has only been caught in glimpses.

Full-tilt, unbridled wrath from God has never been experienced in all of creation, including humanity, and has certainly not encountered the ultimate wrath of God—but they will.

INTENSE JUDGMENT ON SODOM AND GOMORRAH

Then the Lord rained brimstone and fire on Sodom and Gomorrah, from the Lord out of the heavens. 25 *So He overthrew those cities, all the plain, all the inhabitants of the cities, and what grew on the ground.*

—Genesis 19:24-25

So severe was this blast of judgment that nothing remained in Sodom and Gomorrah, not even what grew on the ground. It was a clean sweep; nothing survived. All because the men of Sodom constantly performed wicked deeds.

LOT'S FOOLISH DECISION TO DWELL IN SODOM AND GOMORRAH

Amazingly, Lot may not have known just how evil these men were, and, ignorantly, made this foolish choice to take up his abode among such very wicked men, which occasioned a great deal of grief, trouble, and vexation to Lot; or if he knew it, the prospect of convenience for his cattle and of enriching himself might have tempted him and prevailed over him to take such a treacherous step; whatever the end motivation was for Lot, he was not restrained from dwelling among them, those vile men of Sodom and Gomorrah.

The look on their countenance witnesses against them, and they declare their sin as Sodom; they do not hide it. Woe to their soul! For they have brought evil upon themselves.

—Isaiah 3:9

These men were exceedingly great sinners, guilty of the most heinous and notorious crimes. They were addicted to the most scandalous and unnatural lusts imaginable, and they committed these crimes openly and publicly in the sight of God, in the most daring and vile manner, in direct defiance of God Almighty, without any fear or shame.

The Targum of Jonathan reckons up many of their sins, as defrauding one another in their substance, sinning in their bodies, incest, unclean copulation, shedding of innocent blood, worshiping of idols, and rebelling against the name of the Lord.[1]

WHAT CAUSED THE LORD TO SHARE HIS PLAN FOR SODOM AND GOMORRAH WITH ABRAHAM?

One consideration is that the Lord apparently debated whether to reveal His intentions to Abraham. Here were the reasons God decided to reveal His plans for Sodom and Gomorrah to Abraham.

1. Abraham shall surely become a great and mighty nation, and therefore has the interest of humanity in this act of retribution against Sodom. All that concerns man concerns Him.
2. In Abraham, all the nations of the earth were blessed. Therefore, Abraham would be personally and directly concerned with all the dealings of mercy and judgment among the inhabitants of the earth.
3. God knew Abraham, who was counted a friend of God. "I have known him." The Lord made Himself known to Abraham, manifested His love to him, and renewed him after His own image. As a result, this judgment upon Sodom was to be explained to Abraham, that he might train his household to avoid the sins of this doomed city, to keep the way of the Lord, and to do justice and judgment; so that the intent that the Lord's blessing may continue upon Abraham, as God spoke it over him (*see* Genesis 18:19).

The dreadful judgment of the Lord on Sodom, much like God's judgment on the antediluvian world, which was unleashed through the flood of Noah, serves as a warning example to all who hear of them. It is also a warning to all to continue in righteous justice and judgment, to continue to benefit from the covenant that God gave to Abraham.

GOD'S COVENANT WITH ABRAHAM CAUSED GOD TO SHARE HIS SECRET

Who is the man that fears the Lord? Him shall He teach in the way He chooses. [13] *He himself shall dwell in prosperity, and his descendants shall*

> *inherit the earth.* [14] ***The secret of the Lord is with those who fear Him, and He will show them His covenant.***
>
> —Psalm 25:12-14

Ultimately, God's covenant with Abraham led the Lord to reveal to him what He was about to do to Sodom and Gomorrah. God's secret was available through the promise to Abraham, as part of the covenant God placed upon him.

WHEN PUSHED, GOD WILL RIGHTSIZE WICKEDNESS

When pushed, God will rightsize wickedness. As evil capsizes a population, there will come a point of no return, and God will step in under such extreme circumstances. Much of this is based on the principle of sowing and reaping. God is not mocked; whatever a man sows, so shall he reap (*see* Galatians 6:7).

We see this in scenarios such as the Tower of Babel and Nineveh, which ultimately served humanity's good. Consider also the Philistines, who came against Israel until God embarrassed them through a shepherd boy who struck down their Nephilim champion.

REAPING THE JUDGMENT OF GOD IS NOT EXCLUSIVE TO THE OLD TESTAMENT: HEROD EATEN BY WORMS

> *So on a set day Herod, arrayed in royal apparel, sat on his throne and gave an oration to them.* [22] *And the people kept shouting, "The voice of a god and not of a man!"* [23] *Then immediately an angel of the Lord struck him, because he did not give glory to God. And he was eaten by worms and died.*
>
> —Acts 12:21-23

The judgment of God is certainly not exclusive to the Old Testament; we see how God dealt with King Herod in the New Testament, when the people praised him as a god. In that moment, Herod was struck down and eaten by worms.

Early church historian Josephus wrote about the moment Herod was struck, providing a detailed account of Herod's death based on historical records and reports. His description of Herod being struck down after receiving divine praise and suffering severe abdominal pain for five days is consistent with the biblical account in Acts 12:21-23, though he does not mention the specific detail of worms consuming Herod's flesh.

Instead, Josephus focuses on Herod's royal attire, the crowd's praise, the omen of an owl, and the intense pain in his belly, which he attributes to a fatal illness.

> On the second day of the spectacles he put on a garment made wholly of silver, of a truly wonderful texture, and came into the theater early in the morning. There the silver of his garment, being illuminated by the fresh reflection of the sun's rays, shone out in a wonderful manner, and was so resplendent as to spread awe over those that looked intently upon him. Presently his flatterers cried out, one from one place, and another from another, (though not for his good) that he was a god; and they added, "Be thou merciful to us; for although we have hitherto reverenced thee only as a man, yet shall we henceforth own thee as superior to mortal nature." Upon this the king neither rebuked them nor rejected their impious flattery. But he shortly afterward looked up and saw an owl sitting on a certain rope over his head, and immediately understood that this bird was the messenger of ill tidings, just as it had once been the messenger of good tidings to him; and fell into the deepest sorrow. A severe pain arose in his belly, striking with a most violent intensity. He therefore looked upon his friends, and said, "I, whom you call a god, am commanded presently to

> depart this life; while Providence thus reproves the lying words you just now said to me; and I, who was by you called immortal, am immediately to be hurried away by death. But I am bound to accept what Providence allots, as it pleases God; for we have by no means lived ill, but in a splendid and happy manner." When he had said this, his pain became violent. Accordingly he was carried into the palace, and the rumor went abroad everywhere that he would certainly die soon. The multitude sat in sackcloth, men, women and children, after the law of their country, and besought God for the king's recovery. All places were also full of mourning and lamentation. Now the king rested in a high chamber, and as he saw them below lying prostrate on the ground he could not keep himself from weeping. And when he had been quite worn out by the pain in his belly for five days, he departed this life, being in the fifty-fourth year of his age and in the seventh year of his reign.[2]
>
> —Josephus, *Antiquities* 19.8.2 343-361

FULL-TILT WRATH OF GOD HAS NEVER BEEN EXPERIENCED SINCE THE BEGINNING OF THE WORLD, BUT ULTIMATELY, IT WILL BE

> *For then there will be great tribulation, such as has not been since the beginning of the world until this time, no, nor ever shall be.*
>
> —Matthew 24:21

It may be that the wrath of God was poured out on an ancient world before the time of Adam; it was certainly poured out during the global deluge, the flood of Noah, which wiped nearly every living thing from the face of the earth. However, according to Matthew 24:21, Jesus states that there will be a time of tribulation unlike anything the world has ever seen or will ever see again. No matter what wrath was poured out in the ancient world or in the flood of Noah, nothing will compare to what will transpire at the end of this age.

IF SCHOOLS DESIRE TO TEACH THE HISTORY OF SEXUAL PERVERSION, THEY SHOULD START WITH SODOM AND GOMORRAH

Someone once said that if we are going to teach sexual perversion as part of history in modern schools, we should include Sodom and Gomorrah. As the days of Noah were, so will the coming of the Son of Man be. We are living in a time before the great and terrible day of the Lord. Leading up to that time, the culture is growing increasingly like that of Sodom and Gomorrah.

During this time and season, we see the hour approaching, but we consider the judgment upon Sodom and Gomorrah. In our day and in our time, the gospel of Jesus Christ is the answer that Sodom and Gomorrah lacked. We have the answer, and we, the Church, are empowered to rescue a dying world from a future of wrath without Jesus.

> *Dear reader, Christ in you, the hope of glory, is the answer for everyone you know, rescuing them from this horrific scenario of God's wrath at the end.*

God not only deals directly with a nation or people group but also sends reformers or agents of change, such as prophets, kings, or unique voices, to the generation in which they live. In the following chapter, we examine two figures who brought about significant change in their time.

CHAPTER SIX

JOSIAH AND CYRUS: AGENTS OF NATIONAL REFORMATION

Then he cried out against the altar by the word of the LORD, and said, "O altar, altar! Thus says the LORD: 'Behold, a child, Josiah by name, shall be born to the house of David; and on you he shall sacrifice the priests of the high places who burn incense on you, and men's bones shall be burned on you.'"

—1 Kings 13:2

King Josiah, whose name was prophesied more than 300 years before his birth and between 308-330 years before the prophecy was fulfilled, was commanded to sacrifice the priests of the high places who did evil in the sight of God upon the altar. A strong prophecy of judgment was spoken against occult priests who practiced witchcraft in the high places of worship.

As king, Josiah was among the best, if not the best, of all the Jewish kings since the time of David. He began well, continued well, and would have ended well if he had not gone to war against Pharaoh Neco, in violation of what God was trying to tell him. Yet what Josiah accomplished during his tenure was profound, making him a true reformer of the nation, something every generation can learn from.

THE KING TORE HIS GARMENTS

Josiah was eight years old when he became king, and he reigned thirty-one years in Jerusalem. His mother's name was Jedidah the daughter of Adaiah of Bozkath.

—2 Kings 22:1

Now it came to pass, in the eighteenth year of King Josiah, that the king sent Shaphan the scribe, the son of Azaliah, the son of Meshullam, to the house of the Lord.... [8] Then Hilkiah the high priest said to Shaphan the scribe, "I have found the Book of the Law in the house of the Lord." And Hilkiah gave the book to Shaphan, and he read it. [9] So Shaphan the scribe went to the king, bringing the king word, saying, "Your servants have gathered the money that was found in the house, and have delivered it into the hand of those who do the work, who oversee the house of the Lord." [10] Then Shaphan the scribe showed the king, saying, "Hilkiah the priest has given me a book." And Shaphan read it before the king. [11] Now it happened, when the king heard the words of the Book of the Law, that he tore his clothes.

—2 Kings 22:3, 8-11

Josiah became king at the age of 8 and began his reign. It wasn't until he discovered the Book of the Law, concealed within the house of the Lord, that reformation was born in the heart of this young king. Upon hearing the words of the Law read aloud, Josiah was cut to the heart and tore his clothes in agony because God's Word was not being honored in the land. Josiah took action to bring the nation into compliance with the Law of God.

A GENERATION CUT TO THE HEART

Our day requires those who will discover the Law of God for their generation and be cut to the heart, much like Josiah, who discovered the ancient paths of God's will. First came the prophetic declaration in 1 Kings 13:1-2, which named Josiah more than 300 years before he was born. God calls His voices in advance for the good of His children and of a nation. In our day and in our time, we are walking in this same clarion cry.

In Josiah's day, the prophecy spoken over 300 years in advance about him came to pass when he took action against the wickedness in the land. Like the prophetic declaration over Josiah, God Almighty has purposed the same for His believing Church to rise in this time. He has predestined it! Ephesians 1:5 says, "Having predestined us to adoption as sons by Jesus Christ to Himself, according to the good pleasure of His will." It is thrilling to realize that it is also His good pleasure toward us that we are predestined as sons through adoption by Jesus Christ, His Son.

It is the empowering will of God that we expose every place we tread to the kingdom of God. This is a major part of being predestined for His good pleasure. The kingdom of God is not necessarily a behavior or a physical object; it is righteousness, peace, and joy manifesting in and through the believer. Romans 14:17 says, "For the kingdom of God is not eating and drinking, but righteousness and peace and joy in the Holy Spirit."

PROPHESYING AGAINST AN EVIL OBJECT

> *Then he cried out against the altar by the word of the Lord, and said, "O altar, altar! Thus says the Lord: 'Behold, a child, Josiah by name, shall be born to the house of David; and on you he shall sacrifice the priests of the high places who burn incense on you, and men's bones shall be burned on you.'"*
>
> —1 Kings 13:2

Prophets and believers are empowered by the Holy Spirit to declare life over things that align with God's will and are likewise anointed to prophesy against evil that is destined to produce death and destruction.

Like that altar that had a prophetic declaration against it, saying, "O altar, altar!" Power is released by God's anointed voices, using their authority to proclaim His will on earth as it is in heaven, with utterances that align with Scripture. No force or object in all of creation can withstand God's will being declared with authority against the evil purpose it is intended to bring about.

Josiah was awakened to God's will for his generation and took bold action to enforce it in his nation.

JOSIAH MISSED GOD AT THE END, A WARNING TO THOSE GOD RAISES

> *But as for the king of Judah, who sent you to inquire of the Lord, in this manner you shall speak to him, "Thus says the Lord God of Israel: 'Concerning the words which you have heard—* [19] *because your heart was tender, and you humbled yourself before the Lord when you heard what I spoke against this place and against its inhabitants, that they would become a desolation and a curse, and you tore your clothes and wept before Me, I also have heard you,' says the Lord.* [20] *'Surely, therefore, I will gather you to your fathers, and you shall be gathered to your grave in peace; and your eyes shall not see all the calamity which I will bring on this place.'" So they brought back word to the king.*
>
> —2 Kings 22:18-20

An interesting twist in the story of Josiah is his ending. In 2 Kings 22, we see that Josiah received a prophetic word that, because of his humility and tender-heartedness, he would not experience calamity and would be gathered to the grave in peace. Much of this word came to pass, except the part about being gathered to the grave in peace. Why do I point this out? Because Josiah had a prophetic word about going to the grave in peace, yet when he faced Pharaoh Neco, he pressed on in battle when he should not have. The Lord prophesied to Josiah that there would be calamity upon the kingdom, but that Josiah would not experience it. When Pharaoh Neco came to fulfill what was prophesied, Josiah attempted to intervene, an action that cost him his life.

> *Moreover Josiah put away those who consulted mediums and spiritists, the household gods and idols, all the abominations that were seen in the land of Judah and in Jerusalem, that he might perform the words of the law which were written in the book that Hilkiah the priest found in the house of the Lord.* [25] *Now before him there was no king like him, who turned to the Lord with all his heart, with all his soul, and with all his might, according to all the Law of Moses; nor after him did any arise like him.* [26] *Nevertheless the Lord did not turn from the fierceness of His great wrath, with which His anger was aroused against Judah, because of all the provocations with which Manasseh had provoked Him.* [27] *And the Lord said, "I will also remove Judah from My sight, as I have removed Israel, and will cast off this city Jerusalem which I have chosen, and the house of which I said, 'My name shall be there.'"*
>
> —2 Kings 23:24-27

God was pleased with much of what Josiah had done in the Lord's name, yet God remained angry with Manasseh's actions, which would result in Judah being removed from God's sight. Pharaoh Neco was the instrument who would accomplish this action.

JOSIAH ATTEMPTED TO INTERVENE ON THE ACTIONS OF PHARAOH NECO, WHO WAS APPOINTED BY GOD

> *In his days Pharaoh Necho king of Egypt went to the aid of the king of Assyria, to the River Euphrates; and King Josiah went against him. And Pharaoh Necho killed him at Megiddo when he confronted him.* [30] *Then his servants moved his body in a chariot from Megiddo, brought*

> *him to Jerusalem, and buried him in his own tomb. And the people of the land took Jehoahaz the son of Josiah, anointed him, and made him king in his father's place.*
>
> —2 Kings 23:29-30

> *After all this, when Josiah had prepared the temple, Necho king of Egypt came up to fight against Carchemish by the Euphrates; and Josiah went out against him.* [21] *But* ***he sent messengers to him, saying, "What have I to do with you, king of Judah? I have not come against you this day, but against the house with which I have war; for God commanded me to make haste. Refrain from meddling with God, who is with me, lest He destroy you."*** [22] ***Nevertheless Josiah would not turn his face from him,*** *but disguised himself so that he might fight with him, and did not heed the words of Necho from the mouth of God. So he came to fight in the Valley of Megiddo.* [23] *And the archers shot King Josiah; and the king said to his servants, "Take me away, for I am severely wounded."* [24] *His servants therefore took him out of that chariot and put him in the second chariot that he had, and they brought him to Jerusalem. So he died, and was buried in one of the tombs of his fathers. And all Judah and Jerusalem mourned for Josiah.*
>
> —2 Chronicles 35:20-24

Josiah lost his life after attempting to intervene in Pharaoh Neco's military action. By failing to discern the word of the Lord through Pharaoh Neco, Josiah lost his life, and it appears he altered the prophecy given to him. How did he alter the prophecy that he would go to the grave in peace? By disobeying and failing to discern that God was with Neco. The lesson here is that even when God raises a reformer for a generation, free moral agency is a factor. The will of God does not always come to pass when those God has empowered miss His Word and step out in their own might with their own agenda.

Josiah was a great king who accomplished much for the glory of the Lord, yet he fell into presumption and stepped beyond the Word of the Lord, even in the face of a direct warning. When God raises a leader, that leader must remain sensitive to what He leads them to do at each step and finish strong.

THE CYRUS MANDATE

> *Thus saith the Lord to his anointed, to Cyrus, whose right hand I have holden, to subdue nations before him; and I will loose the loins of kings, to open before him the two leaved gates; and the gates shall not be shut;*
> [2] *I will go before thee, and make the crooked places straight: I will break in pieces the gates of brass, and cut in sunder the bars of iron:* [3] *And I will give thee the treasures of darkness, and hidden riches of secret places, that thou mayest know that I, the Lord, which call thee by thy name, am the God of Israel.*
>
> —Isaiah 45:1-3 KJV

Another profound example of God's prophetic call to bring about a reformer is found in the narrative of Cyrus. Isaiah, the prophet, named Cyrus 150-200 years before he was born. We know that he fulfilled the prophetic word regarding his destiny in Isaiah 44:28 and 45:1-13.

CYRUS THE ANOINTED

According to Isaiah 45:1, God said that a Gentile king would be "anointed" and would be used to "subdue nations." Cyrus fulfilled this prophecy by subduing 46 nations, including the Medes, Babylonians, Lydians, Carians, Caunians, Lysians, Bactrians, Sacae, Parthians, Hyracanians, Chorasmians, Sogdians, Arians of Herat, Zarangians, Arachosians, Satagydians, and the Gandarians.

> *Now in the first year of Cyrus king of Persia, that the word of the Lord by the mouth of Jeremiah might be fulfilled, the Lord stirred up the spirit of Cyrus king of Persia, so that he made a proclamation throughout all his kingdom, and also put it in writing, saying,* [23] *Thus says Cyrus king of Persia: All the kingdoms of the earth the Lord God of heaven has given*

me. And He has commanded me to build Him a house at Jerusalem which is in Judah. Who is among you of all His people? May the Lord his God be with him, and let him go up!

—2 Chronicles 36:22-23

Who says of Cyrus, "He is My shepherd, and he shall perform all My pleasure, saying to Jerusalem, 'You shall be built,' and to the temple, 'Your foundation shall be laid.'"

—Isaiah 44:28

THE ORDAINED RISE OF CYRUS

Cyrus of Persia was one of the greatest conquerors in world history. He inherited the throne of Persia from his father, Cambyses I, in 559. In 556 the Babylonian king Nabonidus, motivated by a dream, abandoned the treaty that his country had maintained with the Medes for over half a century and made a treaty with Cyrus. This gave Cyrus the freedom to move against the Medes (ruled by his grandfather Astyges) whom he conquered in 550.

As a result, the new Medo-Persian Empire was thus formed, with control over the entirety of Iran. By 546 he defeated the Anatolian kingdom of Lydia and Ionia. For the next five years he consolidated his control over the tribes in northeastern Iran. All of this success paved the way for his crowning achievement, the conquest of Babylon in 539 B.C. The whole of the Near East (excluding Egypt) was under the control of the Persians when Cyrus was killed in battle in 530.

THE RELIGIONS OF CYRUS

Cyrus most certainly was not a worshiper of Yahweh. In his inscriptions his polytheism is evident. In one case he requests that all the gods pray for him to Nabu and to Marduk his lord, whom he claimed to worship.

Other indications suggest that Cyrus was a Zoroastrian (a religion based on the teachings of Zarathustra, an Iranian holy man who lived sometime in the early first millennium B.C.). Zoroastrianism flourished during the Achaemenid empire in Iran. There is no concrete evidence for Zoroastrianism until the reigns of Darius I and his successor Xerxes I, the names of Cyrus's children show Zoroastrian influence, and he is known to have set up a fire stand (important in Zoroastrian worship) for the king's daily ritual.[1]

GOD USED CYRUS TO BREAK IN PIECES THE GATES OF BRONZE, AND TO CUT THE BARS OF IRON

I will go before you and make the crooked places straight; I will break in pieces the gates of bronze and cut the bars of iron.

—Isaiah 45:2

Cyrus was anointed by God to accomplish several things. It is fascinating to discover that the reference in Isaiah 45:2 speaks of *gates of bronze* and *bars of iron.*

Greek historian Herodotus described Babylon as having "one hundred gates in the circuit of the wall, all of bronze with bronze uprights and lintels." Large bronze gates have been excavated at the Assyrian-period site of Balawat, giving a glimpse of what the Babylonian walls may have been like. Gates were locked by means of a bar slid across the gateway, and iron would obviously be the most difficult to break.[2]

- "Gates not being shut" was the key to their battle-less victory.
- "Two-leaved gates" were the double gates of Babylon.

Regardless of how impenetrable Babylon's gates would prove to be, God anointed Cyrus to break them. Babylon was under God's judgment, and Cyrus was the weapon God would use to reform the narrative.

THE KING OF BABYLON WAS REJECTED

> *While he tasted the wine, Belshazzar gave the command to bring the gold and silver vessels which his father Nebuchadnezzar had taken from the temple which had been in Jerusalem, that the king and his lords, his wives, and his concubines might drink from them.* [3] *Then they brought the gold vessels that had been taken from the temple of the house of God which had been in Jerusalem; and the king and his lords, his wives, and his concubines drank from them.* [4] *They drank wine, and praised the gods of gold and silver, bronze and iron, wood and stone.*
>
> —Daniel 5:2-4

Everything turned against Babylon at a celebration. Belshazzar ordered the gold and silver vessels his father had taken from the temple to be brought. Not just any temple. This was the temple in Jerusalem, God's Temple!

Everyone in the ancient world understood the significance of sacred vessels. The fact that these had not been melted down suggests they were preserved because of their sacred character; in other words, they were recognized as sacred to the God of Israel. Yet in Belshazzar's eyes, since the god of Babylon was seen as the conqueror, the things belonging to the "conquered" gods would have been taken as booty into the temple of Marduk.

Perhaps the use of the vessels was a way of calling to remembrance the god's previous victories, or perhaps it was an even worse issue: that Belshazzar was so depraved and removed from any form of reverence that he defiled the sacred items from God's Temple merely to impress his guests. Whatever the motive for bringing these items to light, it provoked a response from God Almighty.

THE WRITING WAS ON THE WALL!

They drank wine, and praised the gods of gold and silver, bronze and iron, wood and stone. [5] *In the same hour the fingers of a man's hand appeared and wrote opposite the lampstand on the plaster of the wall of the king's palace; and the king saw the part of the hand that wrote.* [6] *Then the king's countenance changed, and his thoughts troubled him, so that the joints of his hips were loosened and his knees knocked against each other.*

—Daniel 5:4-6

The phrase "the writing is on the wall" comes from this story. Daniel 5:5 says, "the fingers of a man's hand appeared and wrote." A humorous point emerges upon understanding what happened in this narrative. As Belshazzar was blaspheming God by using what was holy for a profane activity, a supernatural hand appeared and must have shaken the room. So great was the shock of this moment that everyone was likely reduced to absolute terror! We recognize this in Daniel 5:6, which says, "Then the king's countenance changed, and his thoughts troubled him, so that the joints of his hips were loosened and his knees knocked against each other."

Simply put, the king had an accident in his robe. He lost control of his bodily functions! The encounter was so shocking that it likely pushed Belshazzar to the brink of a panic attack and a psychotic episode.

THE INSCRIPTION THAT WAS WRITTEN

Then the fingers of the hand were sent from Him, and this writing was written. [25] *"And this is the inscription that was written: MENE, MENE, TEKEL, UPHARSIN.* [26] *This is the interpretation of each word. MENE: God has numbered your kingdom, and finished it;* [27] *TEKEL: You have been weighed in the balances, and found wanting;* [28] *PERES:*

Your kingdom has been divided, and given to the Medes and Persians." [29] *Then Belshazzar gave the command, and they clothed Daniel with purple and put a chain of gold around his neck, and made a proclamation concerning him that he should be the third ruler in the kingdom.*

—Daniel 5:24-29

The Talmud suggests that the writing was vertical and backward: Aramaic, like Hebrew, reads from right to left. Biblical interpreters reversed the chart for Western readers, reading it backward: MeNe, MeNe, Tekel, Peres.

Here is what these words meant:

1. Mene: Numbered, reckoned. "God hath numbered thy kingdom and finished it." Your number is up.
2. Tekel: Weighed. "Thou art weighed in the balances, and art found wanting."
3. Peres (rendered 'upharsin': 'u' is Aramaic for "and"; "pharsin" is the plural form of "peres"): Broken, divided. "Thy kingdom is divided, and given to the Medes and the Persians." (By implying a different vowel, "paras" rather than "peres." It also becomes a play on words; paras was the word for Persia.)[3]

THAT VERY NIGHT, BABYLON WAS CONQUERED, BUT NOT DESTROYED

That very night Belshazzar, king of the Chaldeans, was slain. [31] *And Darius the Mede received the kingdom, being about sixty-two years old.*

—Daniel 5:30-31

This same night, the Persians conquered Babylon! There was no battle! The temple services were not interrupted; Cyrus' attitude was to honor the gods of his conquered. For 200 years, Babylon was the secondary capital of the Persians. A key thing to understand is that Babylon was not destroyed during this takeover.

Scriptural prophecies predict that Babylon will yet be destroyed like Sodom and Gomorrah with hailstones of fire. This leads many scholars and prophecy teachers to believe that Babylon will one day rise to power again to fulfill these scriptures.

GOD'S PERSONAL LETTER TO CYRUS

Because Babylon was not destroyed, Cyrus could boast that the conquest was almost bloodless, with no significant damage to the city. Daniel the prophet (who lived until the third year of Cyrus) presented Cyrus with the writings of Isaiah that include a letter addressed to Cyrus by name, written 150 years earlier, taken directly from Isaiah 44:27, 45:1.[4]

> *Who says to the deep, "Be dry! And I will dry up your rivers";* [28] *Who says of Cyrus, "He is My shepherd, and he shall perform all My pleasure, saying to Jerusalem, 'You shall be built,' and to the temple, 'Your foundation shall be laid.'"*
>
> —Isaiah 44:27-28

The prophecy begins in Isaiah 44:27, "Who says to the deep, 'Be dry! And I will dry up your rivers.'" Drying up the rivers was the method Cyrus used to conquer Babylon. They were able to access the city because of the low water. Isaiah 44:28 shows that Cyrus was predicted by name.

CYRUS MUST HAVE SMIRKED AT THE PROPHECY OF BELSHAZZAR'S LOOSE LOINS MISHAP!

Extra-biblical texts say that Daniel showed Cyrus the prophecies concerning himself and the fall of Belshazzar. The prophecy was fulfilled when God intervened in Belshazzar's blasphemous actions, causing him to soil himself. "Loose the loins of kings," as described in Daniel 5:6 and prophesied in Isaiah 45:1 (KJV), "...and I will loose the loins of kings..." Just imagine the smirk that must have been on Cyrus's face when Daniel read him that verse; that must have been a real moment of humor!

CYRUS RESPONDED TO THE PROPHECY

History records Cyrus' response: he reversed the policies of his predecessors by releasing the captives to go to their own homelands. God uses the authentication of His message by describing things yet to happen, prophecy. Precisely, right 100 percent of the time, and revealed it through Daniel to Cyrus!

In each generation, God calls us to rise and become who we are meant to be. He will intervene and often call the future to a purpose aligned with His plan, raising a man or woman to fulfill His will. For example, God used Cyrus, a man who was not one of His own. God also uses His own, as He did with Josiah.

Our role is to be positioned for the day God has called us to. Make it a goal to be ready in and out of season.

SECTION TWO

THE PRESENT EVIL AGE

CHAPTER SEVEN

THE NEO-BABEL AGENDA

> *Then the devil, taking Him up on a high mountain, showed Him all the kingdoms of the world in a moment of time. 6 And the devil said to Him, "All this authority I will give You, and their glory; for this has been delivered to me, and I give it to whomever I wish. 7 Therefore, if You will worship before me, all will be Yours." 8 And Jesus answered and said to him, "Get behind Me, Satan! For it is written, 'You shall worship the Lord your God, and Him only you shall serve.' "*
>
> —Luke 4:5-8

Repeating cycles are part of Luciferian history. A part of Lucifer's story is his rise and fall, an arc that recurs among his admirers. Followers of the devil may indeed find success through the deceptive assistance of darkness, but will ultimately face the horrific reality that they served the wrong master!

Not only are the plans of darkness to captivate humanity, but, like the Tower of Babel in Genesis 11, nefarious forces seek to defy God's plans for humanity. Goliath, the giant slain by David, was no different, as he defied the armies of the Living God, a direct defiance of the God of Israel. (*See* 1 Samuel 17.)

Society's elites, either subtly or overtly, have accepted the same deal offered to Jesus. This is the source of power and promotion for many who appear on the world stage, including in entertainment and high office. Even the billionaire elites attempt to make decisions for the rest of humanity regarding the environment and daily life. All of these, if not submitted to the Lordship of Jesus Christ, are, in one way or another, working for the deceiver, Satan.

THE HIGH PLACE OF CONTRACTUAL AGREEMENT WITH SATAN

> *The devil led him up to a high place and showed him* ***in an instant*** *all the kingdoms of the world.*
>
> —Luke 4:5 NIV

One point worth considering is that when the devil took Jesus to the top of a high mountain, it happened in a single moment. What was shown to Jesus was like a snapshot, or, as the New International Version of the Bible says, "in an instant." This moment is supernatural and offers insight into how the enemy entices and attracts those hungry for power and access to the highest seats of influence and control. This was a vision, or an interdimensional access to space and time, used by the god of this world, the devil, to show Jesus everything from one location. Consider the supernatural experiences shown to people today and the temptations that accompany them. All of this could be yours; with the devil saying, "I will give it to you," a similar offer would impact a godless person who might be willing to give themselves over to darkness in exchange for earthly power.

WHAT IS THE DEVIL OFFERING WORLD PLAYERS TODAY?

Consider what darkness might offer individuals today. Could it be that the devil, or through his means of power on earth, would cut similar deals with players willing to cooperate? Saying to them, in similar terms, that if they will bow down and worship him, he will give them this part of society, influence in entertainment, breathtaking wealth, or political prowess that carries a dark supernatural strength.

Based on Luke 4, it is safe to say that whatever the darkness has done in the past, it will do in the present and even in the future. This is why, as believers, we must be vigilant, for the devil is looking for someone to devour.

THE DEVIL SEEKS WHOM HE MAY DEVOUR

> *Be sober, be vigilant; because your adversary the devil walks about like a roaring lion, seeking whom he may devour.* [9] *Resist him, steadfast in the faith, knowing that the same sufferings are experienced by your brotherhood in the world.*
>
> —1 Peter 5:8-9

Notice what 1 Peter 5:8 states, "…the devil walks about like a roaring lion, seeking whom he may devour…." First off, the devil goes about roaring. He uses his voice and suggestions to see who will respond to his message. Who will engage with what he is saying—this is the purpose of his voice. We recognize these as the fiery darts of the enemy, hitting us with thoughts and impressions through supernatural influences in our minds and impulses, and through the world around us via media, music, conversations, and what we see and hear.

Second, the devil cannot devour anyone at will! He does not have that authority. He couldn't even devour Job in the Old Testament story. The only way he may devour someone is with that person's permission. This devouring can only happen when a person cooperates with the roar or with his voice. Similar to Adam and Eve in the garden, who listened to the words of a talking serpent instead of obeying God's commands regarding the tree, today, many in positions of power in society follow that same voice and open their lives to be devoured. In this process, these individuals are used for a Luciferian purpose: to carry out the will of darkness upon society, whether on a large or small scale.

DARKNESS SETS OUT TO DISCOURAGE BELIEVERS BY PARADING THE SUCCESS OF THE WICKED

It can be disheartening for believers who are immersed in the system of this world to see the prosperity of the wicked and the elevated status of the godless. Believers are often tempted to imitate those they see in the media and in positions of power. Influencers in entertainment showcase their lavish lives in ways that tempt others with the idea of what they could have if they were like them.

GODLY PROMOTION IS THE HIGHEST PROMOTION AND IS A CLEAN INCREASE

> *The blessing of the Lord makes one rich, and He adds no sorrow with it.*
>
> —Proverbs 10:22

It must be said that God promotes and elevates His people for His purposes in this world as well. That process is called *the blessing of the Lord.* This blessing makes one rich without sorrow. It is a clean increase, filled with joy, to go forward and impact society with the gospel of Jesus Christ and to make disciples of nations. Increase in God's way is a tremendous thing and far surpasses the lying abundance of darkness.

Yet we face a Luciferian system that rewards its followers with riches, influence, and everything the world offers—all that is required is a person's free moral agency and their eternal soul.

HOW THE BELIEVER SHOULD RESPOND TO THE SUCCESS OF WICKEDNESS

The Word of God is clear about the fate of the wicked, and even when it seems that wickedness has the advantage, there is a perspective that must be understood now more than ever.

> *I said to the boastful, "Do not deal boastfully," and to the wicked, "Do not*
> *lift up the horn.* 5 *Do not lift up your horn on high; do not speak with a*
> *stiff neck."* 6 ***For exaltation comes neither from the east nor from the***
> ***west nor from the south.*** 7 ***But God is the Judge: He puts down one,***
> ***and exalts another.***
>
> —Psalm 75:4-7

Psalm 75 clarifies the issue of seeking elevation. For the believer, God grants promotion. Notice that promotion does not come from the east, the west, or the south. The one direction not mentioned is the north! Why? Because that is where promotion comes from—the north, where God is. God is the One who promotes; He is the Judge, lifting one and bringing another down. For those of us who are loyal and follow Him, we can rest in knowing that whatever our portion is, we will be content with it and faithful to carry out what He gives us to do.

THE AGONIZING JOURNEY OF THE RIGHTEOUS WHEN THE WICKED PROSPER, AND A REVELATION OF THEIR END

> *Truly God is good to Israel, to such as are pure in heart.* 2 *But as for*
> *me,* ***my feet had almost stumbled; my steps had nearly slipped.*** 3
> ***For I was envious of the boastful, when I saw the prosperity of***
> ***the wicked.*** 4 *For there are no pangs in their death, but their strength*
> *is firm.* 5 *They are not in trouble as other men, nor are they plagued*
> *like other men.* 6 *Therefore pride serves as their necklace; violence covers*
> *them like a garment.* 7 *Their eyes bulge with abundance; they have*
> *more than heart could wish.* 8 *They scoff and speak wickedly concern-*
> *ing oppression; they speak loftily.* 9 *They set their mouth against the*
> *heavens, and their tongue walks through the earth.* 10 *Therefore his*

> *people return here, and waters of a full cup are drained by them.* [11] *And they say, "How does God know? And is there knowledge in the Most High?"* [12] ***Behold, these are the ungodly, who are always at ease; They increase in riches.*** [13] ***Surely I have cleansed my heart in vain, and washed my hands in innocence.*** [14] *For all day long I have been plagued, and chastened every morning.* [15] *If I had said, "I will speak thus," Behold, I would have been untrue to the generation ofYour children.* [16] ***When I thought how to understand this, it was too painful for me.***
>
> —Psalm 73:1-16

Psalm 73:1-16 highlights how believers may be tempted to think the wicked are being rewarded. Feeling that being a believer puts you at a disadvantage can lead to such thoughts. The psalmist in Psalm 73 shares this perspective from personal experience. Verse 2 indicates that he nearly faltered upon seeing what he saw. In verse 3, it's even clearer that this righteous man envied the boastful and the prosperity of the wicked. He argues that they face no pain in death, live in strength, do not suffer trouble like others, and escape plagues, yet pride is their necklace, and violence covers them like clothing.

The psalmist continues by noting that *the eyes of the wicked bulge with abundance, and they possess more than a heart could wish for.* These same evil individuals scoff and speak wickedly about oppressing others, and they have lofty words. Even more, they set their mouth against the heavens and speak whatever they wish about all that is happening on the earth. A hallmark of these wicked figures is that they take what the righteous regard as the emptying of a full cup accumulated; it is a picture of taking from the good. The psalmist was deeply discouraged, arguing that it seems the wicked have every advantage, which, given their apparent benefits, might cause the righteous to become discouraged and to contemplate why they bother to live righteously and walk before the Lord in righteousness.

A HORRIFYING END TO THE WICKED—TERROR AND DOOM

> ***Until I went into the sanctuary of God; then I understood their***
> ***end.*** 18 *Surely You set them in slippery places; You cast them down to*
> *destruction.* 19 ***Oh, how they are brought to desolation, as in a***
> ***moment! They are utterly consumed with terrors.*** 20 *As a dream*
> *when one awakes, so, Lord, when You awake, You shall despise their image.*
>
> —Psalm 73:17-20

A striking conclusion emerges at the end of this observation. At the very end of it all, the wicked come to a sudden and irreversible end. Observe verse 17, where the psalmist pivots by doing what believers are meant to do—enter the sanctuary, which means meeting with God, your strength and source. Believers who make God their total source and place of dependence have a glorious end, regardless of the trials of life, which do not seem to affect the evil in the same way. Remember, that is only for a short time, and it is a temporary window for evil figures.

Verse 17 begins to make this clear through a revelatory understanding afforded to the psalmist, who realizes that the end of the wicked is shocking and brings doom. He understood their end. Tragically, the righteous psalmist was enlightened about the outcome of evil individuals.

The end of the wicked:

1. God sets them in slippery places.
2. Casts them down to destruction.
3. They are brought down to desolation in a moment—suddenly!
4. They are utterly consumed by terrors—doom is their new reality.

The picture here is of a wicked person who has reveled in their vile ways, dismissing any recourse to God or even caring what God thinks. These actions completely violate God's ways and arrogantly mock and use the righteous for their purposes until the final moment arrives.

LAST MOMENTS OF EVIL PLAYERS

In their last moment, they are overtaken by terror. It is the picture of someone walking along a long dock, when, in one fateful step, the wooden planks give out beneath them. In shock and disorientation, they feel the splash as they plunge into the sea below. In a microsecond, they are underwater. Trying to regain their bearings, they open their eyes, and a great white shark is directly in front of them, its mouth opening wide. Bam, they are consumed. All of this happens in mere seconds. This offers a sense of what the psalmist describes as their end. Horrific and a place of no return. Only doom awaits them forever beyond this moment. This imagery in the Psalms provides insight into why we should continue to serve the Great God of heaven.

LUCIFERIAN PATTERN OF DEFIANCE AND THEIR COSMIC STUNTS

> *And no wonder! For Satan himself transforms himself into an angel of light.*
>
> —2 Corinthians 11:14

Today, there are many such evil postures in our modern world. Luciferians are those who, according to some, believe that Yahweh, the Living God of heaven, was the "villain" in the story of Lucifer's fall. Because of this, they believe the time will come when they can open an avenue, or a portal, to heaven, storm the kingdom of heaven, and overthrow Yahweh. What a surprise that will be if and when they attempt this cosmic stunt. There is no foundation or authority for this belief; it is merely a figment of delusion brought to them by Lucifer himself.

How is it possible that so many people are drawn to Lucifer and deceived? The answer lies in 2 Corinthians 11:14. Satan can transform into an angel of light.

> *Luciferianism,* by definition, *is a belief structure that venerates the fundamental traits that are attributed to Lucifer.* The custom usually reveres Lucifer not as the Devil, but as a savior, a guardian or instructing spirit or even the true god as opposed to Jehovah. Lucifer is described by ***The Satanic Bible*** as one of the four crown princes of hell, particularly that of the East, the "lord of the air," and is called the bringer of light, the morning star, intellectualism, and enlightenment.[1]

Luciferians regard him as the "angel of light," but not in the same way Christians do. Instead, they see him as the bringer of knowledge, enlightenment, and self-empowerment. They view him as a source of light rather than darkness and believe he will guide them. This respect for Lucifer stems from seeing him as a positive force, offering humans potential and guidance on how to increase. Similar to what Satan offered Jesus when he offered Him the kingdoms of the earth, they think he offers good things rather than evil.

THE REMOVAL OF GOD FROM THEIR THINKING OPENS THE DOOR TO LUCIFERIAN IDEOLOGY

> *Because, although they knew God, they did not glorify Him as God, nor were thankful, but became futile in their thoughts, and their foolish hearts were darkened.* 22 *Professing to be wise, they became fools,* 23 *and changed the glory of the incorruptible God into an image made like corruptible man—and birds and four-footed animals and creeping things.* 24 *Therefore God also gave them up to uncleanness, in the lusts of their hearts, to*

> *dishonor their bodies among themselves,* [25] *who exchanged the truth of God for the lie, and worshiped and served the creature rather than the Creator, who is blessed forever. Amen.*
>
> —Romans 1:21-25

Our tech and the world of science want to remove God from the equation in many arenas. There are certainly scientists and technology workers who believe in God. What is shocking is how many seem to be growing ever more distant from the knowledge of God and continue to pursue a carnal, natural way of measuring truth and facts.

Removing God from their thinking is part of the Luciferian agenda. They don't personally remove God Almighty from their thoughts. Still, the cultural tools used by these groups and other elites encourage social campaigns that eliminate God from the hearts and minds of society.

Within the zeitgeist of young people finding their way, questions and disinformation about God, His existence, and relevance are met with as much fodder as possible. This is done intentionally at the expense of so many seeking life's answers. The impact of this godless agenda has affected the Church. Even more significantly, it has directed our nation's leaders, ultimately steering the course of our future generation.

Romans 1:21 says, "...although they knew God, they did not glorify Him as God, nor were thankful, but became futile in their thoughts, and their foolish hearts were darkened." What a shocking point! They knew God yet did not glorify Him as God; they were also *unthankful*. This rendered their thoughts futile. "Futile in their thoughts" is clarified by the Greek word *mataioó*, which means *to make vain or worthless, to cancel out. Destitute of real wisdom, to be or act perversely, foolish.*[2] It describes leaving the right path to follow foolish or bad courses.

Additionally, Romans 1:21 states that their foolish hearts became darkened. We could say the heart, the seat of reasoning and choice, was filled with darkness, sending these darkened hearts into a state of insanity regarding their choices, life decisions, and beliefs.

GENEROUS OR STINGY: A SIGN OF A GOOD EYE OR A BAD EYE

The lamp of the body is the eye. If therefore your eye is good, your whole body will be full of light. [23] *But if your eye is bad, your whole body will be full of darkness. If therefore the light that is in you is darkness, how great is that darkness!*

—Matthew 6:22-23

The lamp of the body is the eye. Therefore, when your eye is good, your whole body also is full of light. But when your eye is bad, your body also is full of darkness. [35] *Therefore take heed that the light which is in you is not darkness.* [36] *If then your whole body is full of light, having no part dark, the whole body will be full of light, as when the bright shining of a lamp gives you light.*

—Luke 11:34-36

Jesus speaks literally of a "single" eye versus a "bad" or "evil" one. A "single" eye normally meant a generous one. A "bad" eye in that culture could mean either a diseased one or a stingy one. Many people believed that light was emitted from the eye, enabling one to see, rather than that light was admitted through the eye; here it seems to be admitted through the eye.[3]

One takeaway from Jesus' language is the contrast between self-centeredness and selflessness. A generous person is selfless, seeking others' good, whereas a stingy person is selfish, seeking only their own good.

JESUS IS THE LIGHT

In Luke 11:34-36, Jesus next exhorted each person to focus their eyes on *the light*: Jesus Himself. The people had requested a sign (*see* Luke 11:16; Luke 11:29), but Jesus explained that the light of His perfect life should be enough of a sign.

These words are very close to Luke 8:16; however, in Luke 8:16, "No one, when he has lit a lamp, covers it with a vessel or puts *it* under a bed, but sets *it* on a lampstand, that those who enter may see the light." The "lamp" that has been lit refers to the person who hears Jesus' message, responds to it, and spreads it to others.

Jesus described His own ministry and message as lighting a lamp that was not hidden or put under a basket, but rather made public, with a message available for all to accept. The lamp is Christ's message, and "light" is the truth of His revelation and guidance (Luke 11:33). The eye represents spiritual understanding and insight, filtered through a person's "good" or "bad."

When eyes are pure, that is, when they operate properly, the illumination makes it easier for the body to function. Those with "pure eyes" are the true disciples who listen to and respond to Jesus' guidance.

By contrast, when eyes are evil, that is, when they are not functioning properly, the result is impaired functioning throughout the rest of the body. Those with "evil eyes" are those who reject Jesus' words; all they have is the darkness and futility of their own evil ways.

REVELATION KNOWLEDGE

> *The spirit of a man is the lamp of the Lord, searching all the inner depths of his heart.*
>
> —Proverbs 20:27

Many things become evident when we recognize that our single-focused eyes on the Lord create light within us—even revelation through His Word.

> *That the God of our Lord Jesus Christ, the Father of glory, may give to you the spirit of wisdom and revelation in the knowledge of Him,* 18 *the eyes of your understanding being enlightened; that you may know what is the hope of His calling, what are the riches of the glory of His inheritance in the saints.*
>
> —Ephesians 1:17–18

Revelation in the knowledge of Him, with the eyes of your understanding enlightened! This is what it means to have light in your eyes, and it all points to knowing Jesus more and more through all He has provided for you!

After all, you have the capacity for God, but this is not enough: Christ must give you light. Ephesians 5:14 says, "Therefore He says: 'Awake, you who sleep, arise from the dead, and Christ will give you light.'"

LIGHT LEADS TO AN ILLUMINATED LIFE AND JOURNEY

But the path of the righteous is like the light of dawn, that shines brighter and brighter until the full day.

—Proverbs 4:18 NASB

Light shines from the path of the righteous! It might be said that the way of the righteous person will shine with understanding and good works that radiate God's goodness and reveal Jesus, even in the darkest circumstances. Think of this: God is light, pure light, and there is not a trace of darkness in Him at all! When we walk with Jesus as our focus, this trait also comes through in the believer's life. First John 1:5 says, "This is the message which we have heard from Him and declare to you, that God is light and in Him is no darkness at all."

LUCIFERIAN LIGHT IS FALSE KNOWLEDGE

Evil is the opposite of light that comes to a person through what they focus on and what they think about. Wickedness has an agenda to extinguish the light or information that the public considers. It seeks to remove all things godly or right. What is concerning is the seduction of information being propagated into the culture. In a time when good is called evil and evil is called good. Once again, these lying counterfeits want the minds and eyes darkened in a generation for their purposes. Remember that Luciferians worship light or higher knowledge, viewing Lucifer as the bearer of light.

NEO-BABEL

Ultimately, the Luciferian agenda is aiming toward a neo-Babel operation. A place where enough people agree with their wicked ideas, or even worship darkness to the point of ushering in a vile access point from the realm of the spirit into the natural. Something that is likely the Tower of Babel's real purpose in Genesis 11. In that valley of Shinar, a tower was built not only for elevation into the sky but also as an access point to the spirit realm.

This is already a point many believe occurs under the guise of science at institutions such as CERN in Switzerland. I discuss CERN, home of the Large Hadron Collider, in greater detail in my book *Punishing the Darkness.* The overall idea is that it is a place where they smash atoms and particles at the molecular level to observe collisions and understand the origins of the universe. What many believe is happening there is far more nefarious.

PORTALS ARE BEING OPENED

> *Then the fifth angel sounded: And I saw a star fallen from heaven to the earth. To him was given the key to the bottomless pit.* [2] *And he opened the bottomless pit, and smoke arose out of the pit like the smoke of a great furnace. So the sun and the air were darkened because of the smoke of the pit.* [3] *Then out of the smoke locusts came upon the earth. And to them was given power, as the scorpions of the earth have power.* [4] *They were commanded not to harm the grass of the earth, or any green thing, or any tree, but only those men who do not have the seal of God on their foreheads.* [5] *And they were not given authority to kill them, but to torment them for five months. Their torment was like the torment of a scorpion when it strikes a man.* [6] *In those days men will seek death and will not find it; they will desire to die, and death*

will flee from them. [7] *The shape of the locusts was like horses prepared for battle. On their heads were crowns of something like gold, and their faces were like the faces of men.* [8] *They had hair like women's hair, and their teeth were like lions' teeth.* [9] *And they had breastplates like breastplates of iron, and the sound of their wings was like the sound of chariots with many horses running into battle.* [10] *They had tails like scorpions, and there were stings in their tails. Their power was to hurt men five months.* [11] *And they had as king over them the angel of the bottomless pit, whose name in Hebrew is Abaddon, but in Greek he has the name Apollyon.*

—Revelation 9:1-11

Revelation 9:1-3 might be the result of a CERN-type experiment that opens gateways to the realm of the spirit, calling it a new dimension. Earth is not prepared for what Revelation 9 and 20 reveal will come upon the world when the abyss is opened.

Ultimately, it's the result of direct satanic scientific meddling, or simply the result of a godless world getting what it has been worshiping. In that moment, the mask will come off, and what has been withheld will no longer remain behind the veil; it will flood the earth with horrific darkness beyond anyone's comprehension.

Opening the bottomless pit would fulfill the attempt at Babel in Genesis 11. Here, there is no restraint on these monstrous creatures and the hellish activities brought forth upon planet Earth. This is a first stage toward the final phase of the Luciferian agenda. The last stage will be the lake of fire for these players and their game—eternal punishment.

In the meantime, we are in the battle to hold back as much of this trash as possible by preaching the gospel, casting out demons, and fulfilling the Great Commission. Both now, as the Church remains, and at the end of Armageddon, we will see massive victory again. The endgame is wonderful for believers in Jesus.

THE CRUCIAL PIECE

The crucial point is that those who do not know Jesus face the all-consuming darkness that will consume them without intervention. The Church's intervention! We are called by God to stand against the hordes of Luciferian and Satanic attacks on society while we are here. As living sacrifices offering the Lord our good and reasonable service, we rescue all we can in the name of Jesus Christ the Lord and declare His Lordship over every place our feet tread.

CHAPTER EIGHT

KINGDOMS COLLIDE IN TERRITORIAL WARFARE

> *And Jesus came and spoke to them, saying, "All authority has been given to Me in heaven and on earth.* [19] *Go therefore and make disciples of all the nations, baptizing them in the name of the Father and of the Son and of the Holy Spirit,* [20] *teaching them to observe all things that I have commanded you; and lo, I am with you always, even to the end of the age." Amen.*
>
> —Matthew 28:18-20

God raises those who will speak to authority in the kingdom for which they are anointed. Kingdoms are a unique concept to ponder. Something I was considering in prayer one morning is this: The Church was a mystery revealed after Jesus. Think about it: in the Old Testament, the Church was neither known nor spoken of overtly. It was concealed in the Old Covenant and revealed in the New Covenant through the death and resurrection of Jesus Christ. What this may reveal is full access to all the dimensions that may play into our position with the Lord in an eternal future.

We will likely be given all knowledge and be able to access all things simultaneously. Compared to this time, when we are limited to a three-dimensional experience, touching the realms of God by faith, yet with limited understanding and reach. On the day the Lord catches us away, all limitations will change because of our exposure to His fullness; we will be in His presence, and revelatory power will overtake us. When we see Him in the light of who He really is, revelation will envelop our being, and a transition will occur. Upon seeing Him in His glorified state, we will be made like Him, for we will see Him as He is.

> *Beloved, now we are children of God; and it has not yet been revealed what we shall be, but we know that when He is revealed,* ***we shall be like Him, for we shall see Him as He is****.*
>
> —1 John 3:2

By stating "…when He is revealed, we shall be like Him, for we shall see Him as He is…," John was letting us in on a revelatory insight, a glimpse into our eternal future. All that Jesus can access, we will enjoy; all that He is capable of knowing, we may very well have that same privilege. The universe and what it truly holds will be opened to us, for we will be like Him.

Even Adam and Eve, who walked with God in the cool of the day, will be redeemed through our tremendous Lord Jesus Christ, long after the tree of the knowledge of good and evil and the tree of eternal life, after they stepped into original sin and everything that was lost in the garden. When Adam was told to be fruitful and multiply and to take dominion over creation, we may be involved in fulfilling that mandate during the Millennial Reign of Jesus.

JESUS IS THE SAME YESTERDAY, TODAY, AND FOREVER!

> *Jesus Christ is the same yesterday, today, and forever.*
>
> —Hebrews 13:8

Jesus is the same yesterday, today, and forever! What was intended for humanity from the very beginning will most likely continue into eternity future, only better. Why better? Because every time the covenant changes with God Almighty, He upgrades it. Jesus came to give us a better covenant, founded on better promises, and this alone sets a precedent and offers a glimpse of what the future holds.

Adam was called to subdue the earth, not just from Eden, which was his headquarters, his matrix of operation. I believe Adam was called to bring Eden to the entire world and potentially beyond.

WHERE DOES EXPLORATION IN THE HEART OF MAN ORIGINATE?

Have you ever wondered why exploration is in the heart of man? Why do we have a space program? Why are we so interested in what lies beneath our oceans, or why do we have a constant need to understand archaeology? Every time a discovery is made, it makes global headlines, and with that comes speculation that only ignites a stronger need to learn more about our ancient past.

All of this searching and the innate desire to know "what's out there" are part of our makeup, and I believe we are still connected to Adam, even though the fall tainted everything, including our history. As mentioned in earlier chapters, much could have been happening before Adam's time, and that too remains a mystery that many capable and highly intelligent scholars ponder with stunning insight into what prehistory might have held.

Saying all of this to highlight that we will have access to everything and might very well be working to complete what was initiated by Adam's mandate to take dominion over all creation. Will we reign with Jesus, not just here on earth, but since Jesus is the Last Adam, will He authorize the greatest exploration and advancement of His kingdom to the farthest reaches of the universe and beyond?

EXPLORATION IS A KINGDOM PIECE DORMANT WITHIN HUMANITY, EXPRESSED THROUGH THE NEED TO DISCOVER

Jesus is the King of kings and Lord of lords—titles that signify rule over territory. A glorious and breathtaking future may lie ahead, in which we, as His people, expand His kingdom to the farthest corners of the universe. It may be that what we call space is not empty at all, and when we are transformed and made like Him, our view of space and time could change so much that the nature of ultimate reality becomes clear to us. We will gain a new understanding through our transformed bodies, enabling us to advance His dominion to places beyond our current five senses.

The planets in our solar system may appear lifeless and simply out there, with no purpose within our current understanding. Still, they may very well be part of God's plan for dominion and kingdom expansion in the eternal future.

Our short lives here and now are for the gospel and His pleasure; yet ultimately, just as the Church was a mystery in the Old Covenant, we may be living with a mystery we have little to no grasp of. One such mystery could be the activities we will participate in throughout the eternal future, advancing the purposes and plans of our Great God of heaven. We may be in for a stunning epic we cannot yet understand, and what surprises await us, I'm certain, will be breathtaking!

THIS CURRENT TERRITORY WAY

What we are facing is a time of territory. As I often say, both God and the devil are territorial, meaning there is a focal point in gaining territory—human beings.

Your mind, your process, and your ability to make decisions and take action in this world are the purpose of the territory war. You are the territory, and your mind is the control center of this operation. Whoever controls the mind controls the individual. We who are redeemed have given our territory to the Lord God of heaven. Those under the dominion of evil have given their territory to the purposes of the devil. There is no middle ground in the equation, and possessing a person's territory ultimately means that there will be a physical outer territory influenced by the people under each system.

Viewing life and society through these lenses clarifies the vital reasons we spread the gospel and must continually bring light to darkness. Yes, to save souls by leading them to the Lordship of Jesus Christ, but also to make an impact on culture through our presence and to protect those without a voice. Justice enters the land when people who submit to God's light go out into the world to preach that light, live that light, and influence everything around them. This is a territory-taking message of eternal significance.

God loves you and wants the territory of your life first for fellowship and family. He also wants to work with you to reclaim His lost creation through evangelism, turning them into family. Additionally, God wants to impact society as a whole with good and push back evil. In the same way, the devil wants the territory as a utility leveraged for his evil agenda, which is focused on hurting the God of heaven in any way he can. Harming humanity is the vengeance the devil carries out, not just out of hatred for people, but out of hatred for God.

Whoever influences a person can alter the terrain. The will of God does not automatically come to pass, nor does the devil's. People are the means by which either kingdom advances.

THE GREAT COMMISSION

A sobering reality becomes clear when we recognize how crucial the Great Commission is: preaching the gospel and making disciples of all nations is not merely a nice Christian formality. It is crucial to usher in the kingdom of God for humanity, and it is also of the utmost importance for changing how society operates. As Proverbs 29:2 says, "When the righteous are in authority, the people rejoice; but when a wicked man rules, the people groan." What must be seen is God's power at work in culture.

The Great Commission is God's mobilization plan to fulfill what Jesus lived, died, and was resurrected for. We, the *Ekklesia*, or the Church, are anointed by Jesus to fulfill His will on earth as it is in heaven. Territory is taken when we preach the gospel and make disciples in all nations. Even more, the culture is influenced. Turning the disobedient toward the wisdom of the just is more than simply preaching the gospel; it means impacting the culture so that even those who do not believe in the Lord are put in a position to cooperate with a just society. This includes protecting the innocent, helping the helpless, feeding the poor, and assisting widows and orphans. Real social justice is found when the righteous reign by majority and do not allow wickedness to run amok in the land. God loves all people, even those who do not serve Him. It is His nature to bring life and life more abundantly to everything influenced by His kingdom and through His people.

CONQUERING POWER THAT BRINGS THE WORLD TO ITS KNEES!

> *For whatever is born of God overcomes the world. And this is the victory that has overcome the world—our faith.*
>
> —1 John 5:4

Believers in Jesus who are active in their faith carry horsepower! I like the rendering of this verse in the Message translation: "The conquering power that brings the world to its knees is our faith."

The word "world" in 1 John 5:4 is the Greek word *kosmos,* meaning *the public.* It's the society you're living in and all its norms, values, and ideology that they're trying to push on you. When you rise in faith, it will bring the wicked, Babylonian, dark, institutionalized demon to its knees. Doing this gains territory in a generation. When that begins to happen, you're starting to radiate the truth that *greater is He who is in you than he that is in the world.*

> *You are of God, little children, and have overcome them,* ***because He who is in you is greater than he who is in the world****.*
>
> —1 John 4:4

Consequently, he who is in the world is talking about the Antichrist. The Antichrist is not standing among us today, but the spirit of Antichrist is here. We are pushing it back and making a way where there seems to be no way. We overcome the Antichrist by the blood of the Lamb. This is what I call "going red"—applying the blood of the Lamb to our lives!

And they overcame him by the blood of the Lamb and by the word of their testimony, and they did not love their lives to the death.

—Revelation 12:11

AS HE IS, SO ARE WE IN THIS WORLD!

Love has been perfected among us in this: that we may have boldness in the day of judgment; because as He is, so are we in this world.

—1 John 4:17

In 1 John 4:17, Jesus speaks of the boldness that will stand against a wicked culture and an evil time. The devil runs the systems of this world, which is why we preach the gospel. The systems of this world need you.

They need you to rise and press back against them with truth as a blazing light in the darkness. God wants you to win even more than you do. We must stand up to the darkness because institutions flooded by the Luciferian system of this age seek to choke out the Word of God. They seek to extinguish the believer's life in God and to bring discouragement or crisis fatigue. We stand up to it by faith. Standing in faith is the power that brings the world to its knees.

GOD'S WILL FOR YOU IS TO BE DELIVERED FROM THIS PRESENT EVIL AGE!

Here is the great news! We are also living in the days of the greatest opportunity, marked by glorious advancement. After all, it is not God's will that His Church leave this world with a whimper and a sigh. In truth, it is God's will that we be delivered from this present evil age.

Who gave Himself for our sins, that He might deliver us from this present evil age, according to the will of our God and Father.

—Galatians 1:4

Consider this: in Galatians 1:4, the apostle Paul wrote that Jesus came to "deliver us from this present evil age," and the most significant point is that it is "the will of God our Father!" If the average believer were asked what the will of God is, they might answer in various ways. Here, we can confidently say it is His will that we be delivered from the present evil age we face. Additionally, the Church, filled with believers, is the decisive factor in how the world will proceed in the present era.

Complete reliance on Jesus Christ and Him as Lord gives you both positional and territorial authority, from which will come the advancement of God's will and mission for your life. The blood of Jesus, in action through His Church, advances the Great Commission. This action and privilege of the Church not only win the lost but also bring about revival, and they are meant to reach beyond the Church and into the culture. After revival, which is necessary, we are destined for more. A cultural impact and a reformation, but not without a preceding revival. It is a revival that awakens the people of God and adds to the number of believers through salvation, who become disciples.

REFORMATION

> *He will also go before Him in the spirit and power of Elijah, "to turn the hearts of the fathers to the children," and the disobedient to the wisdom of the just, to make ready a people prepared for the Lord.*
>
> —Luke 1:17

Again, as I discussed in Chapter Five, using Luke 1:17, we see the words spoken to Zacharias, the father of John the Baptist, who was given a message by an angelic servant of fire. The message stated that John the Baptist would go forward in the spirit and power of Elijah, *"to turn the hearts of the fathers to the children,"* preparing for generational merging. In our day, we could say this would be a form of revival, a way to bring the generations together for the Lord, yet here is an additional outcome—*the disobedient to the wisdom of the just*. This is an accompanying effect of God's people experiencing generational healing or coming together for the Lord Almighty.

A modern revival would reflect this scenario and, as a direct result, bring another social impact. The disobedient would turn to the wisdom of the just. Another way of saying this is that the culture is significantly affected, or that those who are part of the world's system, the disobedient, must come under the guidance or the wisdom of the just.

Think of it! Disobedience may not bring about a heart change; the disobedient represent the massive godless activity of a society, and individuals may not come to the saving knowledge of Jesus Christ. However, the culture and society around us will be safer and far more civil as righteousness reigns in the land. Those who refuse to soften their hearts toward the things of God lose the potency of their rebellious activities on a widespread cultural level.

> *When the righteous are in authority, the people rejoice; but when a wicked man rules, the people groan.*
>
> —Proverbs 29:2

As part of this cultural shift comes social impact. Placing the righteous in authority makes the people rejoice, whereas the obvious folly of wicked rulers in power makes them groan.

THE KINGDOM OF JESUS IS COMING

A future day is destined to arrive. Prophetically speaking, it is the day when Jesus will rule from Jerusalem and begin the greatest rightsizing in world history. Jesus will usher in His kingdom on earth as it is in heaven now. From this day until that day, we are called to rise in faith, and along this journey, the Holy Spirit leads and guides us.

At every point, no matter how challenging society becomes for the believer, we who know the Lord and walk with the Holy Spirit will be led by Him. You will avoid the traps and pitfalls by His supernatural favor, which will carry you through every circumstance. Darkness will surely attempt to foil the righteous. Remember, you are the dominating force as long as you do not shrink back in the face of evil.

As you rise in faith and remain unshaken, momentum and revival will follow. This ultimately leads to reformation, placing the disobedient under the authority of the wise. This applies to you at both the personal and macro levels. You must know your part in the body of Christ through tribal alignment.

> *For as many as are led by the Spirit of God, these are sons of God.*
>
> —Romans 8:14

One of the wonderful things the Holy Spirit does is lead the children of God. This should give you great comfort as you consider the days ahead. He will never leave you nor forsake you. In this epic we are living out, what is most thrilling is that God will ultimately see His kingdom established on earth. Through it all, there will be those led by His Spirit, going from glory to glory, overcoming challenges through the Spirit's guidance, and in a significant partnership with God, the Maker of heaven and earth, as our partner.

This is one reason it is a great commissioning: it means the sending, but it is not the great mission, which would be God alone doing everything single-handedly. Rather, God has chosen to work through His Church. This means we will overcome and walk in every divine occasion He has made available.

> *You, dear reader, will avoid all the snares and evil plans of darkness in the days ahead. You cannot be defeated. Some people don't know how to lose. This trait comes from the Father of heavenly lights, who gives us every good and perfect gift.*

CHAPTER NINE

A BLOOD-BOUGHT BELIEVER CARRIES FORCE FOR CULTURAL IMPACT!

> *...and on this rock I will build My church, and the gates of Hades shall not prevail against it.*
>
> —Matthew 16:18

Believers carry raw spiritual horsepower designed to impact the world around them. Culturally, the Church is empowered not to be overcome by the gates of hell, the devil's system.

A believer has power and authority from the moment of salvation, but most do not consider what gives that authority. It is, in fact, Jesus Christ living in His Church and through us. The foundational mechanism for this ability is that you have a physical body. That's right, possessing a physical body is the power to open or close access to the realm of the spirit.

> *Jesus answered, "Most assuredly, I say to you,* ***unless one is born of water and the Spirit, he cannot enter the kingdom of God****."*
>
> —John 3:5

In reality, spiritual forces cannot simply do whatever they like in the natural realm. They must have access, by permission, through a physical body.

Being born of water is a prerequisite for having authority in this natural world. To enter the kingdom of God, a person must be born of water, meaning they are born as a baby into this natural world. Being born of water means a person has a physical body, and that body gives them the choice to enter the kingdom of God or to serve the kingdom of darkness.

VESSELS OR PHYSICAL BODIES CARRY CARGO

Preaching the gospel to every living person is crucial because those with physical bodies need to hear and obey God's will. When an individual changes the direction of their life and becomes a vessel for the Lord, real change can happen in this world. Interestingly, we are vessels of the Lord when we are born again. Vessels carry cargo; it could be said that believers are carriers of God Almighty to this world.

GOD DOESN'T DO WHATEVER HE WANTS

Have you ever asked the questions, "Why doesn't God enforce His will upon humanity, or take over every television and computer in the world, not allowing anything else to be played but gospel preaching, and bombard every person with nonstop truth about the gospel? Why doesn't God do more?"

Many people respond by saying, "God wants people to choose Him, and He has given us free choice. He didn't make us robots, or it wouldn't be a real relationship." Yes, that is true, but it is not the whole reason God has not taken over the airwaves or performed wild miracles in the heavens, such as projecting the gospel message across the sky 24 hours a day. The reason God doesn't do that, or anything like it, is that He set laws in motion for the world.

GOD OPERATES BY THE LAWS HE SET IN MOTION

Going all the way back to the Garden of Eden, God Almighty gave dominion over the garden to Adam and, ultimately, the whole world. When Adam and Eve listened to the voice of a talking serpent rather than the Word of God, they transferred their authority to that same serpent—the devil.

Jesus came as the Last Adam to undo the disaster created by Adam, Eve, and the serpent. He defeated the devil over death, hell, and the grave, and made a way for humanity to hear the good news and be liberated from the devil's control. What used to be Adam and God walking in the cool of the day, a fellowship, was turned into a hostage situation in which the devil took Adam and Eve hostage. Rather than destroying everything and starting over, God patiently walked out His divine plan of redemption through Jesus Christ.

WHY DID IT TAKE 4,000 YEARS FOR JESUS TO ARRIVE?

It took 4,000 years for Jesus to arrive on the scene. Why didn't God create Jesus right when Adam fell? Why didn't He manifest another Adam on the spot? The answer is that God's access to man had been altered, and the dominion He gave man was now under the dominion of a fallen archangel once known as Lucifer, now Satan.

God directly created Adam because He could. God had not yet established the rules of dominion or given dominion to Adam. After He created Adam and Eve, He gave them dominion, which they then gave over to the devil.

The issue became how to undo the horrific predicament we had been placed in. How could God bring forth a Redeemer, the Last Adam, without having Adam's dominion under His jurisdiction?

What became necessary was to work through the only legal path available, mankind's free will. From that very moment when Adam and Eve fell, God prophesied in Genesis 3:15 (NIV), saying, "...he will crush your head, and you will strike his heel."

God instantly activated a prophetic plan. But again, why couldn't God have made Jesus right there on the spot, just as He had made Adam? It was because of the change that had just taken place, and now there was only one avenue to bring Jesus into the earth. Mankind would have to speak prophetically about Jesus for 4,000 years. Prophets and kings, and through various means, God pressed it upon the hearts of these saints of antiquity to speak out the word regarding Jesus.

THE PROPHESIED WORD BECAME FLESH 4,000 YEARS AFTER THE FALL OF ADAM

Finally, after all the words were released and gathered, the miracle of the virgin birth took place. We can say with confidence that the *Word had become flesh*. (*See* John 1:14.)

The Word became flesh and dwelt among us. Jesus fulfilled the prophetic words spoken throughout the Old Testament, guided by God the Father. God Almighty went to tremendous lengths to bring Jesus into the natural world. It took the words of free moral agents, humans submitted to God, to bring the miracle of Jesus into the natural world. The only way God could win the world back to Him was to enter the world legally.

It took those in the world with physical bodies to hear and cooperate with His will by speaking it into the natural, until finally those words were enough and lasted long enough to bring baby Jesus from the Spirit into the natural.

Free moral agency law still applies today! Only now do we have far greater strength and power to enforce the will of God and manifest His desire in the natural world. We are New Testament believers, and He is residing in us through Christ Jesus, His Son. Not only that, but we have the power of the Holy Spirit working through us by the baptism of His Spirit.

GREATER IS HE WHO IS IN US THAN HE WHO IS IN THE WORLD

That is why we can say with authority that *greater is He who is in me than he who is in the world* (*see* 1 John 4:4). Only believers in the New Testament Church Age can say that. Old Testament believers did not have this privilege. In the Old Testament, you rarely hear about demons or even the devil because there was nothing an Old Testament believer in God could do about them.

UNTIL JESUS, ALL WERE TRAPPED UNDER THE DOMINION OF DARKNESS

All were trapped under the dominion of darkness. God would come mightily upon a prophet or a king to enforce His will in a generation or confront wickedness, but today, in the New Covenant era, we all carry the indwelling power of God through Jesus. We are not under the dominion of evil and darkness; rather, we are here to dispel it by God's authority.

It all hinges on humanity and the physical bodies we possess. While alive, a human being can live for God, the devil, or remain neutral, which ultimately amounts to living for the devil anyway. However, whoever has the reins of that physical body through the influence of thought and action will determine the direction their sphere of influence takes. If the devil has a person's mind and actions, he will take territory and dominion in the place of that person's influence. If God controls a person's mind and actions, it will determine the sphere in which they influence His will on earth.

Ultimately, the greatest territory is the mind, and whoever has a person's heart and mind will advance their spiritual agenda.

WE CAN BE CONFIDENT OF BETTER THINGS IN THE NEW COVENANT!

> *But, beloved, we are confident of better things concerning you, yes, things that accompany salvation, though we speak in this manner.* 10 *For God is not unjust to forget your work and labor of love which you have shown toward His name, in that you have ministered to the saints, and do minister.* 11 *And we desire that each one of you show the same diligence to the full assurance of hope until the end,* 12 *that you do not become sluggish, but imitate those who through faith and patience inherit the promises.*
>
> —Hebrews 6:9-12

Early believers and every believer who walks in the revelation of what they received through salvation in Christ Jesus, our Lord, carry boldness and strength. One way to put it is that their presence demanded an explanation. When mature believers are present, they are different; they walk in authority and fearless faith that overcomes the world. This is why they could lay down their lives in the face of terrifying violence and horrific deaths. A man or woman with this revelation from God is not at the mercy of a culture going mad!

THE PRESENCE OF MATURE BELIEVERS SHOULD DEMAND AN EXPLANATION!

> *Nor will they say, "See here!" or "See there!" For indeed, the kingdom of God is within you.*
>
> —Luke 17:21

> *For the kingdom of God is not eating and drinking, but righteousness and peace and joy in the Holy Spirit.*
>
> — Romans 14:17

The believer needs to understand what Jesus paid for when He died on the cross. Without this understanding, it can lead to a performance-based religion, a system of merit-based toil that lacks true righteousness. Knowing what Jesus provided for you will bring clarity, helping you recognize the free gift you have and what it entails.

Activating the revelation of what Jesus paid for will create boldness in the day of adversity and give power to stand in the midst of a crooked and perverse generation. As Revelation 12:11 states, these are the ones who overcome the evil one by *the blood of the Lamb and the word of their testimony, and they love not their lives even unto the death*! Each mature believer who walks in the finished works of Jesus will experience breathtaking confidence through Christ Jesus living through them.

Hebrews 6:9 amplifies this truth. "But, beloved, we are confident of better things concerning you, yes, *things that accompany salvation....*" To know what accompanies your salvation, you must identify what is included in your salvation.

THINGS THAT ACCOMPANY SALVATION

The things that accompany your salvation are powerful and alive in every believer. What must be understood is that having these things available doesn't ward off the powers of darkness; it is knowing and operating in what you have that terrifies them. A revelation of what you received at salvation is the force that comes alive in a believer and brings the powers of darkness to their knees, even in the face of overwhelming opposition, even to the point of laying down their very lives.

WHAT YOU RECEIVE IN SALVATION IS A LOT MORE THAN FIRE INSURANCE

Most believers don't know what they received with salvation, beyond fire insurance or the assurance that they will not burn in hell and the lake of fire for all eternity. Let's explore what a believer truly has upon receiving salvation by examining the words *sozo* and *soteria*. By understanding the whole meaning of these terms, it becomes clear that believers not only receive fire insurance from hell but also so much more!

SOZO: MEANS SAVED *SOTERIA*: MEANS SALVATION

Two Greek words capture the full scope of our salvation experience—*sozo* and *soteria*. When combined, these two words show that our salvation includes seven key aspects.

SEVEN PARTS TO YOUR SALVATION

1. Saved
2. Delivered

3. To do well, to be prosperous
4. Preserved
5. Protected
6. Healed
7. Made whole

A REVELATION OF JESUS IS CRUCIAL TO OVERCOME DARKNESS IN THIS WORLD

> *For I neither received it from man, nor was I taught it, but it came through the revelation of Jesus Christ.*
>
> —Galatians 1:12

Paul the apostle encountered the revelation of Jesus. It set the course for what he preached, taught, and wrote in the New Testament. He didn't experience a revelation about Jesus; he experienced "the" revelation of Jesus.

What must be added to this understanding is the truth that Jesus paid it all. Religion, or man's attempt and striving to please God based on a person's performance and toil, is the opposite of this. There is a tension between grace and faith in this truth. The revelation of Jesus is what changed Paul's life and ministry. Jesus revealed Himself to Paul not only on the road to Damascus but also through a revelation of Himself, as Paul stated: "I did not receive it from man, nor was I taught it, but it came through the revelation of Jesus Christ." If we compare this to the book of Revelation, we see that John the Revelator experienced a revelation of Jesus Christ, but it was a message about the seven churches and the future. Paul received a revelation of who Jesus is, which empowered his message and doctrine.

> *I have been crucified with Christ; it is no longer I who live, but Christ lives in me; and the life which I now live in the flesh* ***I live by faith in the Son of God****, who loved me and gave Himself for me.*
>
> —Galatians 2:20

Grace is what God accomplished through the redemptive sacrifice of Jesus, who paid with His life and blood. Faith is our part, our response to this free gift. Faith means walking in all that Jesus freely gave us, simply by believing in the One whom God sent. Yet there is a corresponding action in that faith—we are to resist what does not align with what Jesus paid for.

RESIST WHAT DOES NOT ALIGN WITH WHAT JESUS PAID FOR

This is a crucial understanding when discussing suffering and standing firm against sin. When viewing the walk of faith through a religious lens, it is a dreadful perspective; however, when looking at righteousness based on what Jesus did, we can have confidence and strength through faith in His finished work—not our own goodness. Faith, through a revelation of what Jesus did for you, will induce boldness in your life!

Years ago, when reading and hearing stories of early church martyrs, I often asked, "How is it that so many believers would fearlessly give up their lives, even at the threat of being torn apart by lions, burned alive, or subjected to even greater violence?" Many were dying horrific deaths, which, at first glance, would seem terrifying. How could they have been so courageous? What gave them such confidence in those final moments of their lives?

They had a revelation of Jesus; it wasn't just willpower or mental toughness—these saints faced such issues with confidence and joy, coming from a place of knowing what they possessed in Christ and who they were in Him.

RELIGION PREACHES DOING AND TRYING—IN JESUS, EVERYTHING IS DONE, AND THE BELIEVER IS NOW TRUSTING

Many believers think that doing all the right things makes them acceptable to Jesus; however, nothing could be further from the truth. When someone is born again, they become a new creation in Him and are one in the Spirit with Him.

*But he who is joined to the Lord is **one spirit with Him**.*

—1 Corinthians 6:17

Therefore, if anyone is in Christ, he is a new creation; old things have passed away; behold, all things have become new.

—2 Corinthians 5:17

Therefore if any person is [ingrafted] in Christ (the Messiah) he is a new creation (a new creature altogether); the old [previous moral and spiritual condition] has passed away. Behold, the fresh and new has come!

—2 Corinthians 5:17 AMPC

*To the general assembly and church of the firstborn who are registered in heaven, to God the Judge of all, to **the spirits of just men made perfect**.*

—Hebrews 12:23

Old things have passed away; behold, all things are made new! You are a new creation in Christ Jesus—a new kind of being that never existed before.

Knowing this provides the right posture for navigating the present age, the time you are living in. Dear reader, you were born to fulfill God's high calling on your life and to take your place in the present kingdom age, in preparation for the age to come.

JESUS IS THE PROTOTYPE

*For whom He foreknew, He also predestined to be conformed to the image of His Son, that **He might be the firstborn among many brethren**.*

—Romans 8:29

Empowerment through what Jesus paid for makes believers a powerful force in the natural world. Jesus was our *prototype,* the Firstborn among many brethren. What He was, we are to walk in His ways. As He is, so are we in this world (*see* 1 John 4:17).

We are His body, His people; we are not only united with Him in the Spirit but are also a direct extension of Him right now, as He is seated at the right hand of the Father. Together, we form the *Ekklesia*, a governing body in this physical world. While we are here, we enforce the will of God (as it is in heaven) on earth. We preach the gospel, and through it, we influence culture with this kingdom message.

God's cry to the entire world is *Repent and be saved!* God's cry to the Church is to *renew your mind to what you have!*

People who know who they are in Jesus and what they are called to do will influence society; this is when reformation occurs. A society shaped by the gospel is how victory is achieved.

Believers must understand this to be truly effective and to walk confidently in the midst of the present evil age. A revelation of what Jesus provided, followed by living in it, will empower one to engage with a fallen world. The world is dead; believers are alive. A believer with this understanding will be well-equipped in this age, leading up to the very end. This is why Paul was so relentless and confident: his revelatory encounter with the Son of the Living God. Believers should be the same.

THE DEVIL CAN'T BEAT THE CHURCH, SO HE ATTEMPTS TO JOIN IT!

If the spirit of the age cannot get you to compromise through sin or rebellion, and if a believer cannot be defeated that way, what often comes next is to run a believer into the cage of religion. Performance for identity is a deception that works very well in the Church. The devil can't beat the Church, so he attempts to join it. What is the purpose? To interfere with the Church's authority and the Great Commission.

The devil will never be a legitimate part of the Church of Jesus, never. He cannot take the Church head-on in a fight and win, so he is left with deception and various forms of suggestion.

THE DEVIL SOWS MESSAGES AND RELIGIOUS IDEOLOGIES CONTRARY TO THE TRUTH OF THE GOSPEL

> *I marvel that you are turning away so soon from Him who called you in the grace of Christ, to a different gospel,* 7 *which is not another; but there are some who trouble you and want to pervert the gospel of Christ.* 8 *But even if we, or an angel from heaven, preach any other gospel to you than what we have preached to you, let him be accursed.* 9 *As we have said before, so now I say again, if anyone preaches any other gospel to you than what you have received, let him be accursed.*
>
> —Galatians 1:6-9

One of the biggest deceptions is performance-based religion, which distracts from maintaining your faith in Jesus Christ, our Lord. In Paul's letter to the Galatians, we see him confront the religious legalism that had infiltrated the church of Galatia. Paul addresses this issue with force. Why is this so destructive? Because it takes your eyes off what Jesus did for you and shifts the focus to you and what you are doing for Him.

Faith in Jesus is the entirety of the gospel; whenever that shifts to something else, it is a doctrine of demons. That was what Paul was aggressively confronting.

In Galatians 1:6-9, Paul used strong language when he said they were turning from the grace of Christ to a different gospel. He went on to say that some want to pervert or twist the gospel of Christ. In verse 8, he made it glaringly clear by saying, "If we, or an angel from heaven, preach any other gospel to you than what we have preached to you, let him be accursed." Just in case the reader missed what Paul meant, he repeated himself in the following verse! Galatians 1:9 continues, "If anyone preaches any other gospel…let him be accursed."

That word "accursed" in Greek is *anathema,* and it carries the meaning of *estrangement from Christ and His salvation.*[1]

All who go back to keeping the law are under obligation to observe the whole law or be cursed (*see* Galatians 3:1-5, 10-12; Galatians 4:21-5:4).

Some Jewish mystics of the period claimed revelations from angels (especially in apocalyptic literature). Oaths and curses were familiar in ancient religion, magic, and everyday life. Paul may allude here to the curses of the covenant leveled against those who failed to keep Moses' law (Deuteronomy 27–28); more significant is the use of this same word for "curse" in the Septuagint of Deuteronomy 13:1-18: false prophets and those who listened to them were to be destroyed.[2]

Paul was an apostle tasked to proclaim the gospel message. There was a group known as the Judaizers, on the other hand, who were cowardly compromisers who mixed Law and grace, hoping to please both Jews and Gentiles, but never asking whether or not they were pleasing God.[3]

This same issue is at hand today, and we must be vigilant to keep the pure gospel message true to the Scripture for the glory of Jesus Christ. In doing so, we will not allow the devil, through his schemes, to, in a sense, join the Church through a bad understanding, thereby rendering the message powerless.

YOU ARE ANOINTED TO BE THE BEST THERE IS!

It is this truth that will give us boldness in the days of adversity we face. As the world shakes and nations experience greater turmoil, we are called to be the best there is, but this cannot be done by our own strength. It must be done through the revelation of Jesus Christ.

Knowing what salvation brings is a game-changer. Don't try harder by striving, living a life of begging, pleading, crying out with long prayers and vain repetitions, and believing you'll be heard for your many words and emotional outbursts. Instead, develop confidence in what Jesus has already provided. Awakening to this truth makes you very dangerous to the kingdom of darkness.

Without knowing this, your life could be defined by performance-based religion. Jesus is Lord, and He deserves our loyalty and free moral agency under His command. This is how winning is done; this is the way of the believer.

CHAPTER TEN

CHURCH AND THE GOVERNMENT: HOW SHOULD THE CHURCH RESPOND TO EVIL LEADERS?

The kingdom of God is not a democracy; it's a kingdom and a theocracy. A present-day cultural issue is the debate over the Church's role in government and where the line lies. What should the Church be doing and what should it not be doing in relation to government in a nation? In this chapter, I hope to shed some light on this issue, as we are in the Church Age and the Church might be forfeiting some surprising things when it does not have to.

It might also be startling to discover that the Church is supposed to have a voice in every area of society; much of what we can or will say depends on the specific structure of government in the nation where believers reside. Also shocking is the recognition that the Church has a much greater responsibility in a nation than many realize.

THE FIRST-CENTURY ZEALOTS AND A WARNING

The Zealots were a Judean Jewish group who formed a first-century political movement with the primary goal of overthrowing the Roman government. They were, in a sense, Jewish patriots. The word "zealot" comes from the Greek word *zelotes,* which carries the meaning *emulator, zealous admirer or follower.*[1]

According to early church historian Josephus, three main Jewish groups were present during the days of Jesus: the Pharisees, the Sadducees, and the Essenes. I agree with this; however, the zealots were also present at that time and would be considered the fourth group.

The Zealots were founded by Judas of Galilee and Zadok the Pharisee. Josephus mentions that the Zealots "agree in all other things with the Pharisaic notions; but they have an inviolable attachment to liberty, and say that God is to be their only Ruler and Lord."

The Zealots led a rebellion against the Roman imperial cult. In AD 66, they seized Jerusalem during the Great Jewish Revolt. Although they captured the city, they ultimately failed in the revolt. In the fateful year AD 70, the Romans came in great force and destroyed the city of Jerusalem and the temple. Masada became the Zealots' final holdout, but they were ultimately trapped in the mountain fortress and overcome by the Roman military.

JESUS WAS ALMOST FORCIBLY TAKEN AND SET AS KING

> *Therefore when Jesus perceived that they were about to come* ***and take Him by force to make Him king,*** *He departed again to the mountain by Himself alone.*
>
> —John 6:15

After Jesus fed the 5,000, the event had such an impact that the people nearly forced Him to become king of Israel. A mission had been prophesied for the Messiah; however, we know that in His first advent, Jesus came to establish the kingdom of God within men by dying and resurrecting for the sins of mankind. He was also doing the Father's will by establishing the Church, or *Ekklesia.*

SIMON THE ZEALOT WAS A DISCIPLE

Matthew and Thomas; James the son of Alphaeus, and ***Simon called the Zealot.***

—Luke 6:15

When the people wanted to take Jesus and make Him king, He withdrew and went to the mountain by Himself. Making Jesus king certainly reflects what the Zealots would have wanted, yet the text doesn't specify that. One of the disciples Jesus chose was Simon the Zealot. Simon might have agreed with the idea of taking Jesus and forcing Him to be king over Israel. As a former Zealot, Simon could have resonated with the pro-Israel worldview and encouraged this idea.

Again, the text doesn't say this about Simon, but Jesus did depart to be alone. He took none of the disciples with Him. It is purely conjecture, but it wouldn't be a far leap to consider that Jesus might have needed to get away from Simon for a moment, since the former Zealot, now a disciple, might have been suggesting to Jesus that being king was the right move.

JESUS DEPARTED FROM THE PRESS OF THE PEOPLE WHO WOULD MAKE HIM KING PREMATURELY

As much as the Zealots loved their nation, they were not part of the purpose Jesus had in preaching and doing the work of the kingdom. This is a major point we must consider. We are to do what is right in our nation, stand up for the gospel, and pursue what is best for the citizens of any nation. However, in doing so, we must always keep the main thing the main thing. At the end of the age, we will not be asked whether we got our nation on track; the question will be, did we do our part in the Great Commission?

Having said this, let it be known that the Church should be deeply involved in the political world and doing everything in its power to bring righteousness to the land. We, as believers in Jesus, are not to go to the Zealot level; however, we are to sound the alarm, stand for what is right, contend for social issues, and get those closest to biblical truth into seats of power.

PACIFISTS, THE EXTREME OPPOSITE OF ZEALOTS

On another note, it is a dereliction of Christian duty not to stand up for society, especially when it comes to the oppression of the weak and those harmed by a ruthless governing power. What we, as believers, are called to do is not to hide and watch but to be involved at a much higher level than unbelievers, even if it costs us everything.

SAINT TELEMACHUS THE HERMIT MONK STOPPED THE GLADIATOR GAMES IN ROME

In the late 4th or early 5th century, there was a monk named Saint Telemachus, a Christian ascetic who had traveled from the East to Rome. Telemachus entered a Roman stadium during a gladiatorial contest and was horrified by what he witnessed. In an attempt to stop the violence, he descended from the stands and entered the arena, shouting for the combatants to cease in the name of Christ. He was murdered in the arena, yet his sacrifice changed the nation. Here is his story:

> An ascetic hermit from the East and unknown except for his final act, Telemachus journeyed to Rome just in time for the victory celebrations. After years of aggressive invasions from the continent, Rome had finally defeated the Goth king Alaric in northern Italy in 403.
>
> As was common in those times, extravagant gladiatorial contests were held in celebration of military victories. The twenty-year-old emperor Honorius decreed that this particular celebration would be held in the 50,000-capacity Coliseum, a battleground named for the colossal 130-foot statue of Nero nearby, the emperor made

famous for condemning Christians into human torches. If there was one place in all of Rome that a pacifist Christian might consider avoiding, the Coliseum was it. Telemachus, a "rudely clad man of rough but imposing presence," resolved to interrupt, indeed to stop, the bloody contest in the Coliseum.

Thousands had gathered that day. Cries of "habet, hoc habet" erupted from the crowds—"He has had it!" they cried every time a fighter was mortally wounded. In this atmosphere Telemachus jumped from the crowd into the arena itself, no longer spectator but activist, peacemaker, preacher.

"Do not requite God's mercy," he screamed, "in turning away the swords of your enemies by murdering each other!" Certainly the crowd heard him, but the gladiators continued fighting. Telemachus ran between the gladiators, pleading with them to stop. "Sedition! Sedition! Down with him!" roared the crowd.

"This is no place for preaching! The old customs of Rome must be observed! On, gladiators!" Still, Telemachus continued to turn from one encounter to another, stopping gladiators in mid-fight. Then, frustrated by the annoyance of one man interrupting the games, someone pulled a sword and, thrusting it, Telemachus fell. Joining in, the crowd threw stones down from their seats to the arena below.

News quickly spread throughout Rome that the murdered man was the hermit Telemachus. Rome was shocked, as was Emperor Honorius, that such a gentle man had been slain. Telemachus's courage and boldness to speak God's mercy and love changed the games forever. A man bent on peace, Telemachus lost his life fighting in the grandest battleground of Rome. Soon after his death, gladiatorial battles were banned from the Coliseam. Telemachus had achieved the impossible.[2]

Heroes of the faith do not often come as we might expect. Standing for what is right in your generation might cost everything. In Telemachus' case, the price was his life. Yet from his courageous stand for morality, he turned the tide in a nation.

SUBMISSION TO THE GOVERNMENT: THE ROMANS 13 QUESTION

> *Let every soul be subject to the governing authorities. For there is no authority except from God, and the authorities that exist are appointed by God. [2] Therefore whoever resists the authority resists the ordinance of God, and those who resist will bring judgment on themselves. [3] For rulers are not a terror to good works, but to evil. Do you want to be unafraid of the authority? Do what is good, and you will have praise from the same. [4] For he is God's minister to you for good. But if you do evil, be afraid; for he does not bear the sword in vain; for he is God's minister, an avenger to execute wrath on him who practices evil.*
>
> —Romans 13:1-4

One topic that often comes up in conversations about believers and governmental authority is submission to government. Many immediately revert to Romans 13, saying, "God placed these leaders in the positions they are in," and, as a result, adopt a lackadaisical mindset toward governing authorities. What should be considered is that the context of that passage might be shocking in light of what we are about to look at.

ROMANS 13 WAS WRITTEN UNDER A MONARCHY

When Paul wrote Romans 13, the society in which they lived was under a monarchical form of rule. The emperors who ruled with absolute authority often considered themselves gods. This was often followed by demands to be worshiped as a god. Even those who were more benevolent still ruled with complete domination. What they said was what went—period.

What should be considered right out of the gate is that John the Baptist was unafraid of the governing authorities of his day, calling them out for their sinful behavior. Ultimately, this cost him his life. (*See* Matthew 14:1-12 and Mark 6:14-29.)

JESUS CALLED HEROD A FOX

> *On that very day some Pharisees came, saying to Him, "Get out and depart from here, for Herod wants to kill You."* [32] *And He said to them,* ***"Go, tell that fox,*** *'Behold, I cast out demons and perform cures today and tomorrow, and the third day I shall be perfected.'"*
>
> —Luke 13:31-32

When pressed, Jesus rebuked the government by calling Herod a *fox*. Some scholars believe this was a reference to Herod's perverse lifestyle or a gesture toward his deviant, sly behavior in all things. It could have been both! Additionally, in a deeper study, I discovered that the word "fox" refers to a *vixen, a female fox*. One takeaway could be that Jesus was speaking to the real authority behind Herod's madness—Herodias, the wife of Herod's brother Philip, whom Herod had taken as his own.

FOX OR VIXEN

Jesus may have been pointing to her as the real authority in the house. By calling Herod a vixen, Jesus may have been saying, "I'm not talking to you, Herod; I'm talking to the one who is really in charge, the real leader of your perverse household, Herodias." Regardless of what Jesus was saying, He was responding with a strongly negative connotation toward the governing authority of His day. That point is worth considering in light of Romans 13. Setting that aside, we need to take a deeper look at Romans 13 to understand what it says and how it relates to you.

DO NOT RESIST THE ORDINANCE OF GOD

> *Therefore, whoever resists the authority resists the ordinance of God, and those who resist will bring judgment on themselves.*
>
> —Romans 13:2

Romans 13:2 is very clear and straightforward, but context matters. After all, *a text without its context is a pre-text*, as it has been said. When you read a text out of context, you are left with a con.

Verse 3 sheds further light on the subject.

> *For* ***rulers are not a terror to good works, but to evil****. Do you want to be unafraid of the authority? Do what is good, and you will have praise from the same.*
>
> —Romans 13:3

We see that God appoints rulers not for terror but for good works. They are appointed by God for a specific task—to be a terror to evil works.

WHAT HAPPENS WHEN A RULER WHO IS APPOINTED FOR GOOD USES THEIR POSITION FOR EVIL?

> *For* ***he is God's minister to you for good****. But if you do evil, be afraid; for he does not bear the sword in vain; for* ***he is God's minister, an avenger to execute wrath on him who practices evil****.*
>
> —Romans 13:4

In Romans 13:4, we see that rulers are appointed by God to be ministers of good, ultimately to act as avengers, executing wrath on those who practice evil.

Some might ask, "But what happens when a ruler perverts their office of authority? What are believers to do?" Under a monarchy, the only real course of action was to disobey the ruler whenever the Bible or God's commands were violated, even at the risk of their very lives. This is what many of the saints of old did.

They resisted sin to the point of laying down their lives, remaining loyal to Jesus. If a kingdom or empire imposed on the saints was contrary to God's will, believers were to resist by continuing God's work, regardless of any earthly authority's demands, at whatever cost.

IN THE UNITED STATES OF AMERICA, THE MONARCHY IS *WE THE PEOPLE*

Here is the major difference between present-day America and nations that are fundamentally similar. We are not a monarchy; we are a republic, and as such, we are not the subjects of a king or an emperor. Instead, *We the People* are the ones in charge. The political figures in our culture work for the people, according to the Constitution. We, the people, are the boss, and in this unique scenario, we find a very different biblical approach to Romans 13.

As believers, we are to uphold the laws of the land, and if we are going to be biblical, this means it is not just our right—it is our *responsibility* to ensure that those in the high offices of the land adhere to the Founding Fathers' wishes, as clearly laid out in the Constitution and our Declaration of Independence.

A BIBLICAL FIDUCIARY'S RESPONSIBILITY

> *I pledge allegiance to the flag of the United States of America; and to the Republic for which it stands, one Nation under God, indivisible, with liberty and justice for all.*

We have a fiduciary responsibility to our republic to keep it *one Nation under God, indivisible, with liberty and justice for all.* When a political figure engages in corrupt conduct or violates our nation's original purpose, we, the people, must act through voting, legislation, and by making our voices heard to change the wrongful activities of any political figure or voice in high office. It is our civic duty as citizens of a free nation; it is also our biblical duty as believers in this nation.

EACH NATION IS DIFFERENT

Now, if a modern nation in which a believer lives does not have a foundation built on these principles, it leaves no other option but to obey God rather than man. However, where the law of the land does not conflict with the will of God, believers in that nation are to follow that law.

We have been largely duped in America by our culture, through the dumbing down of what we can and cannot do. Leaders in the political realm and those with a cultural agenda will attempt to conceal the truth from the public and lead us to believe that our rights are merely privileges.

IGNORANCE IS CURRENCY FOR EVIL POLITICIANS TO STAY IN POWER

Many hold the fallacious view that our rights are not rights at all but privileges granted to us by our political overlords. Nothing could be further from the truth. In our current day, ignorance is the currency of wicked leaders who want nothing more than to keep our citizens as beggars and underlings to their agendas of control and global dominance.

WHAT DOES NATIONAL REVIVAL LOOK LIKE?

If our leaders are doing wrong, we are to speak out and contend for what is right. Something we often hear is that America needs a revival. Yes, and amen. But what is a national revival?

1. A national revival would be a massive number of people coming to the saving knowledge of Jesus.
2. At the national level, it would mean the nation returning to its original purpose. In the case of the United States of America, it would mean

making the land constitutional again. It would mean training our children in the wishes of the Founding Fathers, shining a light on the reality that America was founded on Christian principles, and bringing us completely back to that.

God will eventually deal with every nation that has come against His saints. Consider the judgment against Rome described in the book of Revelation.

> *Then one of the seven angels who had the seven bowls came and talked with me, saying to me,* ***"Come, I will show you the judgment of the great harlot who sits on many waters."***
>
> —Revelation 17:1

> *I saw the woman,* ***drunk with the blood of the saints and with the blood of the martyrs of Jesus****. And when I saw her, I marveled with great amazement.*
>
> —Revelation 17:6

According to the *IVP Bible Background Commentary,* Rome, whose empire spread throughout the Mediterranean coasts, is portrayed here in Revelation 17 as sitting on many waters (cf. Psalm 65:7; Isaiah 17:12-13). John the apostle, or "The seer of Patmos," speaks of Rome as "the great harlot…drunk with the blood of the saints and the blood of the martyrs of Jesus." Although Rome fell, many Bible prophecy scholars and commentators believe that this great harlot will yet be fulfilled in the end times.

THE LORD'S DAY, JESUS REVEALS A GOVERNMENTAL CONFRONTATION THROUGH THE PROPHETIC EXPERIENCES OF JOHN

> *I was in the Spirit on* ***the Lord's Day****, and I heard behind me a loud voice, as of a trumpet.*
>
> —Revelation 1:10

My friend Rick Renner wrote something tremendous in his masterful book, *A Light in Darkness: Seven Messages to the Seven Churches, volume one*. It gives insight into the Lord's Day in a way only Rick can. This was a day set aside for emperor worship, and Jesus arrived at that exact time to meet with John and made a statement.

> John related that this happened on "the Lord's day." Casual readers take this to mean "Sunday," but it actually has nothing to do with Sunday at all. The phrase "the Lord's day" is a translation of the Greek word *kuriakos,* a specific word that was used primarily to describe *the Emperor's Day.*
>
> It has been proven from ancient inscriptions that the word *kuriakos* was a common word for anything *imperial* and that the first day of each month was designated as an *imperial day* when the ruling emperor was especially celebrated. That day was referred to as *kuriakos* or the *Emperor's Day.*
>
> This means Jesus Christ chose to reveal Himself as the *King of kings* and *Lord of lords* on the very day that the entire Roman Empire was specially celebrating the supposed deity of the wicked Emperor Domitian. It must have struck John that on the same day when the whole world was worshiping a fraudulent, evil human ruler, the *True Ruler* stepped into the forsaken place where John was exiled and revealed Himself in all of His glory to him.[3]

Further insight into John the Revelator's encounter with the Lord on "the Lord's Day." Romans set aside certain days for emperor worship and called them "the Augustean day." One day a month was dedicated to the honor of the emperor in Asia Minor. This is a powerful moment because Jesus stepped onto that holiday to make clear that Domitian, nor any other emperor, is the one to be worshiped—rather, Jesus Christ is the One to be worshiped. His arrival to John on that exact day was His way of saying they are not the King. I AM!

OUTGROWING THE YOKE IS ONE BIBLICAL WAY TO OVERCOME A WICKED RULERSHIP

So it will be in that day, that his burden will be removed from your shoulders and his yoke from your neck, and the yoke will be broken because of fatness.

—Isaiah 10:27 NASB

Wicked rulers are those who pervert their office of power. Nothing new here; Lucifer did the same. He was appointed to a task, yet he turned it to his own desires. Judgment came against him for this mutinous activity. When evil leaders or governments do this, our role is to walk in the blessing to such a degree that we can outgrow their yoke!

Isaiah 10:27 illustrates this scenario. When God's people were oppressed and dominated by a kingdom, they grew. Where it says the anointing, another translation calls it the fatness. It describes an animal's muscular neck that becomes too massive. It first lifts the yoke off the shoulder—30-fold, then loosens it around the neck—60-fold, until finally the yoke is destroyed—100-fold breakthrough, rendered completely useless.

The message is this: we are to outgrow containment! When evil oppresses, it is our job to expand our influence across every sector until the yoke is destroyed. Through sheer presence, influence, and power in society, we smash the yoke. This is a 30-, 60-, and 100-fold action toward the full potential of freedom.

CHAPTER ELEVEN

THE RESTRAINING FORCE HOLDS THE ANTICHRIST BACK UNTIL THE RAPTURE OF THE CHURCH

And He said: "Take heed that you not be deceived. For many will come in My name, saying, 'I am He,' and, 'The time has drawn near.' Therefore do not go after them."

—Luke 21:8

As we approach the end of the age, Jesus forewarned us to be vigilant and keep our hearts and minds on Him. Crisis fatigue is real. The antidote is to rise in faith and stay filled with the Word of God. As I often say while speaking or broadcasting, read the Bible until it talks back to you. Or, as Rick Renner says, "Read the Bible but let it read you!" That is such a powerful thing to do. Let the Bible read you, go to the fabric of your being, and alter all things that are not of God. The Word will wash you, keep you, and strengthen you.

THE NUMBER OF PROPHECIES ABOUT THE FIRST AND SECOND COMING

Many scholars agree that there are approximately 330 prophecies concerning Jesus, and about 110 of them speak of His First Coming. In the Old

Testament, 1,500 verses speak of the Messiah coming in glory and judgment. In the New Testament, the Second Coming, or Second Advent, is mentioned eight times for every one mention of the First Coming of Jesus. Jesus Himself mentioned His Second Coming 20 times, and these mentions coincide with more than 50 admonitions and warnings to watch for His return at the end.

Prayer is the companion to Bible reading and will also keep you strong and free from deception or terror. These are the two issues Jesus brought to light and warned us about. Our Lord would not warn us about something without giving us the tools and means to overcome it.

VAGABOND BELIEVERS WHO WANDER

Then many false prophets will rise up and deceive many.

—Matthew 24:11

Two warnings must be understood as we draw closer to the Lord's appearing. Not being deceived carries various connotations, but I find what Jesus said in Matthew 24 to be of utmost importance. Matthew 24:11 says that many false prophets will rise and deceive many.

One meaning of the Greek word "deceive" is *planao*, which means *to cause to wander.*[1] Believers in Christ face many challenges; nonetheless, it is not easy to deceive a true believer who walks with the Lord. The Holy Spirit is present to guide us into all truth and will help us avoid outright deception; however, there is a caveat. Believers may not turn away from Jesus and His Lordship, but through life's trials, bad experiences, consistently hearing wrong teachings, or false prophets, a believer can step on a path that is off course.

What does this mean? Deceived means to cause to wander, which is one of the worst things for a believer: to walk through life aimlessly, missing their God-ordained target. Darkness might not turn them from the Lord; they might not renounce Christ or do something horrific that affects their eternal relationship with God. Yet they can be rendered ineffective by wandering.

Deception can simply take a believer off course just enough to miss a seasonal target or, God forbid, a lifelong goal.

Offenses, trials, and betrayal can all play a role in this wandering, vagabond believer. The cure is a good connection to a body of believers and regular Bible reading. On a very fundamental level, clarity will remain.

SEE THAT YOU ARE NOT TERRIFIED

> *But when you hear of wars and commotions, do not be terrified; for these things must come to pass first, but the end will not come immediately.*
>
> —Luke 21:9

Luke 21:9 clearly states that, as Jesus describes to the disciples what will happen at the end of the age and the hardships that will befall the earth, He directly tells them, "Do not be terrified." A point we should take to heart as the days ahead intensify with all that the Bible clearly says will happen.

Knowing what Jesus says to us should be a great source of comfort as we move forward in His kingdom purpose. He would not have said these things to us if they were not possible. Rather, with the help of the Holy Spirit, we can walk through any challenge and overcome it each time.

Wars, rumors of wars, nations rising against nations, pestilences, earthquakes, unstable seas, signs in the sun and the moon—none of it is to be feared!

> *Let not your heart be troubled; you believe in God, believe also in Me.*
>
> —John 14:1

Comfort can be found in this verse, where Jesus clearly states, "Let not your heart be troubled." This means you are in control of what your heart feels, and, like an umpire, you allow or do not allow troubles into your heart. If this were not the case, Jesus would never have said it! He did say it, however, and as a result, we have the promise of His Word to stand up under whatever this world throws at us. Rising to victorious living from a heart that is not troubled is a choice we must make every day, and we must not let anything that counters the Word of God and His promises to us affect this reality.

As redemption draws near, we must also understand that the Church, or the *Ekklesia,* is the restraining force that prevents the full-out operation of the Beast and the forces of darkness from gaining free rein of the landscape. Earth and all its inhabitants are shielded from the full force of evil that will break loose once we are removed.

THE RESTRAINING FORCE HOLDING BACK THE ANTICHRIST

> *Let no one deceive you by any means; for that Day will not come unless the falling away comes first, and the man of sin is revealed, the son of perdition,* [4] *who opposes and exalts himself above all that is called God or that is worshiped, so that he sits as God in the temple of God, showing himself that he is God.* [5] *Do you not remember that when I was still with you I told you these things?* [6] *And* ***now you know what is restraining****, that he may be revealed in his own time.* [7] *For the mystery of lawlessness is already at work; only* ***He who now restrains will do so until He is taken out of the way****.* [8] *And then the lawless one will be revealed, whom the Lord will consume with the breath of His mouth and destroy with the brightness of His coming.*
>
> —2 Thessalonians 2:3-8

Second Thessalonians 2:6-7 indicates that a restraining force prevents the man of sin, or Antichrist, from being revealed. There are several viewpoints on what this restraining force is. In Rick Renner's excellent book *The Rapture, the Antichrist, and the Tribulation,* Rick masterfully shines light on the restraining force. Here, I will briefly summarize Rick's points on who or what this restraining force might be.

Rick points out that the common thought is that there are five things it could be.

1. The Roman Senate: Historian and theologian Tertullian suggested in about 200 AD that the restrainer was the Roman Empire, particularly in its role of maintaining law and order. This was a belief that the Roman government of the day kept the rise of the Antichrist at bay. This is flawed, as we know the Roman Empire ceased to exist, the Antichrist did not appear that day when the government was taken away. This cannot be the restrainer for the simple fact that it no longer exists, and it should be said that no government is the answer to restraining the Antichrist, for that matter.

2. The Archangel Michael: It has been suggested that the restrainer is the Archangel Michael. Who is noted for taking a stand to prevent the activities of evil principalities. This is found in places such as Daniel. Also in Jude 9, while Michael debated over the body of Moses. In Revelation 12:7, Michael and his angels fight against the devil and the fallen angels. Michael fights the dragon and holds back the forces of darkness. Michael, however, does not fit the description of "he" in 2 Thessalonians 2:7; he is a singular force and not in the midst of everything in the world at this time.

3. The Preaching of the Gospel: The Gospel is indeed being preached, and it changes the world and nations, but there is a glitch in the idea that the Gospel is the restrainer. It will never be removed. Revelation 7:4-8 tells us that there will be 144,000 Jewish preachers who will preach God's Word even in that dark season of time. Therefore, the preaching of the Gospel cannot be the restraining force.

4. The Holy Spirit: As powerful as the Holy Spirit is, He will not be removed from the earth. The Holy Spirit will still be on earth, acting as the great "Change Agent," even during the Great Tribulation, as some will respond to the preaching of the 144,000, with scores saved during that time (***see*** Revelation 7:9-17). After

all, Jesus said in John 6:44, "No one can come to Me unless the Father who sent Me draws him; and I will raise him up at the last day." If people are going to get saved during the Great Tribulation, the Holy Spirit must remain on earth during that time; He cannot be the restrainer.

5. The Church: In Matthew 16:18, Jesus spoke of the Church's power, even against the gates of hell. He said, "…I will build my church, and the gates of hell shall not prevail against it." Something to remember here is that the rapture of the Church is a core New Testament doctrine and that it will one day be caught away. The Church is also present in every part of society, including the business world, athletics, the arts, education, government, the medical field, and all spheres of life. When considering the restraining force, only the Church can be found in every aspect of society worldwide. Paul tells us the rapture of the Church will occur one day. This clearly means a time is coming when the Church will be suddenly removed and taken out of the way—exactly as Paul states, at that exact synchronized moment, the Lawless One, or the Antichrist, will no longer be restrained. He will be revealed to the world.[2]

WHAT IS THE RESTRAINER?

Of all these possibilities, only one logically fits the identity of the great restrainer that is currently holding back the advent of the Antichrist and the evil that will accompany the end of the age. It is the Church. Yes, the great restrainer is the Church, or *Ekklesia,* founded on the Rock, with Jesus Christ as Lord. All five listed things have a restraining influence on the earth and the affairs of man. Only one of these is the restrainer, the Church, the body of Christ on the earth.

As the restraining force, the Church is the presence of God that holds things back. Jesus has empowered His Church as a direct extension of Himself in this natural world. First John 4:17 says, "…as He is, so are we in this world."

Understanding that the Church is the restrainer should give you boldness! It is a position of authority and dominance that, when realized, causes a believer to walk into the future with confidence rather than shrink back from the present evil age in which we live.

THE RAPTURE OF THE CHURCH

> *For the Lord Himself will descend from heaven with a shout, with the voice of an archangel, and with the trumpet of God. And the dead in Christ will rise first.* [17] *Then we who are alive and remain shall be caught up together with them in the clouds to meet the Lord in the air. And thus we shall always be with the Lord.* [18] *Therefore comfort one another with these words.*
>
> —1 Thessalonians 4:16-18

We will remain the restrainer until we are caught up to meet the Lord in the air. This is known as the *Rapture* of the Church, or *harpazo,* the taking away of the saints.

Some will say the word "rapture" is not in the Bible, but it is. The English word is not found in the King James Version, but the Latin word *rapiemur* appears in the Latin Vulgate, translating the Greek word *harpazo*, meaning *to be seized.*[3] In the King James Version, this word is translated as *caught up*. God's main purpose in taking believers away is to pour out wrath on earth, something He could not do without His people being removed.

WE WILL BE CAUGHT UP!

Here are other examples of being caught up in scripture:

> *I know a man in Christ who fourteen years ago—whether in the body I do not know, or whether out of the body I do not know, God knows—such a one was caught up to the third heaven.* [3] *And I know such a man—whether in the body or out of the body I do not know, God knows—*[4] *how*

> ***he was caught up*** *into Paradise and heard inexpressible words, which it is not lawful for a man to utter.*
>
> —2 Corinthians 12:2-4

> *She bore a male Child who was to rule all nations with a rod of iron. And her Child was* ***caught up*** *to God and His throne.*
>
> —Revelation 12:5

ANOTHER RENDERING IS TAKEN BY FORCE

Here are some scriptural examples of the phrase taken by force:

> *And from the days of John the Baptist until now the kingdom of heaven suffers violence, and the violent* ***take it by force****.*
>
> —Matthew 11:12

> *All things that the Father has are Mine. Therefore I said that* ***He will take of Mine*** *and declare it to you.*
>
> —John 16:15

> *Now when there arose a great dissension, the commander, fearing lest Paul might be pulled to pieces by them, commanded the soldiers to go down and* ***take him by force*** *from among them, and bring him into the barracks.*
>
> —Acts 23:10

DURING THE RAPTURE WE WILL ALL BE CHANGED

> *Now this I say, brethren, that flesh and blood cannot inherit the king-*
> *dom of God; nor does corruption inherit incorruption.* 51 *Behold, I tell*
> *you a mystery:* ***We shall not all sleep, but we shall all be changed—***
> 52 *in a moment, in the twinkling of an eye, at the last trumpet. For the*
> *trumpet will sound, and the dead will be raised incorruptible, and we*

shall be changed. [53] For this corruptible must put on incorruption, and this mortal must put on immortality. [54] So when this corruptible has put on incorruption, and this mortal has put on immortality, then shall be brought to pass the saying that is written: "Death is swallowed up in victory."

—1 Corinthians 15:50-54

In that moment, in the twinkling of an eye, we will be given glorified bodies and leave this earth to meet the Lord in the air. This includes resurrected saints who will come back to life and receive their new, imperishable, glorified bodies. First Corinthians 15:51 reveals that this is a mystery. What was unknown in the Old Testament is made known in the New Testament.

UPON SEEING JESUS IN HIS GLORIFIED STATE, WE WILL BE MADE LIKE HIM!

*Beloved, now we are children of God; and it has not yet been revealed what we shall be, but we know that when He is revealed, **we shall be like Him, for we shall see Him as He is**.*

—1 John 3:2

Imagine that moment! Suddenly, we will be caught up and, upon meeting the Lord in the air, our bodies will undergo a miraculous transformation. We will be made into the same kind of body He has, for we will be made like Him. That is amazing to ponder.

THE RAPTURE AND THE SECOND COMING

Then the Lord will go forth and fight against those nations, as He fights in the day of battle. [4] And in that day His feet will stand on the Mount of Olives, which faces Jerusalem on the east. And the Mount of Olives

> *shall be split in two, from east to west, making a very large valley; half of the mountain shall move toward the north and half of it toward the south.*
>
> —Zechariah 14:3-4

Many debate the difference between the Rapture and the Second Coming, arguing that there is a distinction between the two. One difference that cannot be avoided is that at the Rapture, the Lord meets us in the clouds and in the air. At His Second Coming, the Lord Jesus will descend to earth and stand on the Mount of Olives, which will cause a massive earthquake and the ultimate defeat of His enemies.

Aside from the arguments about the Rapture and the Second Coming, there is the question of when the Rapture will take place.

LIST OF THE MAIN VIEWS ON THE TIMING OF THE RAPTURE OF THE CHURCH

It is my personal belief that the Church will be part of a Pre-Tribulation Rapture. Yet I wanted to point out a variety of viewpoints circulating about when the Rapture will occur.

PRE-TRIBULATION RAPTURE

Pre-Tribulationism holds that the Rapture occurs before the Tribulation. In an instant, the Church will meet Jesus in the air and be taken to Heaven. The period from the Rapture to Jesus' Second Coming lasts seven years. During those seven years, those taken to Heaven will participate in the Judgment Seat of Christ (also known as the Bema Seat of Christ) and the Marriage Supper of the Lamb.

THE BEMA SEAT OF CHRIST

> *But why do you judge your brother? Or why do you show contempt for your brother? For we shall all stand before the judgment seat of Christ.* [11]

For it is written: "As I live, says the Lord, every knee shall bow to Me, and every tongue shall confess to God." [12] *So then each of us shall give account of himself to God.*

—Romans 14:10-12

For we must all appear before the judgment seat of Christ, that each one may receive the things done in the body, according to what he has done, whether good or bad.

—2 Corinthians 5:10

The Judgment Seat of Christ will occur during the seven-year Tribulation. This will differ from the Great White Throne Judgment, reserved for the wicked and unbelievers. According to 2 Corinthians 5:10, everyone in Heaven will appear before the Bema Seat to receive what is due based on their deeds on earth, whether good or bad. Jesus will examine everything we do, including how we treated the resources God gave us, whether we were faithful with our gifts, whether we yielded to the Holy Spirit, and whether we honored Jesus with our lives. The reward will be given based on these answers.

According to the grace of God which was given to me, as a wise master builder I have laid the foundation, and another builds on it. But let each one take heed how he builds on it. [11] *For no other foundation can anyone lay than that which is laid, which is Jesus Christ.* [12] *Now if anyone builds on this foundation with gold, silver, precious stones, wood, hay, straw,* [13] *each one's work will become clear; for the Day will declare it, because it will be revealed by fire; and the fire will test each one's work, of what sort it is.* [14] *If anyone's work which he has built on it endures, he will receive a reward.* [15] *If anyone's work is burned, he will suffer loss; but he himself will be saved, yet so as through fire.*

—1 Corinthians 3:10-15

According to 1 Corinthians 3:10-15, our works on earth will be tested by fire. Items of value, such as gold, silver, or precious stones, will withstand the fire and not be burned. These will earn a reward. However, those whose foundation is built on wood, hay, or straw will have it burned up by the fire. These individuals will still inherit eternal life, but they will suffer a loss of reward.

MARRIAGE SUPPER OF THE LAMB

> *"Let us be glad and rejoice and give Him glory, for the marriage of the Lamb has come, and His wife has made herself ready."* [8] *And to her it was granted to be arrayed in fine linen, clean and bright, for the fine linen is the righteous acts of the saints.* [9] *Then he said to me, "Write: 'Blessed are those who are called to the marriage supper of the Lamb!' " And he said to me, "These are the true sayings of God."*
>
> —Revelation 19:7-9

The Bride (the Church) will take part in the Marriage Supper of the Lamb. John offers a symbolic interpretation of a wedding feast. This feast gathers believers from every nation throughout history, as well as the raptured Church. Christ (the Bridegroom) will be united with the Church (the Bride), and the celebration will be extravagant and grand. Imagine it. The long-awaited event will finally arrive, and people of every tribe and tongue will be able to take part in this joyous occasion. It will be an event like no other. It will also feel like a family reunion, with every moment shared with those who endured till the end.

> *And in this mountain the Lord of hosts will make for all people a feast of choice pieces, a feast of wines on the lees, of fat things full of marrow, of well-refined wines on the lees.*
>
> —Isaiah 25:6

Isaiah 25:6 is a prophetic verse that describes a glorious feast, similar to a wedding reception. Many believe this feast will take place on Earth at the start of the Millennial Reign. Those who survive the Tribulation and the Battle of Armageddon will be present in their natural bodies. Also in attendance will be the Church, those with glorified bodies; Old Testament saints who were resurrected at the Second Coming with glorified bodies; and the Tribulation martyrs. According to Isaiah 25:6, they will enjoy the choicest food and well-aged wine. Father God is the host, and the location is on His mountain, often interpreted as Zion on Earth. The number of people present will be so large that one can only imagine the size of the table!

PARTIAL RAPTURE

> *For the Lord Himself will descend from heaven with a shout, with the voice of an archangel, and with the trumpet of God. And the dead in Christ will rise first.* [17] *Then we who are alive and remain shall be caught up together with them in the clouds to meet the Lord in the air. And thus we shall always be with the Lord.*
>
> —1 Thessalonians 4:16-17

> *Watch therefore, and pray always that you may be counted worthy to escape all these things that will come to pass, and to stand before the Son of Man.*
>
> —Luke 21:36

The Partial Rapture Theory holds that only those considered spiritually prepared will be taken in the Rapture. This understanding emphasizes those who are *watching* and *praying* for Christ's return. Luke 21:36 uses these key words and continues that these will be worthy to *escape* in the Rapture. Those who are left behind would not meet that criterion. They would be living life, doing everything except waiting and being ready for Christ's return.

Other scriptures cited to support this theory include Matthew 24:42, which says, "Watch therefore, for you do not know what hour your Lord is coming." The Parable of the Wise and Foolish Virgins in Matthew

25:1-13 is also cited to emphasize the need for believers to be ready for the Bridegroom's return.

The issues that arise with this theory concern how we gauge readiness and watchfulness. Could this idea become a work-based understanding? Would those who are left behind even be Christians? This suggests that many would be denied the right to the Rapture because they don't understand the concept.

MID-TRIBULATION RAPTURE

Mid-Tribulation views hold that the Rapture of the Church occurs at the midpoint of the seven-year Tribulation. This is considered Daniel's 70th week.

> *Seventy weeks are determined for your people and for your holy city, to finish the transgression, to make an end of sins, to make reconciliation for iniquity, to bring in everlasting righteousness, to seal up vision and prophecy, and to anoint the Most Holy.* 25 *"Know therefore and understand, that from the going forth of the command to restore and build Jerusalem until Messiah the Prince, there shall be seven weeks and sixty-two weeks; the street shall be built again, and the wall, even in troublesome times.* 26 *"And after the sixty-two weeks Messiah shall be cut off, but not for Himself; and the people of the prince who is to come shall destroy the city and the sanctuary. The end of it shall be with a flood, and till the end of the war desolations are determined.* 27 *Then he shall confirm a covenant with many for one week; but in the middle of the week He shall bring an end to sacrifice and offering, and on the wing of abominations shall be one who makes desolate, even until the consummation, which is determined, is poured out on the desolate."*
>
> —Daniel 9:24-27

According to Daniel 9:24-27, the 70th week of Daniel is a key prophecy about the seven-year Tribulation. This period occurs before the Second Coming of Christ. During this time, the Antichrist makes a covenant with Israel. At the midpoint, the Abomination of Desolation, a blasphemous act of idolatry or the desecration of God's Temple, occurs. At that point, the Antichrist assumes full power, and intense persecution begins. Those who hold this view believe that believers will be part of the first 3.5 years of the Tribulation. These years are referred to as the "beginning of sorrows." They believe that at the conclusion of those 3.5 years, the Rapture of the Church will take place. This is because the Church is spared from God's direct wrath, also known as the "Great Tribulation."

The common criticism of this theory is that God's wrath is not intended for believers. According to Revelation 6, the Seal judgments include catastrophic events such as wars, famine, death, and martyrdom. Revelation 6:17 states, "For the great day of His wrath has come, and who is able to stand?" This occurs at the Sixth Seal, well before the midpoint of the Seventh Trumpet. Since believers are promised deliverance from God's wrath, if they are present during the first half, it would contradict God's protection.

PRE-WRATH RAPTURE

Those who follow the Pre-wrath Rapture theory believe Christians will be present for most of the Tribulation. They hold that the Church will be raptured after the Great Tribulation but before the full outpouring of God's wrath, about five to six years into the Tribulation. The view distinguishes the Tribulation from God's wrath. The early events of the seven years include the wrath of man, Satan, and the Antichrist. This timeframe does not include God's direct wrath. It is also when believers will face persecution, and martyrs will be made. According to Revelation 8–16, the wrath of God begins with the Day of the Lord. The "Day of the Lord" is regarded as a period of intense divine judgment that begins with the opening of the Seventh Seal. Following this will be the Seven Trumpets and the Seven Bowls, leading up to Armageddon, the fall of Babylon, and then to God's final wrath before Jesus' return for the Millennial Reign.

According to this theory, there are no biblical distinctions in early Tribulation events between the "wrath of Satan" and the "wrath of God." The timing is also vague, with no scriptural support for the exact timeline.

Thus, the five-to-six-year mark before the Rapture. With this understanding, there are no specific signs to look for that would indicate when the Rapture will take place during that time. This means people won't know what to look for.

POST-TRIBULATION RAPTURE

> *Immediately after the tribulation of those days the sun will be darkened, and the moon will not give its light; the stars will fall from heaven, and the powers of the heavens will be shaken.* [30] *Then the sign of the Son of Man will appear in heaven, and then all the tribes of the earth will mourn, and they will see the Son of Man coming on the clouds of heaven with power and great glory.* [31] *And He will send His angels with a great sound of a trumpet, and they will gather together His elect from the four winds, from one end of heaven to the other.*
>
> —Matthew 24:29-31

> *And I saw thrones, and they sat on them, and judgment was committed to them. Then I saw the souls of those who had been beheaded for their witness to Jesus and for the word of God, who had not worshiped the beast or his image, and had not received his mark on their foreheads or on their hands. And they lived and reigned with Christ for a thousand years.* [5] *But the rest of the dead did not live again until the thousand years were finished. This is the first resurrection.*
>
> —Revelation 20:4-5

Post-Tribulation Rapture is the belief that believers will be raptured at the end of the Great Tribulation. This means Christians will not escape God's wrath but will experience all that it entails. Matthew 24:29-31 is a key supporting passage, often interpreted as referring to the immediate aftermath of the Tribulation. He will send His angels to gather the elect. Revelation 20:4-5 is another set of verses used in the Post-Tribulation viewpoint. They say this refers to the first resurrection after the Tribulation. With this mindset, they align the Rapture with Christ's Second Coming. They conclude this is the same event, not a separate one.

There are several arguments for why the Post-Tribulation Theory is considered inaccurate. One argument is that the Rapture is when Christ comes for His saints and takes them to Heaven, as seen in 1 Thessalonians 4:17. The Second Coming of Christ, by contrast, is when He returns to earth to judge and reign. Scriptures that support this include Revelation 19:11-14, Jude 1:14, and Zechariah 14:5.

Another argument is that if Christ returns at the very end, all believers at that time would inherit glorified bodies, leaving no one to populate the 1,000-year Millennial Kingdom. That would make the devil's release pointless. Who would he need to deceive if everyone already has glorified, pure bodies? It's an interesting thought. One additional argument, though there are still more that can be listed, is that God's Word says believers are "not appointed to wrath" in 1 Thessalonians 5:9 and Revelation 3:10. The Tribulation involves God's wrath as described in the seals, trumpets, and bowls of Revelation. Some say that believers will be protected during this time, but this underestimates the scope of God's judgments and contradicts what the Word has promised: full deliverance for believers.

POST-MILLENNIAL THEORY

Post-Millennialists believe that Jesus will return after the Millennium. They conclude that this period will be a time of peace, righteousness, and gospel prosperity on earth. During the 1,000-year Millennium, the Church will preach the gospel and fulfill the Great Commission in Matthew 28:19. Through these efforts, the world will become "Christianized," and the majority of people will be saved. This time is also called the "Golden Age." They believe that, over time, evil will be defeated as the gospel spreads, creating a world full of believers and thereby removing the devil's influence in society. After the Millennium, Christ will return to an established earth, with the devil overcome. At this point, the final resurrection will occur, followed by judgment and the eternal state of the new heaven and earth.

There are several reasons this concept may be incorrect. One is that it contradicts the Bible's description of the end times as a period of trouble rather than triumph, as in 2 Timothy 3:1-7, which portrays the *last days* as marked by widespread moral decline. Also, 2 Thessalonians 2:1-12 speaks of a *great apostasy* and the rise of the *man of sin,* also known as the Antichrist. He will lead many astray before Christ's return. There are several other arguments; however, the main one that stands out is the set of key scriptures that appear to be at odds with this idea. For example, the devil is supposed to be imprisoned for 1,000 years. According to Post-Millennial Theory, the Church overcomes evil throughout those years; however, if the Church hasn't defeated the devil's influence up to this point, how could it do so thereafter?

AMILLENNIALISM THEORY

> *But if I cast out demons by the Spirit of God, surely the kingdom of God has come upon you.* [29] *Or how can one enter a strong man's house and plunder his goods, unless he first binds the strong man? And then he will plunder his house.*
>
> —Matthew 12:28-29

> *And raised us up together, and made us sit together in the heavenly places in Christ Jesus.*
>
> —Ephesians 2:6

> *Having disarmed principalities and powers, He made a public spectacle of them, triumphing over them in it.*
>
> —Colossians 2:15

Amillennialism holds that the millennium represents the current church age, which began at Christ's resurrection and ascension. Amillennialists believe Christ is already reigning spiritually from heaven through the

Church. Matthew 12:28-29 is cited to show that Satan is currently "bound" in a limited sense since Christ's ministry on earth, enabling the gospel to spread as it did. In Colossians 2:15, Satan's defeat occurred when Jesus died on the cross. According to Ephesians 2:6, saints are now spiritually reigning with Christ. Amillennialists believe the 1,000-year period is symbolic rather than literal. They argue that Revelation uses symbolic numbers; for example, 1,000 often signifies completeness, as in Psalm 50:10: "cattle on a thousand hills." They also believe that Revelation is highly apocalyptic rather than chronological.

There are several reasons this argument may be incorrect. First, if Satan is bound, why is the world growing darker and more evil? Many have said of this idea, "If Satan is bound today, he must have an extremely long chain!" That is true. First Peter 5:8 says, "*Be sober, be vigilant; because your adversary the devil walks about like a roaring lion, seeking whom he may devour.*" This was written after Jesus had ascended to heaven.

If the devil is bound, how could he be roaming around seeking someone to devour? Second, many Old Testament prophecies describe a future, physical earth filled with peace under the Messiah's rule. Isaiah 11:6-9 describes how the wolf and the lamb will dwell together. Zechariah 14:9, 16-19 discusses that the nations would worship Jesus in Jerusalem and that those who don't will face consequences. We know that this is not currently taking place. Again, these are only a few points. Other scriptures that can be used to prove this theory wrong include Isaiah 65:20-25 and Ezekiel 37:24-28. There are others, but I list only a few here.

COMFORT ONE ANOTHER

Therefore comfort one another with these words.

—1 Thessalonians 4:18

When considering your stance on when or if the Rapture occurs, know that these things are not meant to scare you but to prepare you. As 1 Thessalonians 4:18 says, we should comfort one another with these words.

Jesus' appearance should bring hope rather than terror. There is nothing hopeful about enduring the entire Great Tribulation! This is why I take the Pre-Tribulation position.

WHAT ABOUT THE LAST TRUMP?

There is another issue regarding the timing of the Rapture: the discussion of the last trumpet. At first glance, this might suggest that we will go through the Tribulation. My friend and respected Bible teacher, Alan DiDio, has written a masterful book on the Rapture, and while writing it, he asked me whether I had any questions I found interesting. I immediately brought up the last trumpet. What he wrote is both clarifying and helpful, so I wanted to include it here in its entirety:

> *Behold, I shew you a mystery; We shall not all sleep, but we shall all be changed, in a moment, in the twinkling of an eye, at the last trump: for the trumpet shall sound, and the dead shall be raised incorruptible, and we shall be changed* (1 Corinthians 15:51-52 KJV).
>
> When we talk about the *"last trump"* in 1 Corinthians 15, there's often a leap to connect it to the Seventh Trumpet in Revelation 11, as though Paul had this in mind while writing to the Corinthians. But here's the problem with that: Paul wrote his letter to the Corinthians around AD 53, while John received the Revelation of the Seven Trumpets roughly 40 years later, during his exile on the island of Patmos in AD 95.
>
> Imagine if someone in 2025 is watching an old Monty Python skit about SPAM and thinks they're referring to spam emails. We all know that back in 1980, SPAM had nothing to do with the junk cluttering our inboxes, it was just salty, delicious canned meat. This is the mistake people are making by retroactively applying the Seventh Trumpet to Paul's earlier reference.

Paul wasn't talking about John's trumpet because it would have been impossible for him to do so. That would be like hearing someone in a video from 1980 mention "The Cloud" thinking they meant a data storage method instead of a fluffy thing in the sky. The same applies to terms like virus, stream, or tablet. These words carry different meanings today, and trying to apply a modern revelation to an old conversation just doesn't work.

So what could the "*last trump*" refer to? The context points us in a different direction. It's very likely tied to Jewish traditions because Paul expects them to know exactly what he's talking about. Some suggest that this is specifically referring to the Feast of Trumpets, known as Rosh Hashanah. During this feast, the shofar is blown a total of 100 times. The final blast, called the *Tekiah Gedolah* or Great Blast, is known as the last trump. It's the culmination of a series of trumpet calls intended to awaken and gather God's people, symbolizing the completion of God's plan and heralding the coming of the Messiah.

The shofar is blown throughout the Rosh Hashanah service in four segments:

- **30 Blasts** after the Torah Reading: These represent a call to repentance and reflection, as the people of God align themselves with His Word.
- **30 Blasts** during the Musaf Service: Symbolizing the additional offerings given during the Holy Days, they represent an extra measure of devotion, going beyond the norm to seek God's face.
- **30 Blasts** at the End of the Musaf: These blasts symbolize spiritual breakthrough and God's intervention in the lives of His people.
- **The Final 10 Blasts** (Tekiah Gedolah): The culmination of the entire series, this final trumpet sound is seen as the "last trump," signaling the ultimate arrival of the Messiah.

The last trump in Jewish tradition signifies an ending and a beginning. It's a divine wake-up call, a final proclamation that God's purposes are reaching their ultimate fulfillment. When Paul references *"the last trump"* in 1 Corinthians 15:52, it could be that he was pointing to this idea of the culmination of believers being gathered and transformed. The Church is being called home, and the last trump is the heavenly signal for that glorious event.

Ken Johnson, a respected scholar in the study of the Feasts of God, notes in his book *The Rapture,* that Pentecost was historically referred to as the Feast of the First Trumpet, whereas Rosh Hashanah was known as the Feast of the Last Trumpet. This distinction offers deep prophetic significance, connecting the biblical feasts with God's redemptive timeline and helping us understand why Paul referred to the last trump in 1 Corinthians 15:52.

Others suggest that the last trump could be a reference to Numbers 10:1-3, where two silver trumpets were used to call the people together, signaling an assembly or a warning for war. In other places including Joel 2:1 and Jeremiah 4:5-6, the blowing of the trumpet also had the dual purpose to gather God's people and to sound an alarm. In this context, the last trump can be seen as God calling His people to gather, while signaling a final spiritual battle.

Whatever the last trump is, it is certain that it's not the Seventh Trumpet of Revelation. The thought that Paul was referring to a prophetic detail yet to be revealed to John decades later just doesn't align. Rather, this trumpet is most likely deeply tied to the Jewish understanding of culmination and divine gathering, a truth that resonates not only with ancient prophecy but with our blessed hope in Christ's imminent return and the Rapture of His Church.

The last trump is a call to readiness, a call to victory, and ultimately, a call to be in the presence of our Lord forever. So whether we hear that final blast today or tomorrow, one thing is certain: it will be a sound unlike any other, and it will be a sound of completion, a sound of hope, and a sound that will change everything.

—Alan DiDio, *They Lied to You About the Rapture*[4]

ESCALATION BEFORE JESUS APPEARS

Now as He sat on the Mount of Olives, the disciples came to Him privately, saying, "Tell us, when will these things be? And what will be the sign of Your coming, and of the end of the age?" 4 And Jesus answered and said to them: "Take heed that no one deceives you. 5 For many will come in My name, saying, 'I am the Christ,' and will deceive many. 6 And you will hear of wars and rumors of wars. See that you are not troubled; for all these things must come to pass, but the end is not yet. 7 For nation will rise against nation, and kingdom against kingdom. And there will be famines, pestilences, and earthquakes in various places. 8 All these are the beginning of sorrows. 9 Then they will deliver you up to tribulation and kill you, and you will be hated by all nations for My name's sake. 10 And then many will be offended, will betray one another, and will hate one another. 11 Then many false prophets will rise up and deceive many. 12 And because lawlessness will abound, the love of many will grow cold. 13 But he who endures to the end shall be saved. 14 And this gospel of the kingdom will be preached in all the world as a witness to all the nations, and then the end will come."

—Matthew 24:3-14

Then He said to them, "Nation will rise against nation, and kingdom against kingdom. 11 And there will be great earthquakes in various places, and famines and pestilences; and there will be fearful sights and great signs from heaven. 12 But before all these things, they will lay their hands on you and persecute you, delivering you up to the synagogues and prisons. You will be brought before kings and rulers for My name's sake. 13 But it will turn out for you as an occasion for testimony. 14 Therefore settle it in your hearts not to meditate beforehand on what you will answer; 15 for I will

> *give you a mouth and wisdom which all your adversaries will not be able to contradict or resist.* [16] *You will be betrayed even by parents and brothers, relatives and friends; and they will put some of you to death.* [17] *And you will be hated by all for My name's sake.* [18] *But not a hair of your head shall be lost.* [19] *By your patience possess your souls."*
>
> —Luke 21:10-19

As the world escalates, we can rejoice more and more, lifting our hope and expectation that the Lord will make His appearance. Signs of the times are meant for believers to watch earnestly for His arrival. In this same understanding, what is crucial is that we are to occupy ourselves while we anticipate His coming.

OCCUPY UNTIL HE COMES

> *So he called ten of his servants, delivered to them ten minas, and said to them, "**Do business till I come.**"*
>
> —Luke 19:13

> *And he called his ten servants, and delivered them ten pounds, and said unto them, **Occupy till I come**.*
>
> —Luke 19:13 KJV

The Greek word for "occupy" means: *to be doing, to be busy, occupied, to do business, to trade or traffic.* This runs counter to the escapist mentality, which holds that "We'll hide and watch because eventually we will be rescued out of here." Although Jesus will indeed come on a rescue mission to save us just in the nick of time, we are to go forward with the Great Commission and be busy about the Lord's business until He takes us out of here. A very important point to consider is that, right before the Rapture of the Church, we may not be in the Tribulation, even though it might seem like it! The birth pangs spoken of in Matthew 24 will grow stronger and stronger until finally Jesus appears. When Jesus takes His Church, it will be a rescue mission at the last moment.

URGENCY SHOULD BE OUR POSITION UNTIL JESUS APPEARS

Further, we are to occupy by faith, doing all we are anointed to do while we occupy until He appears. In fact, we are to work as if the Lord could appear at any moment and catch us by surprise! Urgency is what this should create in a faith-filled person, not inactivity. God wants us to do business, take ground for His kingdom, win souls, and impact society in accordance with His will.

Conditions will grow more turbulent and violent as we approach His appearing, but this is exactly what Jesus said would unfold before the end of the age. We are to take heart and stand, for the hour is closer than when we first believed.

Once we have been taken from the earth, the man of sin will appear on the world stage. In the meantime, our role is to punish darkness by being salt and light, winning the lost, and impacting the world in every way we can through the glorious truth of Jesus Christ.

THE WEAPON OF PEACE AND JOY

> *For the kingdom of God is not eating and drinking, but righteousness and peace and joy in the Holy Spirit.*
>
> —Romans 14:17

At this time, the weapon of choice is the agency of peace that Jesus gave to us. Carnality and the operations of unbelievers will not move in the supernatural peace of Jesus. You will need this in your life in the days ahead, most certainly.

> *Peace I leave with you, My peace I give to you; not as the world gives do I give to you. Let not your heart be troubled, neither let it be afraid.*
>
> —John 14:27

And the peace of God, which surpasses all understanding, will guard your hearts and minds through Christ Jesus.

—Philippians 4:7

For you shall go out with joy, and be led out with peace; the mountains and the hills shall break forth into singing before you, and all the trees of the field shall clap their hands.

—Isaiah 55:12

Equally important is joy. This is not a description of happiness or situational fulfillment; joy is a spiritual force that, when coupled with peace, creates an unbeatable combination. Going out in joy is a sense of moving forward. Joy is a spiritual, motivating, and supernatural force that sustains you. Peace is the direction. If joy is the gas pedal, peace is the steering wheel.

...Do not sorrow, for the joy of the Lord is your strength.

—Nehemiah 8:10

I will hear what God the Lord will speak, for He will speak peace to His people and to His saints; but let them not turn back to folly.

—Psalm 85:8

Understanding the peace and joy duo will give you revelatory power to overcome in this jacked-up world! It gives you the power to stand. The expression of peace and joy will make you strong, able to lean into storms that would cause others to fall apart.

POWER TO STAND IN THE MIDST OF PURE MADNESS!

But he who endures to the end shall be saved.

—Matthew 24:13

We need to tell our children this in faith, strengthening them, empowering them to move forward, and bringing peace and joy through endurance.

This is what led figures in the early Church to stand against atrocities and to see the goodness of God manifest right in the middle of pure madness.

POLYCARP: "BE STRONG AND PLAY THE MAN"

I'm often reminded of the story of Polycarp, who stood up for the name of the Lord in his day. It must have been peace and joy that carried him to the very end of his life.

In the year 155, the Bishop of Smyrna was Polycarp. He had a prophetic vision of his death. He was then taken to the stadium, where he heard a voice say, "Be strong, Polycarp, and play the man."

Here is the story of a hero of the faith who stood strong in his day.

> *The Martyrdom of Polycarp, Bishop of Smyrna, 155*
>
> From Martyrium Polycarpi *[A letter from the Church of Smyrna. The first Martyrology]*
>
> I. II. [At the festival of Caesar a number of Christians were set to fight the wild beasts.]
>
> III. ... All the crowd, astonished at the noble conduct of the God-beloved and God-fearing race of Christians, cried out, 'Away with the atheists; let search be made for Polycarp.'
>
> V. But the most admirable Polycarp when first he heard of this was not dismayed, but wished to remain in the city. The majority, however, prevailed on him to withdraw. And he withdrew to a small estate not far from the city. There he passed the time with a few companions, wholly occupied night and day in prayer for all men and for the churches throughout the world; as, indeed, was his habit. And while at prayer he fell into a trance three days before his arrest and saw his pillow set on fire. And he turned and said to his companions, 'I must needs be burned alive.'

VI. Now since they that sought him were persistent he departed to another estate. Then straightway they were upon him, and when they did not find him they apprehended two young servants. Of whom one confessed under torture; for it was impossible for him to escape, since they that betrayed him were of his own household. Then the sheriff, who bore by God's appointment the same name (sc. as our Lord's judge), being called Herod, hastened to bring him into the stadium, that he might fulfil his own appointed lot by becoming a partner of Christ, and that his betrayers might undergo the punishment of Judas himself.

VII. So, on the day of the preparation, mounted police with their usual arms set out about supper-time, taking with them the servant, hurrying 'as against a thief.' And at a late hour they came up to the place and found him in a cottage, lying in an upper room. He could have gone away to another farm, but he would not, saying 'The will of God be done.' So, hearing their arrival, he came down and talked with them, while all that were present marvelled at his age and constancy, and that there was so much ado about the arrest of such an old man. Then he ordered that something should be served for them to eat and drink, at that late hour, as much as they wanted. And he besought them that they should grant him an hour that he might pray freely. They gave him leave, and he stood and prayed, being so filled with the grace of God that for two hours he could not hold his peace, while they that heard were amazed, and the men repented that they had come after so venerable an old man.

VIII. When he had brought to an end his prayer, in which he made mention of all, small and great, high and low, with whom he had had dealings, and of the whole Catholic Church throughout the world, the time had come for him to depart. And they set him on an ass and led him into the city. Now it was a high Sabbath. And there met him the sheriff Herod, and his father Nicetes, who removed him into their carriage, and tried to persuade him, sitting by his side and saying, 'Now what harm is there is saying "Lord Caesar," and in offering incense, and so on, and thus saving thyself?' He at first made no reply, but since they persisted he said, 'I do not intend to do what you advise.' Then, failing to persuade him, they began to use threatening words; and they pulled him down hastily, so that he grazed his shin as he descended from the carriage. Without turning back, as if he had suffered no hurt, he went on with all speed, and was led to the stadium, wherein the tumult was so great that no one could be heard.

IX. Now, as he was entering the stadium, there came to Polycarp a voice from heaven, 'Be strong, Polycarp, and play the man.' And no one saw the speaker, but the voice was heard by those of our people who were there. Thereupon he was led forth, and great was the uproar of them that heard that Polycarp had been seized. Accordingly, he was led before the Proconsul, who asked him if he were the man himself. And when he confessed the Proconsul tried to persuade him, saying, 'Have respect to thine age,' and so forth, according to their customary form; 'Swear by the genius' of Caesar,' 'Repent,' 'Say, "Away with the atheists!"' Then Polycarp looked with a severe countenance on the mob of lawless heathen in the stadium, and he waved his hand at them, and looking up to heaven he groaned and said, 'Away with the atheists.' But the Proconsul urged him and said, 'Swear, and I will release thee; curse the Christ.' And Polycarp said, 'Eighty and six years have I served him, and he hath done me no wrong; how then can I blaspheme my king who saved me?'

X. But the Proconsul again persisted and said, 'Swear by the genius of Caesar'; and he answered, 'If thou dost vainly imagine that I would swear by the genius of Caesar, as thou sayest, pretending not to know what I am, hear plainly that I am a Christian. And if thou art willing to learn the doctrine of Christianity, grant me a day and hearken to me:' Then said the Proconsul, 'Persuade the people.' Polycarp replied, 'Thee I had deemed worthy of discourse, for we are taught to render to authorities and the powers ordained of God honour as is fitting. But I deem not this mob worthy that I should defend myself before them.'

XI. Then said the Proconsul, 'I have wild beasts; if thou repent not, I will throw thee to them.' But he said, 'Send for them. For repentance from better to worse is not a change permitted to us; but to change from cruelty to righteousness is a noble thing.' Then said the Proconsul again, 'If thou dost despise the wild beasts I will make thee to be consumed by fire, if thou repent not.' And Polycarp answered, 'Thou threatenest the fire that burns for an hour and in a little while is quenched; for thou knowest not of the fire of the judgement to come, and the fire of the eternal punishment, reserved for the ungodly. But why delayest thou? Bring what thou wilt.'

XII. As he spake these words and many more, he was filled with courage and joy; and his countenance was full of grace, so that no only did it fall not in dismay at what was being said to him, but on the contrary the Proconsul was astonished, and sent his herald to proclaim thrice in the midst of the stadium, 'Polycarp hath confessed himself to be a Christian.' When this was proclaimed by the herald the whole multitude of Gentiles and Jews who dwelt in Smyrna cried out with ungovernable rage and in a loud voice, 'This is the teacher of Asia, the father of the Christians, the destroyer of our gods, that teacheth many not to sacrifice nor worship.' They kept shouting this, asking Philip, the Asiarch, to loose a lion at Polycarp. But he said that it was not lawful for him, since he had finished the sports. Then they decided to shout with one accord that he should be burned alive. For the matter of his vision of the pillow must needs be fulfilled, when he saw it burning while he was at prayer, and turned and said prophetically to his companions, 'I must needs be burned alive.'

XIII. And now things happened with such speed, in less time than it takes to tell; for the mob straitway brought together timber and faggots from the workshops and baths, the Jews giving themselves zealously to the work, as they were like to do.... They were about to nail him to the stake, when he said, 'Let me be as I am. He that granted me to endure the fire will grant me also to remain at the pyre unmoved, without being secured with nails.'

XV. When he had ended his prayer the firemen lighted the fire. And a great flame flashed forth: and we, to whom it was given to see, beheld a marvel.... The fire took the shape of a vault, like a ship's sail bellying in the wind, and it made a wall round the martyr's body; and there was the body in the midst, like a loaf being baked or like gold and silver being tried in the furnace....

XVI. So at length the lawless ones, seeing that his body could not be consumed by the fire, bade an executioner approach him to drive in a dagger. And when he had done this there came out [a dove and] abundance of blood so that it quenched the fire, and all the multitude marvelled at the great difference between the unbelievers and the elect.[5]

IT IS OUR TIME TO STAND. BY THE POWER OF GOD, WE SHALL STAND!

And they overcame him by the blood of the Lamb and by the word of their testimony, and they did not love their lives to the death.

—Revelation 12:11

Polycarp stood firm in the face of adversity. I shared this powerful story from church history to show that there is grace for those who stand in faith and do not shrink back in the face of overwhelming adversity. This serves as a powerful example of not conforming to worldly expectations—an extreme yet meaningful one for us all. We should reflect on this, as sacrificing one's life for faith is still not uncommon even today. Many are still persecuted for their belief in Jesus, even at the cost of their lives. Western society has not experienced this to the extremes the rest of the world has—not yet.

What every believer must be prepared for is to love not their life even unto death. That is part of overcoming the devil and standing as more than a conqueror in this present evil age. You, dear reader, are more than equipped if you walk with the Lord in peace and joy. You will occupy and usher in the appearing of Jesus!

SECTION THREE

THE LAST KINGDOM AND THE AGE TO COME

CHAPTER TWELVE

THE TWO BEAST KINGDOM

Two distinct beasts appear in Revelation 13. First, a beast rises from the sea and is described as having seven heads and ten horns, with ten crowns on its horns and blasphemous names written on its seven heads. It looks like a leopard, with the feet of a bear and the mouth of a lion. Empowered by Satan, who grants this first Beast power, a throne, and great authority—this is what many believe is the Antichrist. The first Beast will rule as the leader of a ten-nation alliance and will hold power for 42 months. Symbolically, the rise from the sea represents a rise from the Gentile world to oppose the things of God and His Church.

THE FIRST BEAST RISING FROM THE SEA—THE ANTICHRIST

Then I stood on the sand of the sea. And I saw a beast rising up out of the sea, having seven heads and ten horns, and on his horns ten crowns, and on his heads a blasphemous name. [2] Now the beast which I saw was like a leopard, his feet were like the feet of a bear, and his mouth like the mouth of a lion. The dragon gave him his power, his throne, and great authority.

—Revelation 13:1-2

> *And four great beasts came up from the sea, each different from the other. [4] The first was like a lion, and had eagle's wings. I watched till its wings were plucked off; and it was lifted up from the earth and made to stand on two feet like a man, and a man's heart was given to it. [5] And suddenly another beast, a second, like a bear. It was raised up on one side, and had three ribs in its mouth between its teeth. And they said thus to it: "Arise, devour much flesh!" [6] After this I looked, and there was another, like a leopard, which had on its back four wings of a bird. The beast also had four heads, and dominion was given to it. [7] After this I saw in the night visions, and behold, a fourth beast, dreadful and terrible, exceedingly strong. It had huge iron teeth; it was devouring, breaking in pieces, and trampling the residue with its feet. It was different from all the beasts that were before it, and it had ten horns. [8] I was considering the horns, and there was another horn, a little one, coming up among them, before whom three of the first horns were plucked out by the roots. And there, in this horn, were eyes like the eyes of a man, and a mouth speaking pompous words.*
>
> —Daniel 7:3-8

This First Beast rises from the sea and is the man of sin, the Antichrist. In Revelation 13:2, notice that the descriptions of a leopard, a bear, and a lion reflect Daniel 7, but they are listed in the opposite order: Daniel 7:3-8 lists them as the lion, bear, and then the leopard. The lion speaks with arrogance and authority, the bear controls extensively, and the leopard conquers with speed!

THE DEADLY HEAD WOUND TO THE BEAST—A GLOBALLY RECOGNIZED ASSASSINATION

> *And I saw one of his heads as it were wounded to death; and his deadly wound was healed: and all the world wondered after the beast.*
>
> —Revelation 13:3 KJV

Tragically, nothing captures the world's attention like the assassination of a world figure. With the assassination comes sympathy and, potentially, an emotional rollercoaster. As the world watches, even obsesses over the apparent death of this figure in Revelation 13:3 from a head wound, an even greater surprise will shock the world. Globally, all will go from watching the assassination to witnessing one of the greatest miracles in modern society. The Beast, or Antichrist, will resurrect.

A DARK MIRACLE

Although it will be a dark miracle, a lying wonder, it will be enough to win the loyalty of the global masses to the Beast. The wounded head, unto death, will be miraculously healed.

Either at the moment the wound occurs or immediately after the incident. Could it be three days after the death that a resurrection might occur while the whole world watches? What will happen will be widely seen and known—the world will see this First Beast recover!

IS THE BEAST'S HEAD WOUND HIS BRAND?

> *Woe to the idol shepherd that leaveth the flock! the sword shall be upon his arm, and upon his right eye: his arm shall be clean dried up, and his right eye shall be utterly darkened.*
>
> —Zechariah 11:17 KJV

Considering that this head wound might become the identifying brand associated with this leader, as seen in Revelation 13:3, 12, and 14, Zechariah 11:17 may refer to the same coming world leader who has an injured arm and an identifying eye. Not only does this passage seem to point to the beast figure in Revelation 13, who was fatally injured in the head, but Zechariah may also shed further light on the issue by suggesting that the wounding might even affect his arm. According to this interpretation, those who identify with him will take the mark of the Beast, aligning with the wound that was healed by receiving the mark on the hand and the forehead. It would seem that humanity will be swayed by the first Beast's attack and recovery.

THE CHURCH WILL NOT BE PRESENT AT THIS TIME

Here is an argument for why the Church will not be present during this time. When the Beast dies and comes back to life, Bible-believing Christians would likely call this out publicly, saying he is fulfilling Scripture as the Antichrist! However, the Church, not present at that time and having been caught up to be with the Lord, would have no say in this event, leaving the people of earth to fall hook, line, and sinker for this moment.

THE WORLD WILL WORSHIP THE FIRST BEAST

> *And they worshipped the dragon which gave power unto the beast: and they worshipped the beast, saying, Who is like unto the beast? who is able to make war with him?* [5] *And there was given unto him a mouth speaking great things and blasphemies; and power was given unto him to continue forty and two months.* [6] *And he opened his mouth in blasphemy against God, to blaspheme his name, and his tabernacle, and them that dwell in heaven.*
>
> —Revelation 13:4-6 KJV

Who is like unto the beast will be the defining statement among the masses who fall to his deception. A world led by their five senses and completely carnal will have no discernment at all. Those who are part of the global community will fall prey to the Beast's presentation. Among the majority of the world, there will be a common thought that no one will be able to defeat him or make war with him. He will meet all of society's needs and expectations for a global leader, for the first season of his power.

There are two identifiers of the Beast:

1. He is wounded in the head.
2. An obnoxious, arrogant, and blasphemous mouth. He boasts and speaks blasphemies.

People are drawn to power, especially when the leader wielding it has a remarkable supernatural aspect. In the case of the Beast, with a wounded head that's recovered, the masses will only fall deeper into his seductive snare. His obnoxious, arrogant, and blasphemous mouth will be overlooked by the awe-inspired audience he accumulates around the world. After a miracle witnessed by the globe, it will be as if nothing he says or does will be questioned—after all, he likely rose from the dead to lead them all to a wonderful future.

> *I was considering the horns, and there was another horn, a little one, coming up among them, before whom three of the first horns were plucked out by the roots. And there, in this horn, were eyes like the eyes of a man, and a mouth speaking pompous words.*
>
> —Daniel 7:8

> *He shall speak pompous words against the Most High, shall persecute the saints of the Most High, and shall intend to change times and law. Then the saints shall be given into his hand for a time and times and half a time.*
>
> —Daniel 7:25

> *Then the king shall do according to his own will: he shall exalt and magnify himself above every god, shall speak blasphemies against the God of gods, and shall prosper till the wrath has been accomplished; for what has been determined shall be done.* [37] *He shall regard neither the God of his*

fathers nor the desire of women, nor regard any god; for he shall exalt himself above them all. [38] *But in their place, he shall honor a god of fortresses; and a god which his fathers did not know he shall honor with gold and silver, with precious stones and pleasant things.*

—Daniel 11:36-38

Following this supernatural recovery, or resurrection, the First Beast, or Antichrist, will rise to complete power on the world stage as the greatest leader, politician, and spokesman society has ever known. He will be awe-inspiring and well-spoken, ushering in a time of peace. All of which is a deception that draws the nations into his nefarious web. The first 3.5 years will be his time to set up a kingdom on earth, with nearly all fawning over his words and actions. This will lead to his big announcement and a shift in the narrative.

HE WILL DEMAND TO BE WORSHIPED AS GOD

Who opposes and exalts himself above all that is called God or that is worshiped, so that he sits as God in the temple of God, showing himself that he is God.

—2 Thessalonians 2:4

A startling discovery is that this First Beast from the sea will oppose and exalt himself above all that is called God. He will declare everything that is worshiped beneath him, sit as God in the Temple of God, and show himself to all humanity as God. This will progress from a time of his seducing the world until he finally declares that he is God and should be worshiped as such.

THE WORLD WILL FOLLOW THE FIRST BEAST DUE TO THE MIRACULOUS

After witnessing what many believe will be the Beast's assassination and his subsequent resurrection, the world will be seduced by the miraculous return of his person. This might occur at the moment of the assassination, or, as I stated earlier, he might come back to life after three days in a truly messianic form. We can only guess, but it would fit the narrative of an Antichrist. Once the First Beast has gained the attention and loyalty of the masses, a shift will occur—he will make war against the Tribulation saints present at this time.

THE FIRST BEAST DECLARES HIMSELF AS GOD

Ezekiel 28:2 prophesies that this figure will lift his heart and say, "I am a god, I sit in the seat of gods, in the midst of the seas." This Beast figure will certainly believe himself to be a god and act accordingly. The prophecy then clarifies this figure's actual station in verse 9. "You are a man, and not a god...." A nice check-up from the neck up for the Beast figure.

Verse 10 says, "...you shall die the death of the uncircumcised by the hand of aliens...." The phrase "you shall die the death of the uncircumcised" implies he is of Jewish origin. The phrase "of the circumcision" is clarified in Daniel 11:36-37.

> *Then the king shall do according to his own will: he shall exalt and magnify himself above every god, shall speak blasphemies against the God of gods, and shall prosper till the wrath has been accomplished; for what has been determined shall be done.* 37 *He shall regard neither the God of his fathers nor the desire of women, nor regard any god; for he shall exalt himself above them all.*
>
> —Daniel 11:36-37

SEXUAL PREFERENCE OF THE BEAST

In Daniel 11, we read, "he shall regard neither the God of his fathers." This again suggests that he will be Jewish. It goes on to say that he will not desire women. An interesting statement. Could he be a homosexual? He very well could be. Additionally, we see that he will have no use for any other god but himself, as he will exalt himself above them all. The Beast in this picture will exalt himself as god above all world religions, and they will follow him! When we see the beheading of saints in the book of Revelation, could it be that Islam has submitted to this man, adjusted their worldview to see the Beast as the fulfillment of what they have been waiting for, and is utilizing their method of beheading for the Beast? It is a likely scenario.

THIS BEAST WILL BE ACCEPTED BY ISRAEL ONLY TO BE BETRAYED BY HIM

> *He has put forth his hands against those who were at peace with him; he has broken his covenant.* [21] *The words of his mouth were smoother than butter, but war was in his heart; his words were softer than oil, yet they were drawn swords.*
>
> —Psalm 55:20-21

This Beast figure is received and accepted by Israel, only to be betrayed by him. By putting forth his hands against those at peace with him, he will break the covenant he made with them. He is a smooth speaker and a deceiver. Yet we see that, even as he makes "peace" with the nations, war was in his heart the entire time. His words are softer than oil, which will woo and draw everyone into his trust and cause all to fall for his demonic flattery. Yet we see that his words were drawn swords, or that he used them for an endgame of death and dominion.

THE BEAST MAKES WAR AGAINST THE SAINTS

> *And it was given unto him to make war with the saints, and to overcome them: and power was given him over all kindreds, and tongues, and nations.*
>
> —Revelation 13:7 KJV

As Revelation 13:7 says, the Beast is able to wage war and overcome the saints during the second half of the Great Tribulation, which the prophet Jeremiah calls "the time of Jacob's trouble" (*see* Jeremiah 30:7). The Antichrist will enter Palestine, take over the temple as his capital, be worshiped there as God, and unleash murderous persecution of the saints. This is a global event lasting 3.5 years. Every people group, every tongue, and every nation will be overtaken by the Beast during this 3.5-year period. We will look more at the time of Jacob's trouble in the coming chapter.

Here are a few other prophetic scriptures that point to this time and the Beast's ability to overcome the saints.

> *As I watched, this horn was waging war against the holy people and defeating them.*
>
> —Daniel 7:21 NIV

> *Because of rebellion, the Lord's people and the daily sacrifice were given over to it. It prospered in everything it did, and truth was thrown to the ground.*
>
> —Daniel 8:12 NIV

> *He will become very strong, but not by his own power. He will cause astounding devastation and will succeed in whatever he does. He will destroy those who are mighty, the holy people.*
>
> —Daniel 8:24 NIV

> *His armed forces will rise up to desecrate the temple fortress and will abolish the daily sacrifice. Then they will set up the abomination that causes desolation.*
>
> —Daniel 11:31 NIV

> *Now when they have finished their testimony, the beast that comes up from the Abyss will attack them, and overpower and kill them.*
>
> —Revelation 11:7 NIV

THE CHURCH HAS A DIFFERENT PROMISE THAN THE OLD TESTAMENT SAINTS AND THE SAINTS IN THE BOOK OF REVELATION

Now, let us compare the saints listed in the previously cited scriptures with those referenced in Revelation 13:7 and with the saints of Matthew 16:18.

> *And I tell you that you are Peter, and on this rock I will build* ***my church,*** *and* ***the gates of Hades will not overcome it****.*
>
> —Matthew 16:18 NIV

The Church mentioned by Jesus is the *Ekklesia*, or the called-out ones, and the gates of hell will not overcome it. How does Revelation 13 depict the Beast overcoming the saints? We must remember that not all saints are the same. The Church is not appointed unto wrath, and the Church will be caught away before the arrival of this world system dominated by the Beast.

The Church, or the *Ekklesia*, differs from the Old Testament saints, and the *Ekklesia* also differs from the saints in the book of Revelation. Consider John the Baptist, who certainly qualifies as a saint. He was in a different category from the New Testament believer.

In Matthew 11:11 NIV, Jesus says of John, "Truly I tell you, among those born of women there has not risen anyone greater than John the Baptist; yet whoever is least in the kingdom of heaven is greater than he."

Regarding John the Baptist and the New Testament believer, John was still under the Old Covenant and was considered the greatest prophet because he was the voice announcing and ushering in the arrival of Jesus. One who is part of the *Ekklesia*, or the kingdom of heaven that Jesus established through His Church after His death and resurrection, has a different promise from that of John the Baptist or anyone under the Old Covenant. When the New Covenant time ends, the Church Age ends, and with it the age of grace. Following this is the Tribulation period. Those who are born again during the Tribulation will not have the same standing as those who were in the Church Age or the age of grace. This difference is one reason the Beast will be given power over these Tribulation saints.

THOSE WHO DWELL ON THE EARTH DURING THE TRIBULATION

> *And all that dwell upon the earth shall worship him, whose names are not written in the book of life of the Lamb slain from the foundation of the world.*
>
> —Revelation 13:8 KJV

Those who worship the Beast during his global reign are what some commentators call earth dwellers. They are people who do not follow Jesus Christ, adopt a new religion in the image of the Beast, and swear their lives to him as an act of worship. Unlike the saints who will find Jesus during the Tribulation, these earth-dwelling people will succumb to every desire of this Satan-possessed Antichrist and believe he is their messiah. Earth-dwelling individuals will be completely sucked into the greatest deception the world will ever know, permanently setting themselves on the road of perdition for all eternity.

THE SECOND BEAST RISING FROM THE EARTH—THE FALSE PROPHET

> *Then I saw another beast coming up out of the earth....*
>
> —Revelation 13:11

What many overlook is that Revelation 13 describes two distinct individuals rather than one. The First Beast is a globally empowered world leader, the Antichrist, whose magnitude of impact leads to his being worshiped as a deity.

There are numerous perspectives and conjectures about the origin of the Second Beast. Some believe that because he comes out of the "earth," he may be Jewish and from Israel.

THE FALSE PROPHET WILL DISPLAY SIGNS AND WONDERS THAT EXCEED THE FIRST BEAST

> *He performs great signs, so that* ***he even makes fire come down from heaven*** *on the earth in the sight of men.* [14] *And* ***he deceives those who dwell on the earth by those signs*** *which he was granted to do in the sight of the beast, telling those who dwell on the earth to make an image to the beast who was wounded by the sword and lived.*
>
> —Revelation 13:13-14

The Second Beast, or false prophet, is from the earth, and will be revealed with signs and wonders that surpass the First Beast profoundly. We see this in Revelation 13, where the Second Beast, or false prophet, will perform "great signs," including making fire come down from heaven in the sight of men. It goes on to say that he deceives those who dwell on the earth by these signs. These signs will be extraordinary in their demonstration, drawing global attention and leading to the worship of the First Beast, or Antichrist.

HIS TWO HORNS AND HIS VOICE

*Then I saw another beast coming up out of the earth, and **he had two horns** like a lamb and spoke like a dragon.*

—Revelation 13:11

These two "horns" mentioned in Revelation 13:11 represent two sources of "authority" or dominion. He "spoke" like the dragon, indicating that he is a "false" leader who appears as a lamb but has the voice of the dragon. A mechanism of the devil is that he is not original in any way. This is why we see him working through this Beast to present imagery of a lamb, yet with the voice of a dragon. The lamb imagery in this picture alludes to his false messianic complex and to the world's perception of him as the messiah. Yet the voice of a dragon is a reminder of the serpent that spoke to Eve in the garden. Words that appease, words that deceive, words that place the global community under his vile spell.

*Now the serpent was more cunning than any beast of the field which the Lord God had made. And **he said to the woman**, "Has God indeed said, 'You shall not eat of every tree of the garden'?"*

—Genesis 3:1

But I fear, lest somehow, as the serpent deceived Eve by his craftiness, so your minds may be corrupted from the simplicity that is in Christ.

—2 Corinthians 11:3

THE FALSE PROPHET WILL CAUSE THE WORLD TO WORSHIP THE ANTICHRIST

*I have come in My Father's name, and you do not receive Me; **if another comes in his own name**, him you will receive.*

—John 5:43

We also observe that this Beast figure is described as the "other beast," whereas throughout Scripture, he is referred to as the "false prophet." He represents the First Beast who was before him and will cause the entire earth to worship the First Beast, even the very image of it.

> *And he exercises all the authority of the first beast in his presence, and causes the earth and those who dwell in it to worship the first beast, whose deadly wound was healed.*
>
> —Revelation 13:12

The Second Beast persuades the whole world to worship the First Beast. Again, the First Beast is identified by his deadly wound that was healed. This could be an assassination, which some speculate could lead to a false resurrection. The First Beast will be possessed by an evil spirit—likely Satan himself.

THE SATANIC TRINITY OFFERING LYING SIGNS AND WONDERS!

> ***The coming of the lawless one is according to the working of Satan, with all power, signs,*** *and* ***lying wonders,*** [10] *and with all unrighteous deception among those who perish, because they did not receive the love of the truth, that they might be saved.* [11] *And for this reason God will send them strong delusion, that they should believe the lie.*
>
> —2 Thessalonians 2:9-11

It appears that Satan, along with the First and Second Beasts, forms the Satanic trinity, a perversion of the Father, Son, and Holy Spirit. The false prophet is mimicking what God did in the Old Testament. We see that the counterfeit will ultimately be fully displayed. Satan's primary skill is deception, and he uses these signs and miracles for his nefarious purpose.

> *But Pharaoh also called the wise men and the sorcerers; so the magicians of Egypt,* ***they also did in like manner with their enchantments****.*
>
> —Exodus 7:11

> *Now as Jannes and Jambres resisted Moses, so do these also resist the truth: men of corrupt minds, disapproved concerning the faith.*
>
> —2 Timothy 3:8

This is the same false-prophet activity—nothing new; it is right out of the same playbook: counterfeit miracles, signs, and lying wonders meant to deceive.

THE THIRD FIGURE IN THIS UNHOLY TRINITY—THE IMAGE OF THE BEAST GIVEN BREATH

> *He was granted power to give breath to the image of the beast, that the image of the beast should both speak and cause as many as would not worship the image of the beast to be killed.*
>
> —Revelation 13:15

Death was the alternative for those who would not worship the image of the Beast. This image of the Beast will be granted breath or animation. Acting as a third part of this blasphemous, unholy trinity, this image of the Beast will speak and breathe, or in layman's terms, come alive on the global stage. A feat that may involve advanced artificial intelligence, transhumanism, or heightened dark supernatural power.

Awe-inspiring supernatural feats, such as the image of the Beast breathing and speaking, will only deepen the masses' belief that this is a god. Consider the falsehood of this vile magic show. It is an evil work to dazzle the five senses and the perception of the world, and perhaps even to strike fear into the audience. Yet even still, there will be those who will be threatened with death if they do not worship this image and take his mark.

Unlike the Beast, who uses deceptive miracles to gain followers, our Lord, the One and Only King, Jesus Christ, also performed many miracles, but He did not rely on them for His authentication. Prophecy from

Scripture was His standard for authentication, not "signs and wonders," as His primary evidence.

When Jesus responded to John the Baptist in prison to the question, "Are you the One, or should we look for another?" He did not perform a special miracle to show John; instead, He quoted prophecies recorded in Scripture and said that these were being fulfilled. A marked difference between Jesus and the two Beasts.

> *Now it came to pass, when Jesus finished commanding His twelve disciples, that He departed from there to teach and to preach in their cities.* [2] *And when John had heard in prison about the works of Christ, he sent two of his disciples* [3] *and said to Him, "Are You the Coming One, or do we look for another?"* [4] *Jesus answered and said to them, "Go and tell John the things which you hear and see:* [5] *The blind see and the lame walk; the lepers are cleansed and the deaf hear; the dead are raised up and the poor have the gospel preached to them.* [6] *And blessed is he who is not offended because of Me.*
>
> —Matthew 11:1-6

A WARNING NOT TO BUILD YOUR FOUNDATION ON SIGNS AND WONDERS

At any point in a believer's walk, it is unstable ground to build a foundation on signs and wonders. Your "experience" is the wrong foundation.

Rather, it is the Word of God that will keep you firmly grounded in your faith and help you avoid being deceived by false signs and wonders. A firm foundation in the Word, coupled with faith, will keep you from being susceptible to all kinds of deception and the never-ending search for more signs and wonders. This is an important warning for every believer, as this false prophet will be a sign-and-wonders expert and a specialist in deception, using them. Carnally minded people want the empirical evidence of a sign and a wonder to dazzle their five senses.

Yet, that is not how faith works. Jesus said, "Blessed are they who believe without seeing" (*see* John 20:29). Matthew 12:38-39 says, "Then some of the scribes and Pharisees answered, saying, *'Teacher, we want to see a sign from You.'* [39] But He answered and said to them, *'An evil and adulterous generation seeks after a sign*, and no sign will be given to it except the sign of the prophet Jonah.'" He called those who wanted to see a sign an evil and adulterous generation.

PARALLEL BETWEEN DANIEL 3 AND REVELATION 13 REGARDING THE IMAGE OF THE BEAST

There is a parallel between Daniel 3 and Revelation 13, where the "image" they make is of the Beast. As in Revelation, the Antichrist figure Nebuchadnezzar made an image to be worshiped. Those who would not, were to be put to death. This is a direct prophetic reflection of what the Antichrist and the false prophet will do in the book of Revelation. That same spirit of Antichrist has been around since the very early days, as demonic strongholds will always point to one thing. The complete and total domination of mankind, or at the very least, to dominate as many people as possible under a false god scenario.

> *Nebuchadnezzar the king made an image of gold, whose height was sixty cubits and its width six cubits. He set it up in the plain of Dura, in the province of Babylon.* [2] *And King Nebuchadnezzar sent word to gather together the satraps, the administrators, the governors, the counselors, the treasurers, the judges, the magistrates, and all the officials of the provinces, to come to the dedication of the image which King Nebuchadnezzar had set up.* [3] *So the satraps, the administrators, the governors, the counselors, the treasurers, the judges, the magistrates, and all the officials of the provinces gathered together for the dedication of the image that King Nebuchadnezzar had set up; and they stood before the image that Nebuchadnezzar had set up.* [4] *Then a herald cried aloud: "To you it is commanded, O peoples,*

nations, and languages, [5] *that at the time you hear the sound of the horn, flute, harp, lyre, and psaltery, in symphony with all kinds of music, you shall fall down and worship the gold image that King Nebuchadnezzar has set up;* [6] *and whoever does not fall down and worship shall be cast immediately into the midst of a burning fiery furnace."* [7] *So at that time, when all the people heard the sound of the horn, flute, harp, and lyre, in symphony with all kinds of music, all the people, nations, and languages fell down and worshiped the gold image which King Nebuchadnezzar had set up.*

—Daniel 3:1-7

This passage in Daniel 3 corresponds to the image of the Beast in Revelation 13:15. Once again, we see the spirit of Antichrist at work in ages past. The Beast will fulfill the aim of this wicked agenda. The same agenda was articulated at the Tower of Babel, as we will examine shortly (*see* Genesis 11), and it is reflected in the image raised by Nebuchadnezzar. All these wicked actions are historical precursors to the image of the Beast and his mark.

Then a third angel followed them, saying with a loud voice, "If anyone worships ***the beast and his image****, and receives his mark on his forehead or on his hand."*

—Revelation 14:9

And the smoke of their torment ascends forever and ever; and they have no rest day or night, who worship ***the beast and his image****, and whoever receives the mark of his name.*

—Revelation 14:11

And I saw something like a sea of glass mingled with fire, and those who have the victory over the beast, over ***his image*** *and over his mark and over the number of his name, standing on the sea of glass, having harps of God.*

—Revelation 15:2

So the first went and poured out his bowl upon the earth, and a foul and loathsome sore came upon the men who had the mark of the beast and those who worshiped ***his image****.*

—Revelation 16:2

Then the beast was captured, and with him the false prophet who worked signs in his presence, by which he deceived those who received the mark of the beast and those who worshiped ***his image****. These two were cast alive into the lake of fire burning with brimstone.*

—Revelation 19:20

THE MARK OF THE BEAST

He was granted power to give breath to the image of the beast, that the image of the beast should both speak and cause as many as would not worship the image of the beast to be killed. 16 ***He causes all, both small and great, rich and poor, free and slave, to receive a mark on their right hand or on their foreheads,*** 17 *and that no one may buy or sell except one who has the mark or the name of the beast, or the number of his name.* 18 *Here is wisdom. Let him who has understanding calculate the number of the beast, for it is the number of a man: His number is 666.*

—Revelation 13:15-18

Of all the issues surrounding end-time prophecy, there is no more notorious subject than the mark of the Beast. What may surprise many is that society will not be tricked into receiving the mark; it is not a pitfall to which the unassuming will unknowingly fall. Not at all, much to the contrary. Receiving the mark will be a conscious decision. It will be a life choice with eternal ramifications.

More than a password or a bank card, this will be an act of absolute worship and allegiance to the Antichrist. Taking the mark will not be a choice made solely out of a need to function in society, although that will be part of it. What the mark will represent is the denial of all other beliefs and the complete acknowledgment that the *man of sin* is God to you. Those who make this eternal choice will irrefutably be set on the road to eternal damnation.

Today, with the rise of technologies, digital assets, and the movement of money toward digitization, many perceive this as the mark of the Beast. However, it is not, at least not yet. All of these may lead to a Beast system, but what sets the mark of the Beast apart is that it will be an act of complete allegiance and worship. It's a system being set up for a world leader to take control of, and upon that moment, he will exalt himself above all that is called God. At this point, the offer will be made to all humanity to take the mark in allegiance to the Antichrist, the world leader.

TAKING THE MARK IS AN ACT OF WORSHIP

So seductive and awe-inspiring will this leader's presence be that the majority of the world at that time will quickly swear their lives to this figure. This figure, the Antichrist, will likely have survived an impossible scenario, having been assassinated in the public eye and miraculously recovering to a degree that can only be explained as a supernatural resurrection. This will be his false messianic rising-from-the-dead moment, a perversion of Jesus' death and resurrection. With this and other supernatural abilities on display by the figure, the world will be seduced and will bow to him as he calls himself God.

At this time, we will see the locking in of a world economic system, empowered and operated through the mark. Our current environment of AI and digitized finance will then become part of this heightened mechanism of global control. Anyone who does not participate in this economy and system will have no access to buying power, whether buying or selling.

In Daniel 3, three Hebrew boys were told that unless they bowed down to an idol, they would be cast into the fire. This will be the same scenario. It was a gesture of worship and submission. They said no and were cast into the fire, only to be accompanied by the pre-incarnate Jesus!

In Revelation, those of us who follow Jesus Christ understand what will happen on earth. Whether you believe the Church will be present or removed before this period, one thing is certain. When the mark appears, it will be an act of worship that rejects all other religions and pledges allegiance to a global ruler.

THE MARK IS A SIGN OF OWNERSHIP ON THE PERSON WEARING IT

The word "mark" here is a *charagma (ca,ragma),* meaning a *brand* or a *seal.*[1] The mark signifies allegiance and ownership, like a brand of recognition or association. It is coupled with worship of the Beast. Taking the mark is an irredeemable, conscious act that, in reality, is the signing of one's life away to darkness for all eternity. What the exact mark actually is does not fully come to light. What we do know is that it will be a distinct sign of allegiance and worship. Followers of the Beast will willingly adopt this brand or mark to demonstrate their allegiance to the Antichrist. Enforcement of the mark, which will control what is bought and sold, is possible and will be enforced because the Beast has economic control over the world.

ARTIFICIAL INTELLIGENCE AND DIGITAL TRACKING

Volumes of ink have been spilled over the topic of 666 in Revelation. Here is the bottom line on the issue. There will be a mark that will not allow commerce without it. In the field of Artificial Intelligence and our rapid technological developments, this is no longer an issue beyond the reach of governments or world powers. Mass surveillance and digital tracking, along with digital currency, are well established and continue to expand. When the Beast takes over the world's system, all of these technologies will be at his disposal. From a position of global influence, with humanity viewing him as a god, the worldwide movement will shift toward adopting his mark as an act of willful servitude and loyalty. Moreover, it will be an act of worship. Denying all other forms of religion to say the Beast is the one true god—a dark day in all of history, for sure.

My response to this time is "Thank You, God, for Jesus!" We have a glorious future in Christ the Lord, and as His Church prepares for Him, we also have the great hope that the *Ekklesia*, the called-out ones, His Church, will not be present when the Beast takes over the world. We are the Church of Jesus Christ, and as a corporate body, we are also what is restraining the appearance of the Antichrist and the false prophet. When the Church is removed, then and only then can the man of sin appear on the world stage.

A TYPE OF ANTICHRIST IN ANTIQUITY

> *He was a mighty hunter before the Lord; therefore it is said, "Like Nimrod the mighty hunter before the Lord."*
>
> —Genesis 10:9

> [Nimrod] said he would be revenged on God, if he should have a mind to drown the world again; for that he would build a tower too high for the waters to reach. And that he would avenge himself on God for destroying their forefathers.
>
> —*Antiquities of the Jews*, Book 1, Chapter 4

According to extra-biblical tradition, Nimrod is said to have led the construction of the Tower of Babel. According to Josephus, the motive for building the Tower of Babel was to protect humanity from another flood. Further, according to Josephus, Nimrod "persuaded [his subjects] not to ascribe [their strength] to God, as if it were through his means they were happy, but to believe that it was their own courage which procured that happiness."[2] Humanism was on full display by Nimrod's leadership, he taught the people following him to believe it was not God who brings fulfillment, or happiness, but their own ability to do so. He might as well have said to each individual, you are a god, and you don't need the God of heaven, as you yourself are the source of your own happiness.

> *Humanism:* Humanitas meant *the development of human virtue, in all its forms, to its fullest extent.* The term thus implied not only such qualities as are associated with the modern word humanity understanding, benevolence, compassion, mercy—but also such more assertive characteristics as fortitude, judgment, prudence, eloquence, and even love of honour. Consequently, the possessor of humanitas could not be merely a sedentary and isolated philosopher or man of letters but was of necessity a participant in active life. Just as action without insight was held to be aimless and barbaric, insight without action was rejected as barren and imperfect. Humanitas called for a fine balance of action and contemplation, a balance born not of compromise but of complementarity.[3]

Humanism is the ultimate reliance on the individual self, with no need for God or any higher power. Self-worship replaces God Almighty in a humanistic society. Ironically, when a figure such as the Antichrist appears, he offers a counterfeit to the emptiness that humanistic philosophy fosters in a person. The missing God-piece will be filled with a false god when conditions are right, and the Antichrist will deceive them through empirical falsehood, meeting them on the carnal level. For example, he will perform lying signs and wonders and, at the beginning, will appear to bring about world peace. The humanist would logically follow this type of figure, as they never knew the One True Living God.

If what Josephus suggested about Nimrod was the case, then Nimrod could be classified as a godless, humanistic anti-Adam. Adam, being an original son of God who was to rule the garden and subdue the earth, was also referred to in the Bible as *the first man, or Adam*. Jesus is the Last Adam.

By referring to Nimrod as the anti-Adam, I mean that he carried the original spirit of the Antichrist and raised himself to pervert God's purpose on earth through rebellion. For rebellion against God is one of the primary purposes of the Antichrist.

> *And so it is written, "The first man Adam became a living being." The last Adam became a life-giving spirit.*
>
> —1 Corinthians 15:45

Ever since the fall of man, many false religions and ungodly belief systems have sought to usurp the God of heaven and to do as they wish rather than to serve and surrender to the Creator. Much of this is due to the nefarious activities of those mutinous fallen angels who acted according to their own will rather than in alignment with God's will. That same spirit has flooded the earth, and we face it today—the spirit of *Antichrist.*

THE SPIRIT OF ANTICHRIST IS ALIVE TODAY

> *Now as He sat on the Mount of Olives, the disciples came to Him privately, saying, "Tell us, when will these things be? And what will be the sign of Your coming, and of the end of the age?"* [4] *And Jesus answered and said to them: "Take heed that no one deceives you.* [5] *For many will come in My name, saying, 'I am the Christ,' and will deceive many.* [6] *And you will hear of wars and rumors of wars. See that you are not troubled; for all these things must come to pass, but the end is not yet.* [7] *For nation will rise against nation, and kingdom against kingdom. And there will be famines, pestilences, and earthquakes in various places.* [8] *All these are the beginning of sorrows."*
>
> —Matthew 24:3-8

> *Little children, it is the last hour; and as you have heard that* ***the Antichrist is coming****, even now* ***many antichrists have come****, by which we know that it is the last hour.* [19] *They went out from us, but they*

were not of us; for if they had been of us, they would have continued with us; but they went out that they might be made manifest, that none of them were of us. [20] *But you have an anointing from the Holy One, and you know all things.* [21] *I have not written to you because you do not know the truth, but because you know it, and that no lie is of the truth.* [22] *Who is a liar but he who denies that Jesus is the Christ? He is antichrist who denies the Father and the Son.* [23] *Whoever denies the Son does not have the Father either; he who acknowledges the Son has the Father also.* [24] *Therefore let that abide in you which you heard from the beginning. If what you heard from the beginning abides in you, you also will abide in the Son and in the Father.* [25] *And this is the promise that He has promised us—eternal life.* [26] *These things I have written to you concerning those who try to deceive you.* [27] *But the anointing which you have received from Him abides in you, and you do not need that anyone teach you; but as the same anointing teaches you concerning all things, and is true, and is not a lie, and just as it has taught you, you will abide in Him.*

—1 John 2:18-27

Matthew 24:7 describes what will happen at the end of the age. It includes false christs, wars and rumors of wars, nation rising against nation, kingdom against kingdom, along with famines, pestilences, and earthquakes in various places.Verse 8 places these events in the timeline, with Jesus calling them the beginning of sorrows. Another way to say it is that these are birth pangs, much like a woman about to give birth.

THE EVIL DUO WILL ONE DAY APPEAR BEFORE THE ENTIRE WORLD

All the world's events are leading to the appearance of the one who will come as the imposter to the Messiah. He will have answers at first, but will then turn against all world religions and declare himself higher than all that is called God. That day will come when the man of sin will suddenly appear on the world stage, in all the aspects of who and what he will represent. We, the redeemed, stand in the way of his nefarious reign on earth.

In the meantime, we are dealing with the spirit of Antichrist, and it is only in spirit because the man of sin cannot manifest until the one who restrains is taken out of the way. Even so, the Antichrist will eventually rise; along the way are those who stand up to the spirit of Antichrist and reclaim the culture. Such is the 144,000 Jewish evangelists.

THE 144,000 JEWISH EVANGELISTS, WHO WILL PREACH THE GOSPEL DURING THE REIGN OF THE ANTICHRIST

> *And I heard the number of those who were sealed.* ***One hundred and forty-four thousand of all the tribes of the children of Israel were sealed****.*
>
> —Revelation 7:4

> *Then I looked, and behold, a Lamb standing on Mount Zion, and with Him* ***one hundred and forty-four thousand****, having His Father's name written on their foreheads.*
>
> —Revelation 14:1

> *They sang as it were a new song before the throne, before the four living creatures, and the elders; and no one could learn that song except* ***the hundred and forty-four thousand who were redeemed from the earth****.*
>
> —Revelation 14:3

Even in the middle of it all, God will empower these 144,000 Jewish evangelists to win the lost! Revelation 7:4 speaks of 144,000 actual people living during the end-times Tribulation. This passage contains no allegory and points to these 144,000 being literal Jews—12,000 taken from each tribe of Israel, according to Revelation 7:5-8. These 144,000 Jews are afforded special protection from God; they are "sealed" and kept safe from divine judgments and the evil reign of the Antichrist. Amazingly, these 144,000 can operate freely during the Tribulation. The context of the word "sealed" refers to the impress of a signet ring; an official who wished to delegate his authority for a task to a representative would allow that subordinate to use his signet ring.

Their mission is to evangelize the post-Rapture world and to declare the uncompromising gospel of Jesus Christ during the Tribulation. These Jewish evangelists will lead multitudes to the saving knowledge of Jesus Christ. Revelation 7:9-10 says, "After these things I looked, and behold, a great multitude which no one could number, of all nations, tribes, peoples, and tongues, standing before the throne and before the Lamb, clothed with white robes, with palm branches in their hands, [10] and crying out with a loud voice, saying, 'Salvation belongs to our God who sits on the throne, and to the Lamb!'"

Consider the mercy of God, that even during the age of Tribulation, the gospel will be heard. The name of Jesus will be proclaimed, offering salvation to all who will receive it. This is when many will become saints during the Tribulation. These are not part of the Church, but they will be saved even during the terrible season of the Antichrist.[4]

GOD'S SERVANTS MARKED AS HIS

One will say, "I am the Lord's"; another will call himself by the name of Jacob; another will write with his hand, "The Lord's," and name himself by the name of Israel.

—Isaiah 44:5

Special protection is given to these 144,000, similar to the way God protected His people in Goshen during the 10 plagues (*see* Exodus 8:28; Exodus 9:4; Exodus 11:7).

The protection these Jewish evangelists have is also mirrored from the Old Testament, in Genesis 4:15, speaking of God's protection of Cain, "And the LORD said to him, 'Therefore, whoever kills Cain, vengeance shall be taken on him sevenfold.' And the LORD set a mark on Cain, lest anyone finding him should kill him." Also in Isaiah 66:19, "I will set a sign among them; and those among them who escape I will send to the nations: to Tarshish and

Pul and Lud, who draw the bow, and Tubal and Javan, to the coastlands afar off who have not heard My fame nor seen My glory. And they shall declare My glory among the Gentiles."

THE 144,000 CARRY GOD'S MARK ON THEIR FOREHEADS

And the Lord said to him, "Go through the midst of the city, through the midst of Jerusalem, and put a mark on the foreheads of the men who sigh and cry over all the abominations that are done within it." [5] *To the others He said in my hearing, "Go after him through the city and kill; do not let your eye spare, nor have any pity.* [6] *Utterly slay old and young men, maidens and little children and women; but do not come near anyone on whom is the mark; and begin at My sanctuary." So they began with the elders who were before the temple.*

—Ezekiel 9:4-6

Revelation 14:1 states that these 144,000 have a mark on their foreheads, a parallel to Ezekiel 9:4-6, where judgment could not begin until the foreheads of the righteous, or those who grieved and mourned over the sin of their land, were marked. The forehead and the hand were the most obvious parts of the body, as they could be readily seen (*see* Exodus 13:9, 16; Exodus 28:38; Deuteronomy 6:8; Deuteronomy 11:18).

THESE 144,000 MAY BE THE FIRST FRUITS OF A FUTURE REDEEMED ISRAEL

And I will pour on the house of David and on the inhabitants of Jerusalem the Spirit of grace and supplication; then they will look on Me whom they pierced. Yes, they will mourn for Him as one mourns for his only son, and grieve for Him as one grieves for a firstborn.

—Zechariah 12:10

> *For I do not desire, brethren, that you should be ignorant of this mystery, lest you should be wise in your own opinion, that blindness in part has happened to Israel until the fullness of the Gentiles has come in.* [26] *And so all Israel will be saved, as it is written: "The Deliverer will come out of Zion, and He will turn away ungodliness from Jacob;* [27] *For this is My covenant with them, when I take away their sins."*
>
> —Romans 11:25-27

Zechariah 12:10 and Romans 11:25-27 are prophecies declaring that Israel would repent and turn back to God. The 144,000 Jews appear to be a "first fruits." We derive this understanding from Revelation 14:4, which states, "These are the ones who were not defiled with women, for they are virgins. These are the ones who follow the Lamb wherever He goes. These were redeemed from among men, being *firstfruits to God and to the Lamb."*

I find it wonderful that the character of God Almighty would raise up the 144,000 right in the face of the Antichrist. It is both a defiance of the Antichrist and God's great mercy toward those who dwell on the earth in those days, so that they might still hear the gospel truth of Jesus Christ. It reminds me of a similar story throughout history in which God appointed those who would resist evil in their generation. Although the story is far different from that of the 144,000, another group stood up against unrighteousness in the name of God and the traditions of their fathers, and in the end were victorious. Let's look at the Maccabees, who rose against national oppression in their day. Something wonderful happens when the righteous stand their ground.

THE COURAGE OF MACCABEES

As stated, history is filled with oppressors met by those who would not back down. In the case of the Maccabees, there is a major type and prophetic instance of an attempted abomination within the temple, something the Antichrist will do again when he appears. God has always had those anointed to resist the system of the Antichrist and will have those anointed to resist during the reign of the actual Antichrist, as we saw with the 144,000 Jewish evangelists.

Historically, the spirit of Antichrist has sought to manifest and seize control of culture at nearly every point in society. Here is an example of the spirit of Antichrist attempting to assert dominance over the Jewish people during the intertestamental period. A powerful lesson in this instance is what happens when people stand up to the nonsense being forced upon them. This could happen during the Tribulation to those who are awake to the Antichrist's deception.

THE MACCABEES RESISTED OPPRESSIVE CULTURAL PRESSURE

The story of the Maccabees is detailed in the Apocrypha. They were a group of Jewish warriors who revolted against the Seleucid Empire, which had imposed an authoritarian Hellenistic (Greek) culture on Judea in the 2nd century BC.

In 167 BC, an uprising began when Mattathias, a Jewish priest, heroically refused to worship pagan gods at the order of the ruling kingdom. Mattathias became so indignant against the demand to make a pagan sacrifice that a Hellenistic Jew stepped forward to make the sacrifice in Mattathias's place. In response, Mattathias threw that man on the altar and killed him out of zeal to not defile the commands of God.

Mattathias died in 166 BC, and his son Judah Maccabee assumed leadership and led the rebellion against the oppressive rulership through guerrilla warfare, even defeating Seleucid forces in several key battles.

Judah gained the name "The Hammer" as "Maccabee" is believed to mean "the hammer" in Aramaic, symbolizing Judah Maccabee's fierce combat style. History knows him as Judah the Hammer Maccabee.

In 164 BC, the Maccabees recaptured Jerusalem and purified the desecrated second temple, where an altar to Zeus had been erected, and pigs were being sacrificed.

This event is the origin of Hanukkah, the Festival of Lights, which celebrates the rededication of the temple and the miracle of the oil that burned for eight days. That Maccabean uprising eventually led to the establishment of the Hasmonean dynasty. Uniquely, the Hasmoneans led Judea as their own independent kingdom from around 104 BC to 63 BC.

What was notable about the Hasmoneans was their combination of the powers of the king and the high priest, a controversial arrangement that ran counter to prevailing contemporary views, which held that the priesthood should be reserved only for descendants of Aaron.

The Maccabees are remembered not only for their military campaigns and victories, but also for an intersection in Jewish history in which they chose to resist assimilation into the pagan practices of the ruling kingdom amid religious persecution.

THOSE WHO RESIST THE ANTICHRIST AND THE FALSE PROPHET

Even in the age of Antichrist, there will be those who, in the spirit of the Maccabees, will stand up like the 144,000, displaying strong defiance and being anointed to do so. It is a lesson for all of history that, whether now or in the face of the ultimate tyranny, people can resist darkness by cooperating with God Almighty and bringing about change.

As the days approach, we are to be vigilant and ready to push back against all forms of evil should Jesus tarry in His appearing. What we do know is that when Jesus returns to deal with the Antichrist and the false prophet finally, it will be a no-holds-barred victory in the Battle of Armageddon.

CHAPTER THIRTEEN

AGE OF THE TRIBULATION AND WRATH

For then there will be great tribulation, such as has not been since the beginning of the world until this time, no, nor ever shall be. [22] And unless those days were shortened, no flesh would be saved; but for the elect's sake those days will be shortened.

—Matthew 24:21-22

Of all Bible prophecy, few topics carry as much weight as the Tribulation. It comprises two segments, each lasting 3.5 years, for a total of seven years. The first half is relatively peaceful, but it radically changes in the second half, known as the time of the Great Tribulation.

This seven-year future period is when God will pour out and finalize His judgment on the unbelieving world. Nothing in all of history, before or after, will compare to the level of wrath unleashed upon the world during the second half of the Tribulation. A common question arises among people I meet or see, and even our daily broadcast evokes it from time to time: Are we in the end times?

ARE WE IN THE END TIMES?

And it shall come to pass in the last days, saith God, I will pour out of my Spirit upon all flesh: and your sons and your daughters shall

> *prophesy, and your young men shall see visions, and your old men shall dream dreams.*
>
> —Acts 2:17 KJV

Let me answer that with an oversimplification, but it might be a useful way to define the last days, which transition into the end times. The last days began at Pentecost and will continue until the very end of the Church Age, when the Church is suddenly removed by the Rapture. The end times begin with the Tribulation, followed by the Great Tribulation.

We have been in the last days for nearly 2,000 years. We are not (at least at the time of this writing) in the end times. Once the Church is taken, you can set your clock for seven years. In these last days, we are in the Age of Grace, the Church Age, where grace reigns, and God views the world, especially the Church, through Christ, His Son.

The Tribulation will be triggered by the removal of the saints in the Church's Rapture. For God has not appointed the Church to wrath.

THE CHURCH IS NOT APPOINTED FOR WRATH

> *For God did not appoint us to wrath, but to obtain salvation through our Lord Jesus Christ.*
>
> —1 Thessalonians 5:9

It is a powerful thing to understand—we are not appointed to wrath. How comforting when looking into the last things. One thing I often say is that if God indeed wanted to send the Church through the Tribulation, He is God, and I would embrace it. Yet we find scriptural truth that shows us the vast love of God for His Church. He has foreordained that the Church will fulfill its purpose of expanding the kingdom and winning as many lost souls as possible to the saving knowledge of Jesus, right up to the end of the age. Wrath is the time when God will entirely crush the enemies of His Son and the Church.

ARE WE ALREADY IN THE TRIBULATION?

Given the time, many would ask, "Are we in the Tribulation now?" Amid the chaos, wars, unrest, earthquakes, and geopolitical turmoil, it is easy to wonder whether that is the case. Observing the Word of God, specifically the book of Revelation, brings clarity. We can determine whether we are in the Tribulation by looking at what will unfold in the terrible days to come. By seeing these unimaginable horrors in the book of Revelation firsthand, the question can be answered rather plainly. No, we are not in the Tribulation yet. After looking at the intensity on display throughout the next several passages, it should be clear that we are not there yet.

THE END OF THE CHURCH AGE IS THE BEGINNING OF THE AGE OF THE ANTICHRIST

The restrainer must be removed before the Beast can take the world stage.

> *And now you know what is restraining, that he may be revealed in his own time.* 7 *For the mystery of lawlessness is already at work; only He who now restrains will do so until He is taken out of the way.*
>
> —2 Thessalonians 2:6-7

We who stand firm in the Lord Jesus, bind ourselves to Him, and commit to His will being accomplished on earth, are what I like to call "Beast-Proof." This means that no matter what, we cannot be overcome by the Beast when he arises.

BEAST GIVEN POWER TO OVERCOME THE SAINTS

> *And it was given unto him to make war with the saints, and to overcome them: and power was given him over all kindreds, and tongues, and nations.*
>
> —Revelation 13:7 KJV

Revelation 13:7 describes an end-times scenario in which the Antichrist will be in power on earth. He will also be granted the ability to make war with the saints—and to overcome them.

THE *EKKLESIA* CANNOT BE OVERCOME!

> *And I also say to you that you are Peter, and on this rock I will build My church, and the gates of Hades shall not prevail against it.*
>
> —Matthew 16:18

During the Tribulation, it will be different from the time we are living in now. We are in the Church Age, and Jesus declared in Matthew 16:18 that "the gates of hell shall not prevail" against His Church. Those saints on the earth at that time will be overcome by the Antichrist. Many speculate that this is because the Church of Jesus Christ will be caught up in the air to meet the Lord before this dreadful time.

> *For the Lord Himself will descend from heaven with a shout, with the voice of an archangel, and with the trumpet of God. And the dead in Christ will rise first.* [17] *Then we who are alive and remain shall be caught up together with them in the clouds to meet the Lord in the air. And thus we shall always be with the Lord.*
>
> —1 Thessalonians 4:16-17

Once again, we must recognize that the Church of Jesus Christ is not appointed for wrath and will be taken away before the great and terrible Day of the Lord. Those who remain will still be able to discover the truth of Jesus; some will give their lives to Him, becoming end-time saints. This, however, is not the experience of believers today. We cannot be overcome by the gates of hell unless we permit it or lie down and fail to enforce our authority.

AGE OF GRACE

This dispensation of grace, also known as the Church Age, corresponds to the New Testament period. In this Age of Grace, we, the corporate body of Christ, have the power to stop the gates of hell. Shortly after the resurrection of Jesus, a significant encounter took place. Acts 2 describes this divine occasion, when the Holy Spirit was poured out in power upon all gathered in the upper room.

Not only did the baptism in the Holy Spirit, which caused the believers to speak in different tongues, occur, but it also marked the arrival of a new power and authority. The Church, born during this event, ushered in the last days and began to enforce something that had never before existed. A united group of people was given the authority of God to enforce what Jesus accomplished.

New terminology was introduced, such as "believers," "brothers and sisters," "baptism in the Holy Spirit," and even the term "the Church," which was brand-new. Never had anyone been empowered by the Holy Spirit in this manner. God came and dwelt among men through Jesus and went a step further by making a way for man to become the habitation of God. Anyone who called on the name of Jesus could be saved! Powerfully united against the present evil age, these brand-new believers, filled with God, became a global force to be reckoned with.

> *...These that have turned the world upside down...*
>
> —Acts 17:6 KJV

BLOOD-BOUGHT BELIEVERS ARE BEAST-PROOF!

> *For God did not appoint us to wrath, but to obtain salvation through our Lord Jesus Christ.*
>
> —1 Thessalonians 5:9

To further make the point that we are not in the Tribulation during the Church Age, consider all the issues that will rapidly unfold during those years. The world will experience earth-shaking events beyond imagination. When you look at what the Bible says about that time, it becomes clear that, now, during the Church Age, we are not seeing wrath.

However, the day will come when the world will know the complete and total wrath of the Lamb. The Seven Seals of the Tribulation, followed by the Seven Trumpets and the Three Woes, and then the Seven Bowls, will completely devastate the entire world.

THE DAY OF THE LORD

Scripture refers to the Tribulation as "The Day of the Lord" or a time in which God's personal will intervenes in history to fulfill His ultimate plan for mankind.

> Besides being a time of judgment, it will also be a time of salvation as God will deliver the remnant of Israel, fulfilling His promise that "all of Israel will be saved" (Romans 11:26), forgiving their sins and restoring His chosen people to the land He promised to Abraham (Isaiah 10:27; Micah 4; Zechariah 13). The final outcome of the day of the Lord will be that "the arrogance of man will be brought low and the pride of men humbled; the Lord alone will be exalted in that day" (Isaiah 2:17). The ultimate or final fulfillment of the prophecies concerning the day of the Lord will come at the end of history when God, with wondrous power, will punish evil and fulfill all His promises.[1]

UNPARALLELED TIME OF DISTRESS AND JACOB'S TROUBLE

"For behold, the days are coming," says the Lord, "that I will bring back from captivity My people Israel and Judah," says the Lord. "And I will

cause them to return to the land that I gave to their fathers, and they shall possess it." [4] *Now these are the words that the Lord spoke concerning Israel and Judah.* [5] *"For thus says the Lord: 'We have heard a voice of trembling, of fear, and not of peace.* [6] *Ask now, and see, whether a man is ever in labor with child? So why do I see every man with his hands on his loins like a woman in labor, and all faces turned pale?* [7] *Alas! For that day is great, so that none is like it; and it is the time of Jacob's trouble, but he shall be saved out of it.'"*

—Jeremiah 30:3-7

At that time Michael shall stand up, the great prince who stands watch over the sons of your people; and there shall be a time of trouble, such as never was since there was a nation, even to that time. And at that time your people shall be delivered, every one who is found written in the book.

—Daniel 12:1

The phrase the time of Jacob's trouble comes from Jeremiah 30:7, which says, "It is the time of Jacob's trouble." This prophetic scripture corresponds with the seven-year Tribulation.

In Jeremiah 30:3-4, the Lord speaks to Jeremiah the prophet about Judah and Israel, and He promises that on a future day He will bring both back to the land He had promised their forefathers. This return will be accompanied by distress. The time of Jacob's trouble—Jacob being a synecdoche, or a metaphor, meaning Israel.

Jeremiah 30:5 explains that this will be a time of great fear and trembling. Jeremiah 30:6 describes this time as childbirth, indicating agony. Thankfully, there is hope for Israel, as the Lord goes on to promise that He will save them. Throughout history, no terror has equaled this time of Jacob's trouble; God will deliver them in the end, as Jeremiah 30:7 indicates.

BLESSINGS FOLLOW THE TIME OF JACOB'S TROUBLE

> *"Therefore do not fear, O My servant Jacob," says the Lord, "Nor be dismayed, O Israel; For behold, I will save you from afar, and your seed from the land of their captivity. Jacob shall return, have rest and be quiet, and no one shall make him afraid.* [11] *For I am with you," says the Lord, "to save you; Though I make a full end of all nations where I have scattered you, yet I will not make a complete end of you. But I will correct you in justice, and will not let you go altogether unpunished."*
>
> —Jeremiah 30:10-11

The Lord makes a strong statement here. He declares that as part of the deliverance from the time of Jacob's trouble, He, the Lord, will destroy the nations that opposed and held Israel and Judah captive. Further, God states that He will never allow Jacob to be completely destroyed. Jacob's trouble is described here as a time of discipline for His people, and it is stated, "Though I make a full end of all nations where I have scattered you, yet I will not make a complete end of you. But I will correct you in justice, and will not let you go altogether unpunished." This time will be unparalleled in all of history, as Jeremiah 30:7 says, "Alas! For that day is great, so that none is like it."

> *For then there will be great tribulation, such as has not been since the beginning of the world until this time, no, nor ever shall be.*
>
> —Matthew 24:21

Jesus uses the same imagery and language here in Matthew 24:21, saying of those days of Great Tribulation, "...such as has not been since the beginning of the world until this time, no, nor ever shall be...." It is worth noting that Jesus' and Jeremiah's statements indicate that this Tribulation will be unlike any other time in history, before or after it.

BIRTH PANGS LEADING UP TO THE TRIBULATION

> *And you will hear of* ***wars and rumors of wars****. See that you are not troubled; for all these things must come to pass, but* ***the end is not yet****.* [7] *For* ***nation will rise against nation****, and* ***kingdom against kingdom****. And there will be* ***famines, pestilences****, and* ***earthquakes in various places****.* [8] *All these are the beginning of sorrows.*
>
> —Matthew 24:6-8

Jesus describes the events and conditions leading up to the Tribulation: wars, rumors of wars, nations rising against nations, kingdom against kingdom, famines, pestilences, and earthquakes in various places. But the end is not yet; these are only the beginning of what is to come—the Tribulation.

The apostle Paul echoes this prophetic insight from Jesus by stating a similar idea in 1 Thessalonians 5.

> *For when they say, "Peace and safety!" then sudden destruction comes upon them, as labor pains upon a pregnant woman. And they shall not escape.*
>
> —1 Thessalonians 5:3

Paul states that they will say, "peace and safety," only to experience destruction that will come upon them suddenly, like labor pains on a pregnant woman, and they will not escape. This scenario describes events that follow the Rapture of the Church (*see* 1 Thessalonians 4:13-18). Among the many issues Jesus listed in Matthew 24, He uses the terminology, "the beginning of birth pangs." Paul also uses the same language of "birth pangs" when describing the events leading up to the Rapture of the Church, which immediately precedes the Tribulation. Birth pangs, or birth pains, are described in detail throughout Revelation, chapters 6 through 12.

One of the main purposes of the Tribulation—"the time of Jacob's trouble"—is to bring Israel back to the Lord (*see* Jeremiah 30:22, Hosea 6:1-2, Zechariah 12:10).

THE TIME OF JACOB'S TROUBLE REVEALS THE CHARACTER OF GOD WHO KEEPS HIS PROMISES

God keeps His promises, brings salvation to those who trust in Christ, and pronounces judgment on sin. In the last days, God will pour out His judgment on a reprobate and wicked world. From Israel's vantage point, the seven-year Tribulation is the time of Jacob's trouble. God will purge His chosen people of the wicked and unbelieving who oppress them.

In His goodness and abundant mercy, God makes a way for salvation through it all, so that all who call upon the name of the Lord shall be saved!

> *And it shall come to pass that whoever calls on the name of the Lord shall be saved. For in Mount Zion and in Jerusalem there shall be deliverance, as the Lord has said, among the remnant whom the Lord calls.*
>
> —Joel 2:32

> *For "whoever calls on the name of the Lord shall be saved."*
>
> —Romans 10:13

THE NATION OF ISRAEL WILL EXPERIENCE INTENSE DISTRESS AND PERSECUTION

As we will see in the Seven Seals, the Seven Trumpets, the Three Woes, and the Seven Bowls, there will be an unprecedented period of intense distress and persecution for the nation of Israel. Because of this, Israel will experience salvation and restoration under the Messiah. During the "time of Jacob's trouble," there will be great suffering, but it will end with God's ultimate deliverance. This fulfills the promise to Jacob, Israel, for their preparation and redemption before the Messiah's return. Jeremiah 30 describes a time so severe that there is none like it. This time begins at the start of the Tribulation and lasts for the entire seven years.

DANIEL'S 70 WEEKS

God, in His mercy, has set a limit on the duration of the Tribulation as Jesus says in Mark 13:19-20 NIV, "Because those will be days of distress unequaled from the beginning, when God created the world, until now—and never to be equaled again. If the Lord had not cut short those days, no one would survive...."

> *Seventy weeks are determined for your people and for your holy city, to finish the transgression, to make an end of sins, to make reconciliation for iniquity, to bring in everlasting righteousness, to seal up vision and prophecy, and to anoint the Most Holy.* 25 *Know therefore and understand, that from the going forth of the command to restore and build Jerusalem until Messiah the Prince, there shall be seven weeks and sixty-two weeks; the street shall be built again, and the wall, even in troublesome times.* 26 *And after the sixty-two weeks Messiah shall be cut off, but not for Himself; and the people of the prince who is to come shall destroy the city and the sanctuary. The end of it shall be with a flood, and till the end of the war desolations are determined.* 27 *Then he shall confirm a covenant with many for one week; But in the middle of the week He shall bring an end to sacrifice and offering. And on the wing of abominations shall be one who makes desolate, even until the consummation, which is determined, is poured out on the desolate.*
>
> —Daniel 9:24–27

Here we see that God spoke to Daniel about the purpose and timing of the Tribulation—70 weeks declared against "your people." The reference is to Daniel's people, the Jews, and the nation of Israel. In Daniel 9:24, we see a period during which God's purpose is "to finish the transgression, to make an end of sins, to make reconciliation for iniquity, to bring in everlasting righteousness, to seal up vision and prophecy, and to anoint the Most Holy."

This is a prophetic snapshot of what will happen as the Tribulation begins and of how the Antichrist will rise. We know that Jesus Christ will be victorious in it all.

The Tribulation, that prophetic seven-year period in the end times, will bring an end to humanity's decadence and depravity as God pours out judgment. During that time, Israel will repent of their sins and receive Jesus as their Messiah, paving the way for a period of great blessing and restoration known as the Millennial Reign of Jesus.

THE SEVEN SEALS OF THE TRIBULATION REVELATION 6–8

The Seven Seals are prophetically described in Revelation and are opened by the Lamb of God, Jesus Christ. These Seven Seals are on a scroll; each one, when opened, unleashes breathtaking judgments on the entire world. Here are all seven concisely laid out.

FIRST SEAL

> *Now I saw when the Lamb opened one of the seals; and I heard one of the four living creatures saying with a voice like thunder, "Come and see."* 2 *And I looked, and behold, a white horse. He who sat on it had a bow; and a crown was given to him, and he went out conquering and to conquer.*
>
> —Revelation 6:1-2

The First Seal to be opened has a rider on a white horse. The rider is depicted with a bow (conquest from afar) and a crown (victory/authority) and goes out conquering. This is often interpreted as the Antichrist or a leader/spirit of false conquest. He brings deceptive and false peace or political/military domination. He marks the beginning of the Tribulation with global power consolidation and deception, setting the stage for escalating chaos.

SECOND SEAL

> *When He opened the second seal, I heard the second living creature saying, "Come and see."* [4] *Another horse, fiery red, went out. And it was granted to the one who sat on it to take peace from the earth, and that people should kill one another; and there was given to him a great sword.*
>
> —Revelation 6:3-4

The Second Seal shows a rider on a red horse. This rider symbolizes bloodshed and removes peace, causing widespread slaughter. The rider carries a sword that brings war and mass bloodshed. By removing peace, people will begin to slaughter one another, leading to widespread conflict and death. This would lead to massive global warfare, possibly a World War III-scale conflict following the Antichrist's rise. The consequence for sin will be revealed as war, a divine judgment. Jesus' prophecy in Matthew 24:6 will be fulfilled: "You will hear of wars and rumors of wars."

THIRD SEAL

> *When He opened the third seal, I heard the third living creature say, "Come and see." So I looked, and behold, a black horse, and he who sat on it had a pair of scales in his hand.* [6] *And I heard a voice in the midst of the four living creatures saying, "A quart of wheat for a denarius, and three quarts of barley for a denarius; and do not harm the oil and the wine."*
>
> —Revelation 6:5-6

The Third Seal has a rider on a black horse. This rider is described with scales (rationing), and food prices have skyrocketed. This indicates a severe famine, with luxuries such as oil and wine reserved for the rich. After the Second Seal of war, economic collapse, hardship, and famine typically follow.

FOURTH SEAL

> *When He opened the fourth seal, I heard the voice of the fourth living creature saying, "Come and see."* [8] *So I looked, and behold, a pale horse. And the name of him who sat on it was Death, and Hades followed with him. And power was given to them over a fourth of the earth, to kill with sword, with hunger, with death, and by the beasts of the earth.*
>
> —Revelation 6:7-8

The Fourth Seal has a rider on a pale/green horse. This rider, named Death, kills a quarter of the entire earth by the sword, famine, plague, and beasts. This widespread death and depopulation from multiple causes, culminating in the first four judgments, "The Four Horsemen," signal the severity of the Tribulations. Death and Hades, the realms of the dead, follow as a consequence of sin.

FIFTH SEAL

> *When He opened the fifth seal, I saw under the altar the souls of those who had been slain for the word of God and for the testimony which they held.* [10] *And they cried with a loud voice, saying, "How long, O Lord, holy and true, until You judge and avenge our blood on those who dwell on the earth?"* [11] *Then a white robe was given to each of them; and it was said to them that they should rest a little while longer, until both the number of*

> *their fellow servants and their brethren, who would be killed as they were, was completed.*
>
> —Revelation 6:9-11

When the Fifth Seal is opened, we see the souls of martyrs under heaven's altar crying out for justice. These are Tribulation saints who were killed for their faith. They are given white robes and told to wait for God's judgment to be poured out on His enemies. Although they cry out for justice and continually ask God, "How long?" God, in His patience and mercy, delays sending judgment until martyrdom is complete. This allows more time for people to repent and turn to Him.

SIXTH SEAL

> *I looked when He opened the sixth seal, and behold, there was a great earthquake; and the sun became black as sackcloth of hair, and the moon became like blood.* [13] *And the stars of heaven fell to the earth, as a fig tree drops its late figs when it is shaken by a mighty wind.* [14] *Then the sky receded as a scroll when it is rolled up, and every mountain and island was moved out of its place.* [15] *And the kings of the earth, the great men, the rich men, the commanders, the mighty men, every slave and every free man, hid themselves in the caves and in the rocks of the mountains,* [16] *and said to the mountains and rocks, "Fall on us and hide us from the face of Him who sits on the throne and from the wrath of the Lamb!* [17] *For the great day of His wrath has come, and who is able to stand?"*
>
> —Revelation 6:12-17

At the opening of the Sixth Seal, a great earthquake occurs, the sun blackens, the moon turns blood-red, the stars fall from the sky, and the sky rolls up like a scroll (which leads some to believe it is a nuclear blast). Additionally, the Sixth Seal causes people to hide in terror from God's wrath. This signals the "great day of wrath" approaching. In this instance, we see the kings and the powerful hiding in caves, asking the mountains to fall on them to shield them from the wrath of the Lamb and the face of God Almighty!

SEVENTH SEAL

> *When He opened the seventh seal, there was silence in heaven for about half an hour.* [2] *And I saw the seven angels who stand before God, and to them were given seven trumpets.* [3] *Then another angel, having a golden censer, came and stood at the altar. He was given much incense, that he should offer it with the prayers of all the saints upon the golden altar which was before the throne.* [4] *And the smoke of the incense, with the prayers of the saints, ascended before God from the angel's hand.* [5] *Then the angel took the censer, filled it with fire from the altar, and threw it to the earth. And there were noises, thunderings, lightnings, and an earthquake.*
>
> —Revelation 8:1-5

At the opening of the Seventh Seal, there will be silence in heaven for half an hour. This interlude, a moment of pause, precedes the introduction of the seven trumpets. There are several interpretations of why this silence occurs. The first is that heaven falls silent in awe before the unveiling of the severe judgments to come. These judgments are more intense than those of the previous seals. This silence would be like the "calm before the storm." Another interpretation is that heaven shows reverence before God's judgment. In Habakkuk 2:20, it says, "The LORD is in his holy temple; let all the earth *keep silence* before him." This silence reflects holy reverence and expectation for the upcoming execution of divine justice. Revelation 8:3-4 offers another explanation for heaven's silence. Immediately after the silence, an angel offers incense with the prayers of God's people. This suggests that the pause allows these prayers to ascend before God, who will answer them through the judgments set to follow. Whatever the reason, there will be an awareness of intense judgment, and all of heaven will be quiet for thirty minutes.

THE SEVEN TRUMPETS REVELATION 8–11

Now the earth will experience Seven Trumpets, sounded by angels and bringing even greater judgments. Notice how these trumpets escalate beyond the dramatic judgments of the Seven Seals, with many of them so terrible that they affect one-third of the earth.

FIRST TRUMPET

> *The first angel sounded: And hail and fire followed, mingled with blood, and they were thrown to the earth. And a third of the trees were burned up, and all green grass was burned up.*
>
> —Revelation 8:7

When the first angel sounds this Trumpet, a catastrophic storm of hail, fire, and blood will devastate the land. This resembles the plagues in Exodus 7:20 and Exodus 9:23-25, but it will burn one-third of the Earth's vegetation. Massive wildfires and atmospheric phenomena will destroy forests and grasslands, causing food shortages, economic ruin, and ecological collapse. This will demonstrate God's control over creation and serve as a warning of His escalating wrath.

SECOND TRUMPET

> *Then the second angel sounded: And something like a great mountain burning with fire was thrown into the sea, and a third of the sea became blood. [9] And a third of the living creatures in the sea died, and a third of the ships were destroyed.*
>
> —Revelation 8:8-9

With the blast of this Trumpet, what appears to be a burning mountain to John falls from the sky and plunges into the sea, turning one-third of the seawater into blood. Some say it is a meteor or asteroid. As a result, one-third of all marine life dies, and one-third of all ships at sea are annihilated. This causes red tides, toxic waters, and global maritime disasters. This attack on the seas affects the source of life and trade, amplifying famine and economic chaos.

THIRD TRUMPET

> *Then the third angel sounded: And a great star fell from heaven, burning like a torch, and it fell on a third of the rivers and on the springs of water.* [11] *The name of the star is Wormwood. A third of the waters became wormwood, and many men died from the water, because it was made bitter.*
>
> —Revelation 8:10-11

At the sound of the Third Trumpet, a meteor or comet, a blazing "star" the Bible calls *Wormwood,* falls from heaven, contaminating one-third of the rivers and other fresh waters. The water becomes bitter, threatening human survival and echoing God's judgment on idolatry. Many will die from the poisonous water and from dehydration.

FOURTH TRUMPET

> *Then the fourth angel sounded: And a third of the sun was struck, a third of the moon, and a third of the stars, so that a third of them were darkened. A third of the day did not shine, and likewise the night.*
>
> —Revelation 8:12

Here, celestial bodies lose one-third of their light. The sun, the moon, and the stars are darkened, shortening daylight and causing global cooling, disrupted ecosystems, and fear. This event resonates with Joel 2:31, which prophetically states, "The sun shall be turned into darkness, and the moon into blood, before the coming of the great and awesome day of the Lord." Matthew 24:29 previews this event: "Immediately after the tribulation of those days the sun will be darkened, and the moon will not give its light; the stars will fall from heaven, and the powers of the heavens will be shaken." At the end of the first Four Trumpets, or natural disasters, an eagle cries "Woe! Woe! Woe" in Revelation 8:13 NIV, announcing worse to come.

TRUMPETS ACCOMPANIED BY THREE WOES

FIFTH TRUMPET (FIRST WOE)

> *Then the fifth angel sounded: And I saw a star fallen from heaven to the*
> *earth. To him was given the key to the bottomless pit. 2 And he opened*
> *the bottomless pit, and smoke arose out of the pit like the smoke of a great*
> *furnace. So the sun and the air were darkened because of the smoke of the*
> *pit. 3 Then out of the smoke locusts came upon the earth. And to them was*
> *given power, as the scorpions of the earth have power. 4 They were com-*
> *manded not to harm the grass of the earth, or any green thing, or any tree,*
> *but only those men who do not have the seal of God on their foreheads.*
> *5 And they were not given authority to kill them, but to torment them*
> *for five months. Their torment was like the torment of a scorpion when it*
> *strikes a man. 6 In those days men will seek death and will not find it;*
> *they will desire to die, and death will flee from them. 7 The shape of the*
> *locusts was like horses prepared for battle. On their heads were crowns of*
> *something like gold, and their faces were like the faces of men. 8 They had*
> *hair like women's hair, and their teeth were like lions' teeth. 9 And they had*
> *breastplates like breastplates of iron, and the sound of their wings was like*
> *the sound of chariots with many horses running into battle. 10 They had*
> *tails like scorpions, and there were stings in their tails. Their power was to*
> *hurt men five months. 11 And they had as king over them the angel of the*
> *bottomless pit, whose name in Hebrew is Abaddon, but in Greek he has*

> *the name Apollyon.* 12 *One woe is past. Behold, still two more woes are coming after these things.*
>
> —Revelation 9:1-12

The First Woe begins with the blast of the Fifth Trumpet. A fallen "star," possibly Satan, opens the abyss, releasing vile demons. These rise and torment unbelievers, those without God's seal, for five months. During this time, the pain caused by these beings is so severe that people will seek death, but will not be able to die. The description says they resemble locusts with scorpion stings, human faces, women's hair, lions' teeth, iron breastplates, and wings like chariots. This depicts something so vile that it not only inflicts terrible pain but also inspires such intense fear from its appearance that the torment alone could drive people to want to die.

SIXTH TRUMPET (SECOND WOE)

> *Then the sixth angel sounded: And I heard a voice from the four horns of the golden altar which is before God,* 14 *saying to the sixth angel who had the trumpet, "Release the four angels who are bound at the great river Euphrates."* 15 *So the four angels, who had been prepared for the hour and day and month and year, were released to kill a third of mankind.* 16 *Now the number of the army of the horsemen was two hundred million; I heard the number of them.* 17 *And thus I saw the horses in the vision: those who sat on them had breastplates of fiery red, hyacinth blue, and sulfur yellow; and the heads of the horses were like the heads of lions; and out of their mouths came fire, smoke, and brimstone.* 18 *By these three plagues a third of mankind was killed—by the fire and the smoke and the brimstone which came out of their mouths.* 19 *For their power is in their mouth and in their tails; for their tails are like serpents, having heads; and with them they do harm.* 20 *But the rest of mankind, who were not killed by these plagues, did not repent of the works of their hands, that they should not worship demons, and idols of gold, silver,*

> *brass, stone, and wood, which can neither see nor hear nor walk.* [21] *And they did not repent of their murders or their sorceries or their sexual immorality or their thefts.*
>
> —Revelation 9:13-21

When the Sixth Trumpet is sounded, the Second Woe begins. Four angels are released from the river Euphrates, and an army of 200 million demons is unleashed. They go out and kill one-third of humanity by breathing fire, smoke, and sulfur. During this Second Woe, billions will die. Even so, survivors refuse to repent. Instead, they continue in their vile and evil ways.

SEVENTH TRUMPET (THIRD WOE)

> *Then the seventh angel sounded: And there were loud voices in heaven, saying, "The kingdoms of this world have become the kingdoms of our Lord and of His Christ, and He shall reign forever and ever!"* [16] *And the twenty-four elders who sat before God on their thrones fell on their faces and worshiped God,* [17] *saying: "We give You thanks, O Lord God Almighty, the One who is and who was and who is to come, because You have taken Your great power and reigned.* [18] *The nations were angry, and Your wrath has come, and the time of the dead, that they should be judged, and that You should reward Your servants the prophets and the saints, and those who fear Your name, small and great, and should destroy those who destroy the earth."* [19] *Then the temple of God was opened in heaven, and the ark of His covenant was seen in His temple. And there were lightnings, noises, thunderings, an earthquake, and great hail.*
>
> —Revelation 11:15-19

With the blast of the Final Trumpet, the Third Woe takes place. Unlike the previous six trumpets, which bring catastrophic judgments on the earth, this one shifts dramatically to celebration and proclamation in heaven. We are shown loud, powerful voices declaring that the kingdom of the world has become the kingdom of the Lord and the Messiah. This marks the end of human rebellion and Satan's dominion over the world. Verses 16-18 describe the worship of the 24 elders, who prostrate themselves before God and praise Him for taking His "great power" and beginning His final reign. Verse 19 continues with the opening of the temple, revealing the ark of the covenant. This opening is accompanied by cosmic signs: lightning, thunder, earthquake, and hail. The Seventh Trumpet is the climax of the Trumpet series, shifting from judgment to triumph. However, what follows is the final series of God's judgments during the Tribulation period, known as the "seven last plagues" or the Seven Bowls of God's wrath.

THREE WOES COULD BE PART OF ONE MASSIVE EVENT—AN ASTEROID STRIKING EARTH

Before examining the Seven Bowls, I note that the Three Woes accompanying Trumpets Five through Seven are unique in that some believe they may all be part of a single, giant event. It is believed that what we are observing is the impact of one or two asteroids or meteors striking earth. So devastating is this event that it leads to several related global crises. Like dominoes in motion, once this burning mountain hits the earth, accompanied by another star hitting the sea, what could be a picture of global fallout is what we are being shown.

If anyone were to consider the question, are we living in the Tribulation, or is this the end-times Tribulation narrative right now? We can confidently answer no, based on what we see in the Seven Seals, the Seven Trumpets, and the Three Woes. Each of these earth-shaking judgments is globally impactful. It is a wonder that anyone would survive the Tribulation at all! The world as we know it will be completely gone, leaving the earth itself in utter ruin.

THE SEVEN BOWLS
REVELATION 15–16

The Seven Bowls represent the final judgment on those who have hardened their hearts, blasphemed God, and refused to repent. These Bowls echo the plagues on Egypt in the book of Exodus, symbolizing God's sovereign judgment against evil. Unlike the earlier Seven Seals and Seven Trumpets, which were partial judgments, the Bowl judgments are swift, total, and complete. This will culminate in the declaration, "It is done!"

> *Then one of the four living creatures gave to the seven angels seven golden bowls full of the wrath of God who lives forever and ever.* 8 *The temple was filled with smoke from the glory of God and from His power, and no one was able to enter the temple till the seven plagues of the seven angels were completed.*
>
> —Revelation 15:7-8

In Revelation 15:7, seven angels emerge from the heavenly temple, each receiving a golden Bowl filled with God's wrath. Verse 8 says the temple will be filled with smoke from God's glory, and no one can enter until the seven plagues are completed. This shows that God's judgments are irrevocable once begun.

FIRST BOWL

> *So the first went and poured out his bowl upon the earth, and a foul and loathsome sore came upon the men who had the mark of the beast and those who worshiped his image.*
>
> —Revelation 16:2

With the pouring of the First Bowl over the earth, ugly, painful, festering, and malignant sores break out on the people who bear the mark of the Beast and worship his image. This judgment specifically targets the followers of the Antichrist. It also reveals that believers will be protected because they won't bear the mark of the Beast or worship the Antichrist.

SECOND BOWL

Then the second angel poured out his bowl on the sea, and it became blood as of a dead man; and every living creature in the sea died.

—Revelation 16:3

The Second Bowl is poured out over the sea. Immediately, the sea turns into blood like that of a dead person. As a result, every living creature in the sea dies. This Bowl of judgment affects all ocean life globally.

THIRD BOWL

Then the third angel poured out his bowl on the rivers and springs of water, and they became blood. [5] And I heard the angel of the waters saying: "You are righteous, O Lord, the One who is and who was and who is to be, because You have judged these things. [6] For they have shed the blood of saints and prophets, and You have given them blood to drink. For it is their just due." [7] And I heard another from the altar saying, "Even so, Lord God Almighty, true and righteous are Your judgments."

—Revelation 16:4-7

The third angel pours out his Bowl onto the rivers and springs of water, and they turn to blood. The angel of the waters declares God's justice by punishing those who shed the blood of the saints and prophets. This act embodies divine justice, as the wicked are made to drink blood instead of water. All water, both fresh and salt, will become undrinkable, symbolizing total corruption and divine retribution.

FOURTH BOWL

Then the fourth angel poured out his bowl on the sun, and power was given to him to scorch men with fire. [9] And men were scorched with great heat, and they blasphemed the name of God who has power over these plagues; and they did not repent and give Him glory.

—Revelation 16:8-9

With the pouring of the Fourth Bowl, the sun is given power to scorch men with fire and intense heat. Even under this severe judgment, people will continue to curse God and refuse to repent or give God glory. This reveals that no matter what people go through, if their hearts are hardened, they won't repent and turn to God. It's surprising to think that this would be the case. It would seem that, in the face of all the terrible things taking place, people would humble themselves and turn to God, who would then protect them. However, this is not the case. Instead, they curse God and refuse Him.

FIFTH BOWL

> *Then the fifth angel poured out his bowl on the throne of the beast, and his kingdom became full of darkness; and they gnawed their tongues because of the pain.* 11 *They blasphemed the God of heaven because of their pains and their sores, and did not repent of their deeds.*
>
> —Revelation 16:10-11

The fifth angel poured out his Bowl on the Beast's throne. Consequently, its kingdom was plunged into darkness. Their previous sores, combined with the extreme darkness, caused such fear and pain that they began to gnaw their tongues. Again, instead of turning to the Lord and repenting, they blasphemed God. They allowed the pain of their sores to dictate their response.

SIXTH BOWL

> *Then the sixth angel poured out his bowl on the great river Euphrates, and its water was dried up, so that the way of the kings from the east might be prepared.* 13 *And I saw three unclean spirits like frogs coming out of the mouth of the dragon, out of the mouth of the beast, and out of the mouth of the false prophet.* 14 *For they are spirits of demons, performing signs, which go out to the kings of the earth and of the whole world, to gather them to the battle of that great day of God Almighty.* 15 *"Behold, I am coming as a thief. Blessed is he who watches, and keeps his garments, lest he walk naked*

> *and they see his shame."* [16] *And they gathered them together to the place called in Hebrew, Armageddon.*
>
> —Revelation 16:12-16

The Sixth Bowl is poured out on the great river Euphrates, drying up its waters. This prepares the way for the kings from the east. Demonic spirits like frogs emerge from the mouths of the dragon (Satan), the Beast, and the false prophet. They perform miraculous signs to gather the world's kings for battle at Armageddon. Jesus offers a parenthetical warning and tells those who stay awake that they are blessed.

SEVENTH BOWL

> *Then the seventh angel poured out his bowl into the air, and a loud voice came out of the temple of heaven, from the throne, saying, "It is done!"* [18] *And there were noises and thunderings and lightnings; and there was a great earthquake, such a mighty and great earthquake as had not occurred since men were on the earth.* [19] *Now the great city was divided into three parts, and the cities of the nations fell. And great Babylon was remembered before God, to give her the cup of the wine of the fierceness of His wrath.* [20] *Then every island fled away, and the mountains were not found.* [21] *And great hail from heaven fell upon men, each hailstone about the weight of a talent. Men blasphemed God because of the plague of the hail, since that plague was exceedingly great.*
>
> —Revelation 16:17-21

For the Final Bowl, the angel pours it into the air. A voice from the throne says, "It is done!" Flashes of lightning, thunder, and the greatest earthquake occur. This earthquake is so massive that every island and city will be destroyed, hailstones weighing about a hundred pounds will smash through nearly every standing structure, and plagues of unspeakable proportions will invade the planet.

Consider the implications of this—an earthquake so massive that, by its sheer magnitude, all islands in the sea, along with the mountains, will be rendered nonexistent! One could only surmise from this picture that no standing structure will remain on earth. Nothing has ever compared to this type of event in all of written history. There is no equivalent to this in terms of devastation.

In verse 21, the Final Bowl continues, sending huge hailstones, each about 100 pounds, to the earth, crushing everything in their path and leaving no survivors. These hailstones carry severity to a level that surpasses the hail in Exodus 9:24, "So there was hail, and fire mingled with the hail, so very heavy that there was none like it in all the land of Egypt since it became a nation." This level of weather, which has never occurred in history and will never happen again, is what the world will experience with this catastrophic hail.

In the end, the ultimate travesty is not the wrath and judgment being poured out, but humanity's refusal to repent, even amid destruction that is extreme or devastating. This indicates that people remain unrepentant throughout, underscoring that they deserved the judgment to begin with. Then it all comes to an end at the mother of all battles—Armageddon.

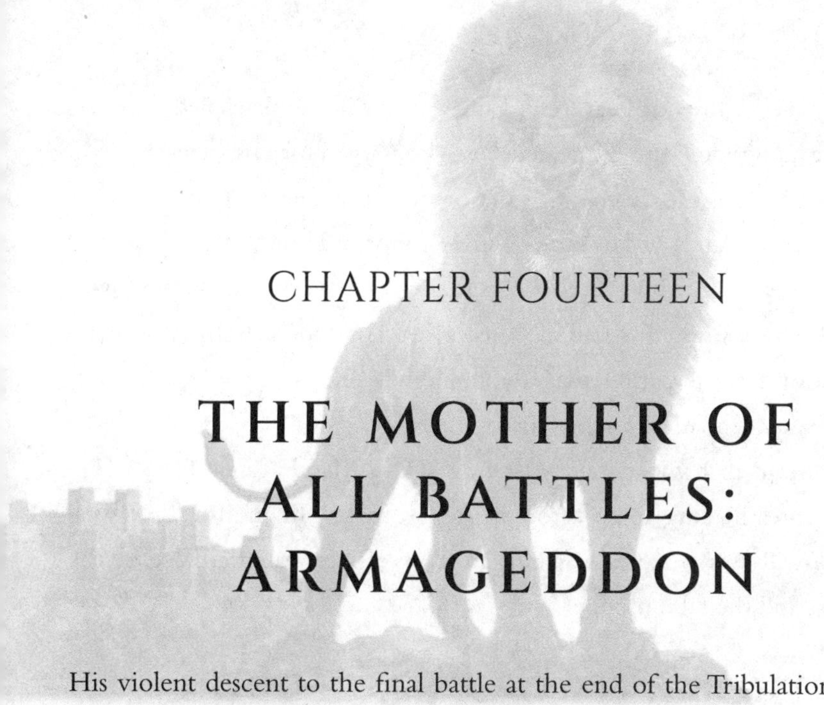

CHAPTER FOURTEEN

THE MOTHER OF ALL BATTLES: ARMAGEDDON

His violent descent to the final battle at the end of the Tribulation will be a far cry from the first time Jesus came to earth. King Jesus will not arrive as a baby or as the kind shepherd figure so many are familiar with. Not on this day; it will be the greatest display of horrific militarized might the universe has ever witnessed. His arrival marks the end of all celestial war crimes against God Almighty and the judgment of all unrepentant malevolent intentions by all humanity in cooperation with the Antichrist—He is coming to finish the judgment that original sin started. Even after thousands of years, God went to great lengths to offer humanity repentance so that they might avoid the wrath that would inevitably follow. Here we see the Lion of the Tribe of Judah, coming in power to execute expedient judgment against all gathered at the Battle of Armageddon.

> *Now Enoch, the seventh from Adam, prophesied about these men also, saying, "Behold, the Lord comes with ten thousands of His saints,* 15 *to execute judgment on all, to convict all who are ungodly among them of all their ungodly deeds which they have committed in an ungodly way, and of all the harsh things which ungodly sinners have spoken against Him."*
>
> —Jude 1:14-15

The angelic hosts of heaven and the saints will be marshaled together and arrive alongside Him. Every believer who longed for His appearing will come with Him as He descends to the battlefield at Megiddo. Jude tells us that tens of thousands of His saints will accompany Him. What a profound thought: we will be with the Lord as He arrives. We will exit heaven with Him and have a front-row seat as Jesus makes His approach. In a moment, when Jesus intersects with Armageddon, He will unleash a pulverizing, battlefield-wide decimation against His enemies.

No one in that wicked army will be able to stand against Him as He unleashes breathtaking force through the sword of His mouth. The *Word made flesh* will now be turned against an army of reprobate flesh, led by the Antichrist and the false prophet.

THE BATTLE OF ARMAGEDDON

> *Then the sixth angel poured out his bowl on the great river Euphrates, and its water was dried up, so that the way of the kings from the east might be prepared.*
>
> —Revelation 16:12

Notably, the powers of darkness will always seek annihilation whenever they have the opportunity. We observe this in the deceptive operation that follows the drying of the River Euphrates. Kings of the east will be able to come across.

UNCLEAN SPIRITS RESEMBLING FROGS

> *And I saw three unclean spirits like frogs coming out of the mouth of the dragon, out of the mouth of the beast, and out of the mouth of the false prophet.* [14] *For they are spirits of demons, performing signs, which go out to the kings of the earth and of the whole world, to gather them to the battle of that great day of God Almighty.* [15] *"Behold, I am coming as a thief.*

> *Blessed is he who watches, and keeps his garments, lest he walk naked and they see his shame."* [16] *And they gathered them together to the place called in Hebrew, Armageddon.*
>
> —Revelation 16:13-16

These unclean spirits may be what they are listed as, or they may be manifestations of demonic entities in the natural world. Some have suggested they might even be a form of fake aliens, which will go out and lie to the world, deceiving many nations into gathering for battle against God's people and God Himself. They will all be assembled in the fateful valley of Megiddo for the Last Battle, *the mother of all battles* that will bring an end to the Great Tribulation—the Battle of Armageddon.

THE MOTHER OF ALL BATTLES

A mighty force will gather to wage war against God and His righteous ones. What happens on that day will be the greatest battle the world has ever seen, and it will end with relative ease. King Jesus will arrive in full glory and splendor to defeat these hordes of evil.

> *Now I saw heaven opened, and behold, a white horse. And He who sat on him was called Faithful and True, and in righteousness He judges and makes war.* [12] *His eyes were like a flame of fire, and on His head were many crowns. He had a name written that no one knew except Himself.* [13] *He was clothed with a robe dipped in blood, and His name is called The Word of God.* [14] *And the armies in heaven, clothed in fine linen, white and clean, followed Him on white horses.* [15] *Now out of His mouth goes a sharp sword, that with it He should strike the nations. And He Himself will rule them with a rod of iron. He Himself treads the winepress of the fierceness and wrath of Almighty God.* [16] *And He has on His robe and on His thigh a name written: KING OF KINGS AND LORD OF LORDS.* [17] *Then I saw an angel standing in the sun; and he cried with a loud voice, saying to all the birds that fly in the midst of heaven, "Come*

and gather together for the supper of the great God, [18] that you may eat the flesh of kings, the flesh of captains, the flesh of mighty men, the flesh of horses and of those who sit on them, and the flesh of all people, free and slave, both small and great."

—Revelation 19:11-18

IMAGINE THE SHOCK THESE ENEMIES WILL FEEL AS THEY REALIZE JESUS IS ABOUT TO ANNIHILATE THEM

Picture Jesus landing amid the apocalyptic scene of Armageddon in the valley of Megiddo; He will deliver immediate judgment. His appearance will be shocking as He lands with garments dipped in blood; again, this will not be His own blood, but rather the blood of His enemies! Can you imagine what will go through the minds and hearts of His opponents? Sneering and arrogance might be their initial reaction when confronted with the Son of the Living God returning for judgment against His enemies. Still, in short order, their arrogant faces will turn from confidence to terror as they realize they are about to be consumed by the wrath of the Lamb.

At this moment, Jesus will be overwhelmingly victorious and, in the same instance, capture the Beast and the false prophet. They may be on display for some time before being cast alive into the lake of fire. Could this be a form of wartime tribunal where all the nations and all the people will hear of their heinous crimes against God and humanity? It very well could be.

WHAT JESUS STARTED IN THE REALM OF THE SPIRIT HE WILL FINISH AT ARMAGEDDON

Having wiped out the handwriting of requirements that was against us, which was contrary to us. And He has taken it out of the way, having

> *nailed it to the cross.* [15] *Having disarmed principalities and powers, He made a* ***public spectacle*** *of them, triumphing over them in it.*
>
> —Colossians 2:14-15

What Jesus initiated in the spiritual realm will be completed in the natural realm at Armageddon. Following the cross, Jesus descended and proclaimed the gospel to those in prison, or, as we might say, to those in Abraham's bosom, or Paradise. He also confronted dark powers during this time.

The term "public spectacle" in Colossians 2:14-15 was used in early history to describe the defeat of one kingdom by another. It was a Roman practice to display their captives and the spoils of conquered enemies in public during their triumphal processions.

It was common to parade defeated kings and dignitaries through the streets. This practice alluded to the Roman emperors' victories, spoils, and triumphs. When they had obtained a victory, the senate decreed a triumph for them. The emperor was drawn in an open chariot, and the captives, stripped of their armor, had their hands tied behind them and were led before him, exposed to public view and disgrace. At the same time, the people shouted and cheered as he passed through the city of Rome, receiving all the marks of honor and respect.

Even more extreme, some believe the captives were stripped naked, their eyes gouged out, and their thumbs and big toes cut off. Regardless, these malevolent powers that had ruled humanity without reprieve were now at a humiliating end. This practice made quite a statement, and that is exactly what Jesus was doing—making a permanent and breathtaking statement. If the more brutal aspect of parading enemies through the streets has any validity, it would imply that these enemies were completely exposed.

Additionally, they would never see again, walk right again, or properly hold a weapon. It was in this state that these defeated foes would be put on display, paraded through the streets of the victorious city. In the realm of the spirit, this played out with equal severity to the kings and opponents put on display by the Romans' cruelty.

JESUS HUMILIATED HIS ENEMIES IN THE SPIRIT REALM—AT ARMAGEDDON, HE WILL PHYSICALLY DESTROY THEM

A moment of pure humiliation and degradation is what these enemies of Jesus were subjected to. This represents the highest order of humiliation, and it is exactly what Jesus did to His adversaries in the realm of the unseen. He defeated them at the crucifixion, then descended to make an open display of these spiritual forces, and on the third day He was resurrected! Armageddon will be the final confrontation with His enemies—what He accomplished in the realm of the Spirit will be completed in the natural for every eye to see. Now at Armageddon, Jesus returns to finish the job.

CAST ALIVE INTO THE LAKE OF FIRE

> *And I saw the beast, the kings of the earth, and their armies, gathered together to make war against Him who sat on the horse and against His army.* [20] ***Then the beast was captured****, and with him the false prophet who worked signs in his presence, by which he deceived those who received the mark of the beast and those who worshiped his image.* ***These two were cast alive into the lake of fire burning with brimstone****.* [21] *And the rest were killed with the sword which proceeded from the mouth of Him who sat on the horse. And all the birds were filled with their flesh.*
>
> —Revelation 19:19-21

After the Beast and the false prophet are captured, we know for certain that they will be thrown alive into the lake of fire! Their judgment and punishment will be carried out publicly before the entire human race.

The lake of fire is known as the second death because it occurs after physical death. Hell is an immediate place of containment and punishment, and it is temporary because it will eventually be cast into the lake of fire. However, the lake of fire represents a whole new level of eternal punishment. Understanding what the lake of fire is or where it is located yields few answers, as the Bible offers only brief descriptions of it.

WHAT IS THE LAKE OF FIRE?

It might be a place that can be understood only when the veil of this natural reality is lifted by death, revealing spiritual understanding. Some have suggested it might be a star or the highest level of punishment, a special dimension beyond death and beyond hell, a place reserved for eternity. Once hell is cast into it, it will remain there for all eternity. Only then will we likely grasp what the lake of fire truly is and where it is. What we do know is that the lake of fire will last forever. There is no escape for those within it after the judgment of the second death.

The lake of fire will receive the Antichrist and the false prophet after Armageddon, but will await the arrival of Satan and those condemned to hell.

Across all eschatological perspectives, what we know is this: *Jesus wins.* He always has and always will. Our role is to stay with Him now and in the future.

JUDGMENT OF THE SHEEP AND GOATS

> *When the Son of Man comes in His glory, and all the holy angels with Him, then He will sit on the throne of His glory.* 32 ***All the nations will be gathered before Him****, and* ***He will separate them one from another, as a shepherd divides his sheep from the goats****.* 33 *And He will set the sheep on His right hand, but the goats on the left.* 34 *Then the King will say to those on His right hand, "Come, you blessed of My*

> *Father, inherit the kingdom prepared for you from the foundation of the world:* 35 *for I was hungry and you gave Me food; I was thirsty and you gave Me drink; I was a stranger and you took Me in;* 36 *I was naked and you clothed Me; I was sick and you visited Me; I was in prison and you came to Me."* 37 *Then the righteous will answer Him, saying, "Lord, when did we see You hungry and feed You, or thirsty and give You drink?* 38 *When did we see You a stranger and take You in, or naked and clothe You?* 39 *Or when did we see You sick, or in prison, and come to You?"* 40 *And the King will answer and say to them, "Assuredly, I say to you, inasmuch as you did it to one of the least of these My brethren, you did it to Me."* 41 *Then He will also say to those on the left hand, "Depart from Me, you cursed, into the everlasting fire prepared for the devil and his angels:* 42 *for I was hungry and you gave Me no food; I was thirsty and you gave Me no drink;* 43 *I was a stranger and you did not take Me in, naked and you did not clothe Me, sick and in prison and you did not visit Me."* 44 *Then they also will answer Him, saying, "Lord, when did we see You hungry or thirsty or a stranger or naked or sick or in prison, and did not minister to You?"* 45 *Then He will answer them, saying, "Assuredly, I say to you, inasmuch as you did not do it to one of the least of these, you did not do it to Me."* 46 *And these will go away into everlasting punishment, but the righteous into eternal life.*
>
> —Matthew 25:31-46

At this time, the Sheep and Goats Judgment will also occur. Jesus addresses this in the Olivet Discourse. This judgment occurs at the beginning of the Millennial Kingdom, following the catastrophic events of Armageddon. All those on the earth at this time, after Armageddon, will be gathered before the Lord. Our Lord will begin to separate them, as a shepherd separates sheep from goats. The sheep will be on His right and the goats on His left. Those saved during the Tribulation are part of the sheep; those who survived the Tribulation without receiving Jesus as their Lord are the goats.

THE SHEEP

On His right hand are those blessed by God the Father and given an inheritance from Him. When this takes place, the reason is stated in verses 35-36 NIV, which say, "for I was hungry and you gave me something to eat, I was thirsty and you gave me something to drink, I was a stranger and you invited me in, I needed clothes and you clothed me, I was sick and you looked after me, I was in prison and you came to visit me." Jesus describes the righteous as not understanding, as shown by their asking, "When did we see You hungry or thirsty or a stranger or needing clothes, or sick or in prison, and did not help You?" It was a natural response, since they had never seen Him in any of these conditions. In verse 40, Jesus explains it to them clearly, "I tell you the truth, whatever you did for one of the least of these brothers of mine, you did for Me."

THE GOATS

Now the attention turns to those on Jesus' left hand. The goats, cursed with eternal hellfire, are told in verse 41 to "Prepare for the devil and his angels." These goats were given the opportunity to minister to the Lord, but refused; they did nothing. In verse 44 NIV, the goats make the same case, "Lord, when did we see you hungry or thirsty or a stranger or needing clothes or sick or in prison, and did not help you?" Jesus gives the same answer, "I tell you the truth, whatever you did not do for one of the least of these, you did not do for Me."

In verse 46, Jesus brings the discourse to a close by drawing a contrast: "these (goats) will go away to eternal punishment, but the righteous (sheep) to eternal life."

By comparison, we see the difference between those who are redeemed and saved and those who are completely lost. At face value, salvation appears to be determined by good works. However, when compared with the rest of Scripture, it is clear that we are saved by grace through faith, not by good works. That said, a true believer, a sheep, will, by nature, act on what Jesus laid out for each class of people. Good works are not the cause of one's salvation, but they are the effect of it!

At the heart of the issue of sheep and goats is the idea that if you are God's, you will love others. Good deeds are a direct result of our relationship with Jesus Christ, the Good Shepherd. If you are in Christ, you want to treat others with kindness, serving and caring for them, and displaying the God-kind of love toward them. The goats, those who are unregenerate, live lives in direct opposition to this behavior. Although "goats" can perform kind actions and be charitable, if they do not have hearts connected with God Almighty through Christ Jesus, His One and only Son, even their most charitable actions are not for the right purpose, which is to honor God.

There are also considerations about this passage as it relates to the nations and how they deal with the weak and their actions toward the nation of Israel. God judges individuals and nations for their actions regarding His ways.

GOATS ARE A PART OF THE ANTICHRIST SYSTEM

The system of the Antichrist and his false prophet, along with all their followers, will rule for a time on the earth; those who serve it will be counted as goats. Even today, we see the spirit of Antichrist at work in so many in positions of authority. It will all come to a sudden and terrifying end for them all, those who oppose the Lamb of God. Even so, Armageddon will be unlike anything the world has ever seen and will mark the turning point toward one of the most fascinating times the Bible speaks of—the Millennial Reign of Jesus Christ.

Dear Reader, your life makes a difference in this world. The impact of your presence as you follow Jesus brings light into darkness, even when Jesus tarries or doesn't appear when many believe He will. Take heart! You are on the winning side of this cosmic war, which began before recorded time. Your future is so bright you will have to put on sunglasses to see it clearly!

Jesus is Lord!

CHAPTER FIFTEEN

MILLENNIAL REIGN: THE KINGDOM ON EARTH AS IT IS IN HEAVEN

When everything culminates in a grand finale after the Battle of Armageddon, Jesus will take His rightful place as King, reigning from Jerusalem. For believers, looking ahead to this future should be a source of great hope, as it anticipates what lies ahead. King Jesus' physical reign on planet Earth will last 1,000 years. Unlike elections, where we have a president or leader in office for a few years, only to be replaced by a new one, this is the beginning of Jesus' eternal reign.

A glimpse into the Millennial Reign of Jesus brings about the culmination of life on earth and offers the closest thing we have to understanding how God intended to live with us on this planet. The Millennial Kingdom of Christ represents a high purpose, both as a fulfillment of what Adam was likely designed to accomplish and as the restoration of the earth following the Great Tribulation.

The Millennial Kingdom is measurable, follows the Kingdom of God, and is embodied in Jesus Christ. On His first visit to the earth, He brought grace; at His Second Coming, He will execute breathtaking justice in wrath and usher in the Millennium. Jesus mentioned His glorious return during His trial before the Sanhedrin in Mark 14:62: "*Jesus said, 'I am. And you will see the Son of Man sitting at the right hand of the Power, and coming with the clouds of heaven.'*" He also referred to the Millennial Kingdom when He taught His disciples to pray, "Your kingdom come" (*see* Luke 11:2-4 and Matthew 6:9-15).

ON EARTH AS IT IS IN HEAVEN

Your kingdom come. Your will be done on earth as it is in heaven.

—Matthew 6:10

Matthew 6:10 describes the Kingdom coming to earth as it is in heaven. The ultimate fulfillment of this reality will occur during the Millennial Reign of King Jesus, also called the Millennium.

THE MILLENNIAL KINGDOM

Tragically, there is considerable controversy surrounding this time. There are many views, some defensible, on various aspects of end-time prophecies. Still, this common divergence—*denying a literal Millennium*—is particularly dangerous because it appears to be an attack on the very character of God!

It does violence to His many explicit promises and commitments that pervade both the Old and New Testaments. The Old Testament is replete with commitments to a literal Messiah who ultimately rules the world through Israel from His throne in Jerusalem.

PROPHECIES ABOUT THE MESSIAH AND THE SECOND COMING

There are at least 1,845 references to the Second Coming in the Old Testament, and 17 books give it prominence. The ancient rabbinical aspirations were dominated by it. In fact, this obsession obscured their recognition of the Messiah when He made His initial appearance. The ancient rabbis firmly believed that the Messiah would come militarily, take over, and establish His earthly kingdom. The expectation was that the Messiah would overthrow Rome and give Israel authority over the world. In this picture, they were correct; they were just incomplete, as they did not discern that Jesus would first come as a Lamb, then as the Lion to rule the nations.

There are at least 318 references in 216 chapters of the New Testament, and 23 of its 27 books give prominence to Christ's Second Coming.

BINDING OF SATAN

> *Then I saw an angel coming down from heaven, having the key to the bottomless pit and a great chain in his hand.* [2] *He laid hold of the dragon, that serpent of old, who is the Devil and Satan, and bound him* ***for a thousand years;*** [3] *and he cast him into the bottomless pit, and shut him up, and set a seal on him, so that he should deceive the nations no more till the thousand years were finished. But after these things he must be released for a little while.*
>
> —Revelation 20:1-3

At the moment Jesus finishes the Battle of Armageddon, an angel from heaven takes Satan and casts him into the bottomless pit, where he will be chained for a thousand years. During this time, he cannot commit his nefarious deeds against the living. The bottomless pit, or the abyss, is a holding place or prison for the devil and his demonic cronies. This location will remain sealed until the end of the 1,000-year reign.

EZEKIEL'S TEMPLE

> *And the man said to me, "Son of man, look with your eyes and hear with your ears, and fix your mind on everything I show you; for you were brought here so that I might show them to you. Declare to the house of Israel everything you see."*
>
> —Ezekiel 40:4

At the beginning of the Millennial Reign, right after Satan is bound and thrown into the bottomless pit, a temple will be built. Ezekiel 40:4 sets the stage for the vision he was to receive concerning this temple. He was told to pay attention and declare everything he saw to the house of Israel. Ezekiel 40–48 presents an extremely detailed vision of the Millennial Temple, often called Ezekiel's Temple. This temple will be built in Jerusalem, near the site of previous temples. Ezekiel was given the measurements of gates, courts, chambers, altars, and much more.

> *Afterward he brought me to the gate, the gate that faces toward the east. [2] And behold, the glory of the God of Israel came from the way of the east. His voice was like the sound of many waters; and the earth shone with His glory. [3] It was like the appearance of the vision which I saw—like the vision which I saw when I came to destroy the city. The visions were like the vision which I saw by the River Chebar; and I fell on my face. [4] And the glory of the LORD came into the temple by way of the gate which faces toward the east. [5] The Spirit lifted me up and brought me into the inner court; and behold, the glory of the LORD filled the temple.*
>
> —Ezekiel 43:1-5

The temple will be constructed and ready for use immediately at the start of the Millennium. Ezekiel 43:1-5 reveals that the glory of God will come from the east. God's Voice will be like the sound of many waters. The earth will be full of His glory. Verse 5 continues by saying that *the glory of the Lord filled the temple*. Not only will Jesus be physically present, but the manifest glory of God will be ever tangible. The glory of God is the visible manifestation of His infinite worth, attributes such as beauty and perfection, and His character. The glory can be described as the radiance of God's holiness and greatness. All of these are revealed through creation, actions, and Jesus Christ.

THE ROLE OF THE LEVITICAL PRIESTS FROM THE LINE OF ZADOK

> *"But the priests, the Levites, the sons of Zadok, who kept charge of My sanctuary when the children of Israel went astray from Me, they shall come near Me to minister to Me; and they shall stand before Me to offer to Me the fat and the blood," says the Lord* God. *16 "They shall enter My sanctuary, and they shall come near My table to minister to Me, and they shall keep My charge. 23 ...And they shall teach My people the difference between the holy and the unholy, and cause them to discern between the unclean and the clean. 24 In controversy they shall stand as judges, and judge it according to My judgments. They shall keep My laws and My statutes in all My appointed meetings, and they shall hallow My Sabbaths."*
>
> —Ezekiel 44:15-16, 23-24

The sons of Zadok are a priestly lineage. They remained faithful to God when others strayed. As a result, they will be rewarded with service as priests in the holy temple in Jerusalem. Ezekiel 44:23 says they will be teachers. They will show people what is holy and what isn't, and what is unclean and what is clean. Those who survive the Tribulation and those born during the Millennium will still need to be taught the things of the Lord. These priests will also bring offerings, judge disputes according to God's laws, and guard the entrance to the temple and the holy place.

ANIMAL SACRIFICES REINSTATED AS A REMINDER OF WHAT JESUS DID

In Ezekiel 43:18-27, the Lord instructs the Zadok priests to offer sacrifices to Him. These sacrifices are not intended to forgive people's sins. Many view them as memorials rather than acts of atonement, or as commemorations of Christ's sacrifice. This memorial is similar to the Lord's Supper and Communion. We take Communion now to remember what Jesus did on the cross for our sins and how He made a way to eternal life with Him. The sacrifices during the Millennium will serve as a continual reminder of the most selfless act in history. Animal sacrifices will teach those in earthly bodies that sin is offensive to a righteous and holy God.

1,000 YEARS RULING AND REIGNING FROM JERUSALEM

> *And in that day it shall be that living waters shall flow from Jerusalem, half of them toward the eastern sea and half of them toward the western sea; in both summer and winter it shall occur.* [9] *And the* LORD *shall be King over all the earth. In that day it shall be—"The* LORD *is one," and His name one.*
>
> —Zechariah 14:8-9

> *He will be great, and will be called the Son of the Highest; and the Lord God will give Him the throne of His father David.* [33] *And He will reign over the house of Jacob forever, and of His kingdom there will be no end.*
>
> —Luke 1:32-33

> *For He must reign till He has put all enemies under His feet.* [26] *The last enemy that will be destroyed is death.* [27] *For "He has put all things under His feet." But when He says "all things are put under Him," it is evident that He who put all things under Him is excepted.*
>
> —1 Corinthians 15:25-27

After Jesus defeats the evil forces, He will begin His 1,000-year reign from Jerusalem. He will rule with righteousness and justice, bringing peace to earth. Jerusalem will be both a political and spiritual center. Luke 1:32 reveals that Jesus will sit on David's throne and rule with the saints. First Corinthians 15:25 speaks of this time, stating that Jesus *must reign* until He puts all enemies under His feet. This includes the enemy of "death."

And He has on His robe and on His thigh a name written: KING OF KINGS AND LORD OF LORDS.

—Revelation 19:16

Kings and lords both do something—they rule over territory. Notice that it says Jesus is the King of kings and the Lord of lords. Jesus has the name above all names, and everything and everyone will be under His complete reign and authority.

WILL KING DAVID RULE WITH JESUS?

Instead, they will serve the LORD their God and David their king, whom I will raise up for them.

—Jeremiah 30:9 NIV

I will place over them one shepherd, my servant David, and he will tend them; he will tend them and be their shepherd. [24] *I the LORD will be their God, and my servant David will be prince among them. I the LORD have spoken.*

—Ezekiel 34:23-24 NIV

David My servant shall be king over them, and they shall all have one shepherd; they shall also walk in My judgments and observe My statutes, and do them. [25] *Then they shall dwell in the land that I have given to Jacob My servant, where your fathers dwelt; and they shall dwell there, they, their children, and their children's children, forever; and My servant David shall be their prince forever.*

—Ezekiel 37:24-25

Afterward the children of Israel shall return and seek the LORD their God and David their king. They shall fear the LORD and His goodness in the latter days.

—Hosea 3:5

Many scholars believe that King David will be resurrected and will rule under Jesus during the Millennial Reign. This view is based on several Old Testament prophecies. These passages describe a future time when "David" will reign alongside the Lord. They use the name "David" directly rather than "son of David" or "branch of David." According to the listed scriptures, David is called a shepherd, a king, God's servant, and a prince. Second Samuel 7:16 says, "And your house and your kingdom shall be established forever before you. Your throne shall be established forever," suggesting that a literal resurrected David will fulfill God's unbreakable covenant promises.

GLORIFIED SAINTS WILL RULE WITH JESUS

Until the Ancient of Days came, and a judgment was made in favor of the saints of the Most High, and the time came for the saints to possess the kingdom. [27] *...Then the kingdom and dominion, and the greatness of the kingdoms under the whole heaven, shall be given to the people, the saints of the Most High. His kingdom is an everlasting kingdom, and all dominions shall serve and obey Him.*

—Daniel 7:22, 27

*Do you not know that the **saints will judge the world**? And if the world will be judged by you, are you unworthy to judge the smallest matters?*

—1 Corinthians 6:2

*And I saw thrones, and they sat on them, and judgment was committed to them. Then I saw the souls of those who had been beheaded for their witness to Jesus and for the word of God, who had not worshiped the beast or his image, and had not received his mark on their foreheads or on their hands. **And they lived and reigned with Christ for a thousand years**.*
[5] *But the rest of the dead did not live again until the thousand years were finished. This is the first resurrection.* [6] *Blessed and holy is he who has*

> *part in the first resurrection. Over such the second death has no power, but they shall be priests of God and of Christ, and* ***shall reign with Him a thousand years****.*
>
> —Revelation 20:4-6

The saints of old, the raptured believers, and those who were martyred will rule and reign with Jesus in Jerusalem. Daniel 7:22 says this will be the time *for the saints to possess the kingdom.* The new kingdom will be their inheritance. These believers will reap what they sowed while alive. According to 1 Corinthians 15:36, "what you sow is not made alive unless it dies." This means that while alive on earth, believers had a choice to crucify and die to the flesh, pick up their cross, and follow Jesus. This was a form of sowing into their future, or their eternal life. The reward will be a glorified body and the kingdom of the Most High, an everlasting kingdom.

SOWING AND REAPING TODAY BRINGS ETERNAL REWARDS

The concept of sowing and reaping begins now and brings another form of eternal reward, namely, rule and responsibility, in the age to come. Rules and responsibilities are determined by faithfulness in this age.

> *Therefore He said: "A certain nobleman went into a far country to receive*
> *for himself a kingdom and to return.* 13 *So, he called ten of his servants,*
> *delivered to them ten minas, and said to them, 'Do business till I come.'* 14
> *But his citizens hated him, and sent a delegation after him, saying, 'We*
> *will not have this man to reign over us.'* 15 *And so it was that when he*
> *returned, having received the kingdom, he then commanded these servants,*
> *to whom he had given the money, to be called to him, that he might know*
> *how much every man had gained by trading.* 16 *Then came the first, saying,*
> *'Master, your mina has earned ten minas.'* 17 *And he said to him, 'Well*
> *done, good servant; because you were faithful in a very little, have authority*
> *over ten cities.'* 18 *And the second came, saying, 'Master, your mina has*
> *earned five minas.'* 19 *Likewise he said to him, 'You also be over five cities.'*

> 20 *Then another came, saying, 'Master, here is your mina, which I have kept put away in a handkerchief.* 21 *For I feared you, because you are an austere man. You collect what you did not deposit, and reap what you did not sow.'* 22 *And he said to him, 'Out of your own mouth I will judge you, you wicked servant. You knew that I was an austere man, collecting what I did not deposit and reaping what I did not sow.* 23 *Why then did you not put my money in the bank, that at my coming I might have collected it with interest?'* 24 *And he said to those who stood by, 'Take the mina from him, and give it to him who has ten minas.'* 25 *(But they said to him, 'Master, he has ten minas.')* 26 *'For I say to you, that to everyone who has will be given; and from him who does not have, even what he has will be taken away from him.* 27 *But bring here those enemies of mine, who did not want me to reign over them, and slay them before me.'"*
>
> —Luke 19:12-27

AUTHORITY GRANTED OVER TERRITORY

This parable compares faithfulness with minas and how it translates into cities. The stewards' use of the amount they were given was proportional to the level of authority they would have over the cities. This parable holds and may give us insight into what eternity might look like. What we do in this life with what we have been entrusted to steward is the measure by which we will be rewarded. This is a sobering truth and should not be taken lightly. Pay attention to the reward—authority over a territory. Jesus is the King of kings, ruling over territories. This is a governmental position. In eternity, our faithfulness will determine the territory over which we will rule as kings.

> *For the kingdom of heaven is like a man traveling to a far country, who called his own servants and delivered his goods to them.* 15 *And to one he gave five talents, to another two, and to another one, to each according to his own ability; and immediately he went on a journey.* 16 *Then he who had received the five talents went and traded with them, and made another five talents.* 17 *And likewise he who had received two gained two more*

also. [18] *But he who had received one went and dug in the ground, and hid*
his lord's money. [19] *After a long time the lord of those servants came and*
settled accounts with them. [20] *So he who had received five talents came and*
brought five other talents, saying, "Lord, you delivered to me five talents;
look, I have gained five more talents besides them." [21] *His lord said to him,*
"Well done, good and faithful servant; you were faithful over a few things,
I will make you ruler over many things. Enter into the joy of your lord." [22]
He also who had received two talents came and said, "Lord, you delivered
to me two talents; look, I have gained two more talents besides them." [23]
His lord said to him, "Well done, good and faithful servant; you have been
faithful over a few things, I will make you ruler over many things. Enter
into the joy of your lord." [24] *Then he who had received the one talent came*
and said, "Lord, I knew you to be a hard man, reaping where you have not
sown, and gathering where you have not scattered seed. [25] *And I was afraid,*
and went and hid your talent in the ground. Look, there you have what is
yours." [26] *But his lord answered and said to him, "You wicked and lazy*
servant, you knew that I reap where I have not sown, and gather where I
have not scattered seed. [27] *So you ought to have deposited my money with*
the bankers, and at my coming I would have received back my own with
interest. [28] *So take the talent from him, and give it to him who has ten*
talents. [29] *'For to everyone who has, more will be given, and he will have*
abundance; but from him who does not have, even what he has will be
taken away. [30] *And cast the unprofitable servant into the outer darkness.*
There will be weeping and gnashing of teeth.'"

—Matthew 25:14-30

In Matthew 25:14-30, it's a similar parable to Luke 19:12-27; Matthew talks about talents and Luke minas. The reward for those who doubled their minas or talents was to rule over cities or to receive many other benefits. The man who earned ten cities was also given the talent from the person who hid it. This symbolizes being rewarded with something many would consider unearned. However, because of his faithfulness with the five, the master recognized that and felt he was worthy of another talent. The master knew he could trust this servant with one more thing, believing he might increase its value as he did with the others.

KINGS AND PRIESTS

> *...but they shall be **priests** of God and of Christ, and shall reign with Him a thousand years.*
>
> —Revelation 20:6

> *And have made us **kings** and **priests** to our God; and we shall reign on the earth.*
>
> —Revelation 5:10

According to Revelation 20:6 and Revelation 5:10, these saints will be kings and priests of God. Revelation 1:6 supports this notion, saying, "and has made us kings and priests to His God and Father, to Him be glory and dominion forever and ever. Amen." They will be found worthy to co-rule with Jesus and to serve as a royal priesthood, helping administer God's kingdom on earth. This will be necessary because there will be those (the sheep) who didn't die during the Tribulation and who chose Christ. The kings and priests will help teach the new generations born to those with natural, physical bodies about Christ and how to function in the new world, a world without the influence of evil.

MORTALS AND IMMORTALS COEXISTING

> *No more shall an infant from there live but a few days, nor an old man who has not fulfilled his days; for the child shall die one hundred years old, but the sinner being one hundred years old shall be accursed.*
>
> —Isaiah 65:20

During the Millennial Reign, mortals and immortals, those with glorified bodies, will dwell together on earth. Mortal survivors, believers who came through the Tribulation, will have natural bodies, live long lives, reproduce, and can even die. However, people will have an increased lifespan during this time. According to Isaiah 65:20, dying at 100 is considered youthful. This could allude to sin still existing and leading to consequences, even during the blessed kingdom era. This contrasts with the current life expectancy, in which youth are under the age of 18. This might also be a subtle reference to the modern study of life extension, or de-aging sciences. Who's to say that this wouldn't play a part in living tremendously long lives?

Unfortunately, during this time, people will still have the capacity and inclination to sin. Just because the devil will be bound doesn't mean humanity will lose its free will. Those with mortal bodies will still be born with a "sin nature" or a "carnal nature." They will learn the truth from the immortal believers and then choose how to respond and live.

UNIVERSAL KNOWLEDGE OF GOD

> *They shall not hurt nor destroy in all My holy mountain, for the earth shall be full of the knowledge of the* Lord *as the waters cover the sea.*
>
> —Isaiah 11:9

> *No more shall every man teach his neighbor, and every man his brother, saying, "Know the* Lord*," for they all shall know Me, from the least of them to the greatest of them, says the* Lord*. For I will forgive their iniquity, and their sin I will remember no more.*
>
> —Jeremiah 31:34

> *For the earth will be filled with the knowledge of the glory of the* Lord*, as the waters cover the sea.*
>
> —Habakkuk 2:14

There will be a deep knowledge of God that will fill the earth. Jeremiah 31:34 states that people of all ages will know God. They will understand God directly, with righteous governance, reversed curses, and a transformed nature under Christ's rule. Those born during this time will know God, but they will still need to learn about Jesus and all He did. Once again, the priests and kings who will rule and reign with Jesus in Jerusalem will teach them this.

WORSHIP WILL BE PART OF LIFE

> *And it shall come to pass that everyone who is left of all the nations which came against Jerusalem shall go up from year to year to worship the King, the LORD of hosts, and to keep the Feast of Tabernacles.*
>
> —Zechariah 14:16

> *Now it shall come to pass in the latter days that the mountain of the LORD's house shall be established on the top of the mountains, and shall be exalted above the hills; and all nations shall flow to it. [3] Many people shall come and say, "Come, and let us go up to the mountain of the LORD, to the house of the God of Jacob; He will teach us His ways, and we shall walk in His paths." For out of Zion shall go forth the law, and the word of the LORD from Jerusalem.*
>
> —Isaiah 2:2-3

> *Thus says the LORD of hosts: "Peoples shall yet come, inhabitants of many cities; [21] the inhabitants of one city shall go to another, saying, 'Let us continue to go and pray before the LORD, and seek the LORD of hosts. I myself will go also.' [22] Yes, many peoples and strong nations shall come to seek the LORD of hosts in Jerusalem, and to pray before the LORD." [23] Thus says the LORD of hosts: "In those days ten men from every language of the nations shall grasp the sleeve of a Jewish man, saying, 'Let us go with you, for we have heard that God is with you.' "*
>
> —Zechariah 8:20-23

Jesus will be ever-present in Jerusalem. He will reign and dwell in a magnificent temple—Ezekiel's Temple. People will come from all the nations and make their way to the mountain of the Lord. Many will say to one another, "Let us go up to the mountain of the Lord." Worship will be a staple among the nations. Jesus living among the people will be so surreal that the masses will want to go. Ezekiel 43 says that God's direct glory will illuminate the New Jerusalem. This concept reveals God's intimate presence through Jesus, thus establishing His kingdom on earth.

People will come to worship and celebrate the Feast of Tabernacles. "The Feast of Tabernacles, also known as the Feast of Booths and *Sukkot*, is the seventh and last feast that the Lord commanded Israel to observe and one of the three feasts that Jews were to observe each year by going to 'appear before the LORD your God in the place which He shall choose.'"[1] During the Millennial Reign, they will celebrate this feast in Jerusalem or on the mountain of the Lord. The Feast of Tabernacles symbolizes the perfect peace, prosperity, and God's dwelling, "the Tabernacle," with humanity. This will be a time of global rejoicing. They will remember God's many provisions and celebrate the physical reign of Jesus.

> *In that day "HOLINESS TO THE LORD" shall be engraved on the bells of the horses. The pots in the LORD's house shall be like the bowls before the altar.* 21 *Yes, every pot in Jerusalem and Judah shall be holiness to the LORD of hosts. Everyone who sacrifices shall come and take them and cook in them. In that day there shall no longer be a Canaanite in the house of the LORD of hosts.*
>
> —Zechariah 14:20-21

According to Zechariah 14:20-21, even everyday items, such as horse bells, pots, and bowls, will bear the words "Holiness to the Lord." The world will be saturated with God's presence. This marks the perfect and pure worship of the Lord and fulfills prophecies about a restored, holy Israel and a unified global worship.

THOSE WHO REFUSE TO WORSHIP

And it shall be that whichever of the families of the earth do not come up to Jerusalem to worship the King, the LORD of hosts, on them there will be no rain. [18] *If the family of Egypt will not come up and enter in, they shall have no rain; they shall receive the plague with which the LORD strikes the nations who do not come up to keep the Feast of Tabernacles.* [19] *This shall be the punishment of Egypt and the punishment of all the nations that do not come up to keep the Feast of Tabernacles.*

—Zechariah 14:17-19

People will have the choice to worship the Lord. Throughout the Millennium, some will choose not to worship, and as a result, they will face consequences. According to Zechariah 14:17-19, the rain will not come to their location. This underscores the importance of nations coming to the Feast of Tabernacles. If one chooses not to go and celebrate, they will face drought. Rain represents blessing, favor, provision, and spiritual nourishment. Rain is essential for life and growth. Without it, it would be considered a plague that God would use to strike those who disobey.

WHAT DOES LIFE IN THE MILLENNIUM LOOK LIKE?

For behold, I create new heavens and a new earth; and the former shall not be remembered or come to mind. [18] *But be glad and rejoice forever in what I create; for behold, I create Jerusalem as a rejoicing, and her people a joy.* [19] *I will rejoice in Jerusalem, and joy in My people; the voice of weeping shall no longer be heard in her, nor the voice of crying.*

—Isaiah 65:17-19

Many wonder what the Millennial Reign will be like. Isaiah 65:17 speaks of a New Heaven and Earth. This differs from Revelation 21, which states that a New Heaven and Earth are created. We know this because during the Millennium, there will still be death, whereas in the New Earth described in Revelation 21, death will have been defeated, and no one will die again. Another difference is that in Isaiah 65:19, the New Earth is surrounded by "coastlands," whereas in Revelation 21:1, the world at that time will no longer have a sea.

The days of weeping and crying will be over. These emotions will be replaced with joy. Jesus will rejoice in Jerusalem and find joy in His people. Think about those words. Jesus will rejoice when the day of prophecy finally comes, and He will find joy in having His people present with Him, ruling and reigning. Imagine that! Throughout history, Jesus has watched as the devil and his minions not only corrupted but also harassed and deceived the masses. Jesus was present when all the prophecies were spoken and written on the page, foretelling a future time when He will reign in Jerusalem for a thousand years. After thousands of years of waiting, it will finally come, and Jesus will have joy in that moment. This is a sobering thought, knowing that Jesus has been waiting for the fulfillment of prophecy as we are.

> *No more shall an infant from there live but a few days, nor an old man who has not fulfilled his days; for the child shall die one hundred years old, but the sinner being one hundred years old shall be accursed.*
>
> —Isaiah 65:20

As previously stated, death will still be present among those with natural bodies. However, dying young would be considered accursed. Premature death will end, as will infant mortality. It is stated that someone who dies at 100 years old is considered a child. This could mean that people will live into their hundreds. Could those born at the beginning of the Millennium potentially live to be close to a thousand years old? It seems highly possible.

> *They shall build houses and inhabit them; they shall plant vineyards and eat their fruit.* [22] *They shall not build and another inhabit; they shall not plant and another eat; for as the days of a tree, so shall be the days of My people, and My elect shall long enjoy the work of their hands.* [23] *They shall not labor in vain, nor bring forth children for trouble; for they shall be the descendants of the blessed of the* LORD, *and their offspring with them.* [24] *It shall come to pass that before they call, I will answer; and while they are still speaking, I will hear.*
>
> —Isaiah 65:21-24

In Isaiah 65:21-24, we see that life will continue as it used to, with people building houses, planting vineyards, and eating their fruit. The difference is that these things will not be done in vain. People will live in the homes they build and enjoy the fruit of their labor, and it won't be taken from them or given to someone else.

PEACE AMONG THE ANIMALS

> *The wolf also shall dwell with the lamb, the leopard shall lie down with the young goat, the calf and the young lion and the fatling together; and a little child shall lead them.* [7] *The cow and the bear shall graze; their young ones shall lie down together; and the lion shall eat straw like the ox.* [8] *The nursing child shall play by the cobra's hole, and the weaned child shall put his hand in the viper's den.*
>
> —Isaiah 11:6-8

> *"The wolf and the lamb shall feed together, the lion shall eat straw like the ox, and dust shall be the serpent's food. They shall not hurt nor destroy in all My holy mountain," says the* LORD.
>
> —Isaiah 65:25

Not only will there be peace among the people, but there will also be peace among the animals. Those who were once predators will now lie with those they once hunted. Isaiah 11:5 and 65:25 both speak of the wolf and the lamb living together, not as predator and prey, but as cohabitants of the New Earth. Isaiah 11 continues by saying that a child, even a nursing child, will play near the cobra's hole. This represents the most innocent of beings, a nursing child, who will be able to come close to what was, at one point, a very poisonous creature. There will be no fear, and no harm will come from the animals to one another or to humanity.

SATAN RELEASED AT THE END OF THE MILLENNIUM

> *Now when the thousand years have expired, Satan will be released from his prison* [8] *and will go out to deceive the nations which are in the four corners of the earth, Gog and Magog, to gather them together to battle, whose number is as the sand of the sea.*
>
> —Revelation 20:7-8

At the end of Christ's 1,000-year reign, Satan will be released from his prison, the abyss, and will have one more chance to deceive the nations in the four corners of the earth, or Gog and Magog. It's amazing to think that the devil will deceive so many people that their number is like the sand of the sea, too many to count. Remember, these people were in the very presence of Jesus for 1,000 years. They experienced the fruit of the Spirit in the purest form. A sad reality is that these same people will have the same awe-deprivation as those who were present when Jesus walked on the earth 2,000 years ago. Those alive during that time saw Jesus heal the sick, raise the dead, and cast out demons, yet they still raised their fists and shouted, "Crucify Him." This could be a similar case at the end of the Millennium, when the devil is released. People of that time experienced Jesus and heard the stories of old, yet they became so accustomed to it that they took for granted who Jesus is and what He did for them.

The devil will deceive those with natural bodies who were born during that time, and the number of such people could be in the billions. We aren't certain how long a period Satan will have to do this or whether he will be working alone. Revelation 20:3 says, "...But after these things he must be released for a little while." A little while could mean a few days or a handful of years.

> *And unless those days were shortened, no flesh would be saved; but for the elect's sake those days will be shortened.*
>
> —Matthew 24:22

Matthew 24:22 speaks of the days being shortened for the elect's sake during the Great Tribulation. Revelation 20:3 describes Satan as being bound and then released for a "little while." These two scenarios reflect God's timing and protection for His people. We can speculate that since God shortened the days during the Tribulation, He won't allow the devil to deceive for long. It's fair to say that at this point, the Lord is sick of the devil's work and ready to bring destruction upon all things evil. It is worth noting that Armageddon is not the final battle; the battle at the end of the Millennial Reign will be. In the finality of all things, the earth will once again rise in defiance of Jesus and the saints.

GOD HIMSELF FIGHTS THE FINAL BATTLE FOR ALL ETERNITY!

> *They went up on the breadth of the earth and surrounded the camp of the saints and the beloved city. And fire came down from God out of heaven and devoured them.*
>
> —Revelation 20:9

Once the devil has done his deceptive work on earth, he gathers all those who chose his side and surrounds *the camp of the saints and the beloved city*. At this moment, Father God steps in and, in a grand finale, puts a stop to this evil event, destroying them all by sending fire from heaven. The Old Testament narrative of God appearing to destroy rebellious or evil people is multiplied here.

In the Old Testament, it was often a whole location, such as Sodom and Gomorrah, or a specific group of people. But in this moment, when the saints and the beloved city are surrounded, God will execute the ultimate judgment and destroy every single person who is against Him and His people.

This is the final battle to end all battles forever! God steps in as if to say, "Jesus, You paid the ultimate price and defeated the enemies at Armageddon. My saints who lived and died in faith also stood strong through all the centuries of difficulty and have overcome. Now it's Dad's turn...." God Almighty Himself will intervene in a highly personal way to engulf these rebellious adversaries once and for all. This is indeed the end of all hatred against God.

THE FINAL JUDGMENT OF THE GREAT WHITE THRONE

> *The devil, who deceived them, was cast into the lake of fire and brimstone where the beast and the false prophet are. And they will be tormented day and night forever and ever.*
>
> —Revelation 20:10

> *Then I saw* ***a great white throne*** *and Him who sat on it, from whose face the earth and the heaven fled away. And there was found no place for them.*
> 12 *And* ***I saw the dead, small and great, standing before God, and books were opened****. And another book was opened, which is the Book of Life. And the dead were judged according to their works, by the things which were written in the books.*
> 13 *The sea gave up the dead who were in it, and Death and Hades delivered up the dead who were in them. And* ***they were judged, each one according to his works****.*
> 14 ***Then Death and Hades were cast into the lake of fire. This is the second death****.*
> 15 ***And anyone not found written in the Book of Life was cast into the lake of fire****.*
>
> —Revelation 20:11-15

It can be difficult to grasp the idea that the devil will reach his eternal fate and never again deceive a single person. Since the beginning of humanity, people have faced temptations, fear, deceit, and more. We have not known life without these things, let alone been free of a sinful nature. During the Millennial Reign, people will experience life without these things; however, they will still have their sinful nature, which is why it will be easy for the devil to build an army.

Lucifer will be cast into the lake of fire and brimstone and tormented day and night forever! There will be no moment of release from the torment. Not only will this be a physical punishment and destruction, but another form of his torment will also be an eternal separation from God. This punishment fits the crime. It's reasonable to say that, given everything he did against God and humanity, he earned what is coming his way.

This Great White Throne Judgment is different from the Judgment Seat of Christ, where Jesus judges the righteous for their rewards. In this scenario, those not found in the Book of Life will be judged without mercy for every evil thing they have done, because they rejected it. At the end of this undeniably terrible day, we see that hell itself is thrown into the lake of fire. People have at times erroneously stated that hell is not forever, and they are correct. Hell will come to an end in its present form when it is cast into the lake of fire entirely. God will have the final say, and in that moment all those who rejected Him, hated Him, and chose to follow darkness will discover a reality completely removed from God Almighty—forever.

Then comes what God the Father and Christ Jesus the Son have longed for since the very beginning of creation. A future together with their children, those who longed for His appearing and served Him in this life. What comes next is an eternity without end.

CHAPTER SIXTEEN

ETERNITY INCOMING FOREVER AFTER THE END

Eternity is coming, and grasping it is not something a natural human being is equipped to do. The word "forever" is not comprehensible to any mortal. Not really. Forever is not simply a long time. It would seem that time is not the relevant issue when dealing with eternity future; rather, what might be at play is a different dimensional reality altogether. A point where we step into a whole new experience far beyond what our finite senses can grasp.

UNDERSTANDING ETERNITY MIGHT BE THE EQUIVALENT OF A DOG LOOKING AT A CLOCK

Imagine a dog looking at a clock. It would see the clock, maybe be amused by it, filled with head-tilting curiosity, but unable to determine what it was or how it operated. This crude comparison illustrates how mankind might try to understand eternity future. Mankind has ideas about their eternal future; they might believe they know what it means to live forever in a kingdom that will never end, but do they really? I don't think so.

THE NOTION THAT AFTER DEATH IS NOTHING

Once, I was asked to officiate a loved one's funeral. Some of my family members believed that once a person dies, they cease to exist. That's it, lights out, everything goes black, nothing more. While speaking, I mentioned that some people believe this. I said, "Please, everyone in this room, close your eyes and imagine nothing." The best a person can do is imagine blackness, yet blackness is still something. After asking the audience to imagine nothing, I went on to say, "Nice try, but if you're honest, you can't imagine nothing, not really, not in its purest form. Why? Because human beings were created from the very beginning to live forever!" The reality is that whether a person is saved or not is an eternal matter. Yes, the natural body dies, but not the inner person, not the spirit, which lives forever. The question is where?

That is why death is such a difficult thing. It feels wrong; it doesn't fit the internal narrative. Again, this is because Adam and Eve were created never to die. After their original sin, they were removed from the garden, and the curse came upon humanity. Yet their origin, their God-breathed part, their life force, comes from the Source of all things, God Almighty. A person doesn't know the hour or minute of their death, and this uncertainty is tied to that eternal spark within them. What is true is that every living person will live for all eternity—somewhere.

THE APOSTLE PAUL VISITED THE THIRD HEAVEN

> *I know a man in Christ who fourteen years ago—whether in the body I do not know, or whether out of the body I do not know, God knows—such a one was caught up to the third heaven.* [3] *And I know such a man—whether in the body or out of the body I do not know, God knows—*[4] *how he was caught up into Paradise and heard inexpressible words, which it is not lawful for a man to utter.*
>
> —2 Corinthians 12:2-4

Consider the apostle Paul's statement about his experience of going to the Third Heaven. He stated that it was unlawful for him to discuss it, which was his primary response to what he witnessed. By saying it was not lawful, he meant he lacked the natural ability to describe what he perceived, as if trying to explain the color purple to a blind person.

THOSE WHO HAVE HAD A NEAR-DEATH EXPERIENCE AND VISITED HEAVEN

When attempting to grasp eternity future, I suspect that by finding small, suggestive yet revelatory glimpses in the Word of God, we can see that what awaits us in its fullness is not comprehensible to any human.

Yes, we know of people who have visited heaven; even my wife, Heather, has her own experience with it, as she wrote in her book, *Unlocking Heaven's Truth: What I Experienced Between Life and Death*. She details her account after breaking her neck in a gymnastics accident, in which she left her body and met the Lord, even having a conversation with Him in heaven.

There are numerous personal accounts of visiting heaven, and I mention this to acknowledge that such experiences occur, as seen in the case of biblical figures such as the apostle Paul. Yet, as legitimate as it is, the fact that there are accounts of those who have gone to heaven and come back from it needs an addendum. Here is what I mean: heaven is not our final destination, and what many have experienced there is a temporary, although glorious, location; it is still not final.

HEAVEN IS NOT THE FINAL DESTINATION FOR BELIEVERS!

It is important to understand that heaven and earth are not the final destinations of believers, for each will be done away with, and the New Heaven and the New Earth will come into existence by the power and will of God Almighty. The Bible and modern accounts of visits to heaven describe it as a temporary place.

We will not be there in the long, eternal future. Most people refer to going to heaven as the final place after they graduate into eternity, and this is correct in the age we are currently living in. Still, the complete picture is not taught enough, revealing how magnificent the future eternity will actually be for the believer. This leads me to consider that what awaits us is truly a surprise our wonderful God is holding back to unveil at that time.

WHAT IS FOREVER?

Forever may not be a long line that never ends. It might be a sudden, supernatural exposure to everything all at once—all of history, past, present, and future. A sudden induction into the multidimensional realm of the spirit may await us. One reason we will receive glorified bodies is not only for the Millennial Reign of Jesus, but also to rule and reign in eternity.

As mentioned earlier, when we see the Lord, we will be made like Him, for we will see Him as He is. Among many reasons, the paramount reason for assuming glorified bodies is to operate in the new dimensional space, which corporeal flesh cannot live in or withstand. Speaking from conjecture, God might even be waiting to create a new dimensional reality once this world and all the prophecies concerning it are finalized. At that point, our great God may speak once again, creating a new space and reality that includes the New Jerusalem, New Heaven, and New Earth as part of the new scenario He has waiting for us.

GOD IS MULTIDIMENSIONAL BECAUSE HE CREATED IT ALL!

God is multidimensional as it stands, and He is the Author of all things created. When He has completed every word and promise in His Word and sustains them forever, there will be nothing to hold Him back from expanding beyond what He has already done and fulfilled, allowing us to accompany Him as kings and lords into the magnificence of what He is planning.

Once again, parables like those about the minas and the talents offer glimpses into eternity, revealing that those who are faithful with their portion will receive more in the future. In the case of the minas, the reward of faithfulness is to rule cities. Those cities are likely in eternity, and the parable offers a glimpse of an expansive future of reigning over territories for the glory of Almighty God and His Son, Jesus Christ.

NO EYE HAS SEEN, NOR EAR HEARD

> *But as it is written: "Eye has not seen, nor ear heard, nor have entered into the heart of man the things which God has prepared for those who love Him."* [10] *But God has revealed them to us through His Spirit. For the Spirit searches all things, yes, the deep things of God.*
>
> —1 Corinthians 2:9-10

"No eye has seen, nor ear heard, nor has it entered the heart of man the things which God has prepared for those who love Him." Does this mean we have never seen it in the Bible, and that no one has ever supernaturally witnessed what is to come, at least not fully? The answer is likely yes.

Well beyond the Millennial Reign and the Great White Throne Judgment comes the new. All things made new means there will be things we are not familiar with, leading us to encounter that existence with God, and, at long last, the mystery of so many things will be as nothing as we walk forward in that plane of glory and in the intention of God's will.

A NEW HEAVEN AND A NEW EARTH, ARE ONLY A GLIMPSE INTO ETERNITY FUTURE

> *Now I saw a new heaven and a new earth, for the first heaven and the first earth had passed away. Also there was no more sea.*
>
> —Revelation 21:1

After everything John had seen on the island of Patmos, from the Rapture to the Tribulation, the wrath of God, all the judgments that took place, and the Millennial Reign, imagine what he felt when he saw the New Heaven and Earth. Revelation 21 details what will take place after the Millennial Reign, and the devil is thrown into the lake of fire for eternity. The Old Earth will pass away, and there will be no more sea. Some believe the reason there will be no more seas is that there will be no more barriers between nations and people groups. We will all be united and not divided by anything, let alone a sea. Other interpretations hold that seas represent evil, chaos, division, and danger. Throughout history, the waters have claimed many lives through their intense storms and the dangers they pose. Both thoughts seem relevant.

THE HOLY CITY—THE NEW JERUSALEM

> *Then I, John, saw the holy city, New Jerusalem, coming down out of heaven from God, prepared as a bride adorned for her husband.* [3] *And I heard a loud voice from heaven saying, "Behold, the tabernacle of God is with men, and He will dwell with them, and they shall be His people. God Himself will be with them and be their God.* [4] *And God will wipe away every tear from their eyes; there shall be no more death, nor sorrow, nor crying. There shall be no more pain, for the former things have passed away."*
>
> —Revelation 21:2-4

Continuing in Revelation 21, the New Jerusalem, also known as the Holy City, the Tabernacle of God, the City of God, and several other names, comes down from heaven, and its Creator is God. It is portrayed as a beautiful, pure bride who has meticulously prepared for the arrival of her husband.

This new city will be God's tabernacle and will dwell with humanity. God Himself will dwell with His people. There will be no more separation. Up to this point, we have needed a Mediator, Jesus, to access the Father. In the New Jerusalem, He will be with us. No Mediator required. It will be as in the days of the Garden, when Adam walked with God.

Revelation 21:4 reveals that God will wipe away every tear. There will be no more sadness, mourning, or pain. All of these will pass away. Imagine a world without these hurts. Up to that point, people have endured some of the worst pains, excruciating enough to make them shed countless tears. The God of heaven will wipe them all away. What a feeling that will be.

IT IS DONE!

> *Then He who sat on the throne said, "Behold, I make all things new." And He said to me, "Write, for these words are true and faithful."* [6] *And He said to me, "It is done! I am the Alpha and the Omega, the Beginning and the End. I will give of the fountain of the water of life freely to him who thirsts."*
>
> —Revelation 21:5-6

God says, "Behold, I make all things new." The previous world, with all its sorrows, will be forever gone. Only the new things will become the new normal. Sin, death, pain, and everything evil will be finished forever. As God said, "It is done." What powerful words those are. Similar to when Jesus said, "It is finished," as He died on the cross (*see* John 19:30), He overcame the devil and made a way for humanity to be saved.

At the Lord's words of "It is done," He will bring all the prophetic words to fruition, and we will reside with Him forever and ever.

OVERCOMERS WILL RESIDE WITH GOD

> *He who overcomes shall inherit all things, and I will be his God and he shall be My son.* [8] *But the cowardly, unbelieving, abominable, murderers, sexually immoral, sorcerers, idolaters, and all liars shall have their part in the lake which burns with fire and brimstone, which is the second death.*
>
> —Revelation 21:7-8

Those who overcome all the evils of their lives, the devil, and his schemes will have access to God for all eternity. He will be their God, and they will be His. The opposite is true for those who didn't overcome but succumbed to Satan and his evil plans. They will take part in the second death, where they will be thrown into the lake of fire with Satan and his vile creatures who chose him over the Father.

THE HOLY CITY AND THE GLORY OF GOD

> *Then one of the seven angels who had the seven bowls filled with the seven last plagues came to me and talked with me, saying, "Come, I will show you the bride, the Lamb's wife."* [10] *And he carried me away in the Spirit to a great and high mountain, and showed me the great city, the holy Jerusalem, descending out of heaven from God,* [11] *having the glory of God. Her light was like a most precious stone, like a jasper stone, clear as crystal.*
>
> —Revelation 21:9-11

The angel who poured out the Seven Bowls of the seven plagues approached John and showed him the Bride (the Church), prepared and adorned for Christ. This signifies purity and a relationship with God, the Father, and Jesus, the Son. God's presence and glory will illuminate the city with such radiance that it will resemble a crystal-clear precious stone. The glory of the Lord is the visible manifestation of God's beauty, holiness, love, greatness, power, and wisdom. His splendor, majesty, and radiance will be present as we experience His true glory in the New Jerusalem.

THE TWELVE GATES AND THE CITIES' MEASUREMENTS

> *Also she had a great and high wall with twelve gates, and twelve angels at the gates, and names written on them, which are the names of the*

> *twelve tribes of the children of Israel: [13] three gates on the east, three gates on the north, three gates on the south, and three gates on the west. [14] Now the wall of the city had twelve foundations, and on them were the names of the twelve apostles of the Lamb. [15] And he who talked with me had a gold reed to measure the city, its gates, and its wall. [16] The city is laid out as a square; its length is as great as its breadth. And he measured the city with the reed: twelve thousand furlongs. Its length, breadth, and height are equal. [17] Then he measured its wall: one hundred and forty-four cubits, according to the measure of a man, that is, of an angel. [18] The construction of its wall was of jasper; and the city was pure gold, like clear glass. [19] The foundations of the wall of the city were adorned with all kinds of precious stones: the first foundation was jasper, the second sapphire, the third chalcedony, the fourth emerald, [20] the fifth sardonyx, the sixth sardius, the seventh chrysolite, the eighth beryl, the ninth topaz, the tenth chrysoprase, the eleventh jacinth, and the twelfth amethyst. [21] The twelve gates were twelve pearls: each individual gate was of one pearl. And the street of the city was pure gold, like transparent glass.*
>
> —Revelation 21:12-21

The construction of the city walls, gates, and foundations is awe-inspiring and admirable. Each of the twelve gates will be inscribed with the names of the twelve tribes of Israel. This is a tribute to the patriarchs of Israel and shows that God will never revoke the status of His chosen people, Israel. Angels will be stationed at each gate. The gold, precious stones, and gates made of a single pearl show the intricate detail God takes in creating this final Jerusalem. These materials are the finest known to man and, obviously, to God as well. The imagery is elegant and conveys value. God spares no expense in creating something so elaborate and beautiful.

THERE IS NO TEMPLE BECAUSE GOD AND THE LAMB ARE ITS TEMPLE

> *But I saw no temple in it, for the Lord God Almighty and the Lamb are its temple.* [23] *The city had no need of the sun or of the moon to shine in it, for the glory of God illuminated it. The Lamb is its light.* [24] *And the nations of those who are saved shall walk in its light, and the kings of the earth bring their glory and honor into it.* [25] *Its gates shall not be shut at all by day (there shall be no night there).* [26] *And they shall bring the glory and the honor of the nations into it.* [27] *But there shall by no means enter it anything that defiles, or causes an abomination or a lie, but only those who are written in the Lamb's Book of Life.*
>
> —Revelation 21:22-27

There will be no temple, because we will dwell with God directly. There will be no need for a sun or moon, because the glory of God illuminates the city and the Lamb is its light. The nations will bring glory and honor to the Lord for redeeming their lives. From that time forward, nothing that defiles or causes abomination will ever enter that wonderful place. Only those whose names are written in the Lamb's Book of Life will enjoy that time and eternity to come.

THE ALPHA AND OMEGA

Even amid all this descriptive splendor, there is little said about what will come after the end of Revelation. God has chosen not to reveal what lies beyond the introductory picture of the New Heaven and Earth and the New Jerusalem.

Remember, it is our Lord who declares in Revelation 22:13-14, "I am Alpha and Omega, the Beginning and the End, the First and the Last. Blessed are those who do His commandments, that they may have right to the tree of life, and may enter in through the gates into the city." He is the First and the Last. He is preparing something that will astonish us. We see glimpses at the end of Revelation, yet God Almighty has chosen not to reveal what else awaits!

OPERATING IN ETERNITY FUTURE WITH THE CURSE ABOLISHED, MEANS ANYTHING IS POSSIBLE!

> *And **there shall be no more curse**, but the throne of God and of the Lamb shall be in it, and His servants shall serve Him.* [4] *They shall see His face, and His name shall be on their foreheads.* [5] *There shall be no night there: **They need no lamp nor light of the sun, for the Lord God gives them light. And they shall reign forever and ever**.*
>
> —Revelation 22:3-5

Think of all the things we believe in here in this fallen world. Faith is often a battleground between our soulish experiences and what the Word says about a matter. We often see victories, but they come only through focused, intentional effort that keeps our faith strong. It takes effort to starve our doubts and align with God's Word to attain what God has promised in any issue.

Now imagine believing for something without the curse present. No demons, no more unbelief, no more resistance, just pure agreement with God's power and promise in an environment free of any Satanic pushback, allowing faith to flow completely unhindered. In that place, anything and everything you think, imagine, or believe for will manifest instantly.

Why? Because you are in God's complete, total, and perfect will and environment, which He created purely for that purpose. Whatever you think or imagine will be His will, given the perfection of our completed standing, including a glorified body.

TRAVEL AT THE SPEED OF THOUGHT

My wife, Heather, said that during her visitation to heaven, whenever she thought of going to a place she wanted to see, she would find herself already there. Other accounts of their time in heaven describe the same kind of motion. We will likely travel at the speed of thought and build anything that aligns with God's character and His will, making nothing impossible. Nothing will be withheld, whether locationally or structurally, if it is part of your thought or desire.

JESUS CREATED THE WORD AT GOD'S DIRECTION BECAUSE WE WILL BE LIKE HIM. WILL WE BE ALLOWED TO BUILD THINGS?

> *The Lord possessed me at the beginning of His way, before His works of old.*
> 23 *I have been established from everlasting, from the beginning, before there*
> *was ever an earth.* 24 *When there were no depths I was brought forth, when*
> *there were no fountains abounding with water.* 25 *Before the mountains*
> *were settled, before the hills, I was brought forth;* 26 *while as yet He had*
> *not made the earth or the fields, or the primal dust of the world.* 27 *When*
> *He prepared the heavens, I was there, when He drew a circle on the face of*
> *the deep,* 28 *when He established the clouds above, when He strengthened*
> *the fountains of the deep,* 29 *when He assigned to the sea its limit, so that*
> *the waters would not transgress His command, when He marked out the*
> *foundations of the earth,* 30 *then I was beside Him as a master craftsman;*
> *and I was daily His delight, rejoicing always before Him,* 31 *rejoicing in His*
> *inhabited world, and my delight was with the sons of men.*
>
> —Proverbs 8:22-31

God, who calls those things that be not as though they are (*see* Romans 4:17), will allow us into His domain, operating in a pure state like Jesus.

Consider Proverbs 8, which speaks of God creating the world through wisdom, who was daily His delight. Jesus was the voice through which God spoke the universe into existence.

Now, consider the future eternity. What might God allow His kings and lords to accomplish with that same ability? This is only conjecture, but it is a fascinating idea. God Almighty allowed Paul to see heaven but not eternity future. He also allowed John the Revelator to see the end of the age and a glimpse of the coming kingdom, which will sit at the precipice of eternity future.

Yet John did not see the details of eternity future. He witnessed its beginning, knowing it would last forever. Yet the daily operations and mechanics of it all, extending into the eons and potentially multidimensional possibilities, were not fully disclosed.

SUPERNATURAL LIGHT FROM GOD

Eternity's future is a subject about which we have limited information, but it is worth considering. This is because the vast majority of a person's existence will be lived out forever in the eons of eternity. A glimpse of this is found in Revelation 22:5, which reads, "They shall reign forever and ever." This is a statement regarding the kings and lords who are simply believers in eternity future. Adam and Eve were most likely going to continue expanding their responsibility into the universe.

The Tower of Babel might have been a perversion of man's desire to go beyond what we know in our natural world. Considering that the sun will no longer be present and God Almighty will be the light who illuminates the entire world, this could be a dimensional scenario in which the light of God not only gives us tangible illumination but also is an omnipresent light with us everywhere. That is not only supernatural but also a dimensional mechanism.

HUMAN BEINGS DESIRE TO EXPLORE THE COSMOS—IT IS A REMNANT DESIRE FROM ADAM'S ORIGINAL MARCHING ORDERS TO TAKE DOMINION OVER CREATION

> Flying in space is not necessary, I don't think. It's something that we have in us. We, uh, we go out at night and we look up into the sky. We see things that we don't know what they are about. Uh, we are curious. We want to see infinity perhaps almost to visit infinity. To me, it's an intangible but it's a part of being a human being is this feeling of it's part of it's there. It's there to see to go to see to touch to smell to understand.[1]
>
> —Apollo Astronaut Michael Collins

Consider mankind's interest in early expeditions or space exploration. We have a desire to expand, study, and develop. Could it be that this internal drive to know more about the great beyond is a piece within us that still needs to be fulfilled? A missing element in reaching beyond the known and attaining knowledge of the unknown?

We might be stepping into the future of why God created the universe in the first place—for His children to occupy and develop it! Of course, this is all speculation and conjecture, yet it is a real consideration.

> *And have made us kings and priests to our God; and we shall reign on the earth.*
>
> —Revelation 5:10

The understanding that humanity was not created to live in heaven is a powerful game-changer once the implications sink in. It's true; we were created to live on the earth and to take dominion over it. Revelation 21:1 says there will be a New Earth. It's possible that the New Earth will be a staging ground for kings and lords to rule and reign. This would complete what God started with Adam, picking up where Adam left off after a 6,000-year interruption. God so wanted His creation and family with Him for all eternity that He sent Jesus to ensure we had the opportunity. What a wonderful God we serve.

ADDITIONAL REFERENCES TO REIGNING WITH THE LORD FOREVER

> *Instead of Your fathers shall be Your sons, whom You shall make princes in all the earth.*
>
> —Psalm 45:16

> *Let* ***the saints be joyful in glory****; let them sing aloud on their beds.* [6] *Let the high praises of God be in their mouth, and a two-edged sword in their hand,* [7] *to* ***execute vengeance on the nations, and punishments on the peoples****;* [8] *to bind their kings with chains, and their nobles with fetters of iron;* [9] *to execute on them the written judgment—this honor have all His saints. Praise the Lord!*
>
> —Psalm 149:5-9

Psalm 149 may offer insights into what saints will do in eternity future. First, they will be joyful in glory, possibly a reference to being in God's eternal light after the end. It also points to the honor given to saints, or we might say kings and lords—the execution of vengeance on the nations and punishments on the peoples. We know that saints will judge angels, and they may very well be ruling over territories and nations in eternity future. We cannot say with absolute authority, but we can speculate that we will be ruling, as the terminology suggests, as kings and lords.

> *For the nation and kingdom which will not serve you shall perish, and those nations shall be utterly ruined.* [13] *"The glory of Lebanon shall come*

to you, the cypress, the pine, and the box tree together, to beautify the place of My sanctuary; and I will make the place of My feet glorious. [14] *Also the sons of those who afflicted you shall come bowing to you, and all those who despised you shall fall prostrate at the soles of your feet; and they shall call you The City of the Lord, Zion of the Holy One of Israel.*

—Isaiah 60:12-14

But the saints of the Most High shall receive the kingdom, and possess the kingdom forever, even forever and ever.

—Daniel 7:18

Until the Ancient of Days came, and a judgment was made in favor of the saints of the Most High, and the time came for the saints to possess the kingdom.

—Daniel 7:22

This is a faithful saying: For if we died with Him, we shall also live with Him. [12] *If we endure, we shall also reign with Him. If we deny Him, He also will deny us.*

—2 Timothy 2:11-12

And he who overcomes, and keeps My works until the end, to him I will give power over the nations—[27] *"He shall rule them with a rod of iron; They shall be dashed to pieces like the potter's vessels"— as I also have received from My Father.*

—Revelation 2:26-27

To him who overcomes I will grant to sit with Me on My throne, as I also overcame and sat down with My Father on His throne.

—Revelation 3:21

And have made us kings and priests to our God; and we shall reign on the earth.

—Revelation 5:10

Will the kingdom expand? Is that why planets are void? Are they waiting to be given dominion over? Some religious views teach that as a doctrine. That is certainly not what I am saying here. But it does lead to speculation about our eternal future. In God's character, we will be doing things with responsibility. What we do know is that eternity future is waiting for us like a gift to be unwrapped. God is saving His best for last and into infinity.

GOD HAS A DIVINE PLAN FOR EVEN IN DEATH AND BEYOND

The prophet Daniel was told by the messenger that the end would come and was shown what his eternity would look like. Daniel 12:13 says, "But you, go your way till the end; for you shall rest, and will arise to your inheritance at the end of the days." A powerful scripture nearly leaped off the page at me one day. It was Psalm 48, which closes by speaking of God as our Guide even to death. A knowing rose in me, recognizing that God will lead us even in death, and in my inner man, I knew He would continue even after crossing the threshold of mortality as we enter eternity.

> *For this is God, our God forever and ever; He will be our guide even to death.*
>
> —Psalm 48:14

Additionally, Psalm 17 speaks to those who are His (God's), alluding to death, that when the psalmist would awake, he would awake to the likeness of God. This speaks of awaking in eternity after death and being in His likeness. For when we see Him, we will be made like Him, for we shall see Him as He is.

> *As for me, I will see Your face in righteousness; I shall be satisfied when I awake in Your likeness.*
>
> —Psalm 17:15

THE PROVING GROUND FOR WHAT WE WILL DO IN ETERNITY FUTURE HINGES ON WHAT WE DO HERE AND NOW

In our day and time, we are to exercise the kingdom of God everywhere we go. The powers of darkness are helpless against the blood-bought company of believers who are exercising their authority and positioning. Our future is glorious, yet here, now, and today, we fight. For the future of our children, as Psalm 102:18 states, "*This will be written for the generation to come.*" Our obedience to honor and walk in all that God has for us to build future generations is practice for reigning in eternity.

JESUS IS COMING SOON!

> *And behold, I am coming quickly, and My reward is with Me, to give to every one according to his work.* 13 *I am the Alpha and the Omega, the Beginning and the End, the First and the Last.*
>
> —Revelation 22:12-13

Jesus is coming back soon! So today, remember this: even on a bad day, you are anointed to be the best there is! We must keep watching, keep discerning, because Jesus is really returning soon!

For Jesus,
Joseph Z

NOTES

CHAPTER ONE

1. The phrase avenger of blood: *IVP Bible Background commentary:* Psalm 9:12. avenger of blood. See the comment on Numbers 35:9-34 for a discussion of the responsibility of the family to avenge a death. It is possible that a more general function is intended in this psalm, since it does not use the same technical term used in the Numbers passage. See Genesis 4:14-15 and Genesis 9:5-6.
2. *Albert Barnes' Bible Commentary,* Isaiah 63:1; https://www.bibliaplus.org/en/commentaries/4/albert-barnes-bible-commentary/isaiah/63/1.
3. Joseph Z, *Breaking Hell's Economy: Your Guide to Last Days Supernatural Provision* (Harrison House Publishers, 2022), 307-310. Kindle Edition.

CHAPTER TWO

1. https://www.gotquestions.org/old-earth-creationism.html.
2. https://biblehub.com/hebrew/3117.htm.
3. https://biblehub.com/topical/b/blameless.htm.
4. https://www.vocabulary.com/dictionary/wickedness.
5. https://www.merriam-webster.com/dictionary/violence.

6. https://www.collinsdictionary.com/us/dictionary/english/proud.
7. https://av1611.com/kjbp/kjv-dictionary/corrupt.html.
8. https://www.dakebibleboard.com/viewtopic.php?t=5930.
9. https://www.nps.gov/subjects/geology/radiometric-age-dating.htm; https://www.nps.gov/subjects/geology/radiometric-age-dating.htm#:~:text=Radiometric%20dating%20calculates%20an%20age,is%20identical%20to%20an%20electron.
10. https://nhm.org/stories/oldest-fossils-far.
11. https://en.wikipedia.org/wiki/Geologic_time_scale.
12. https://www.usgs.gov/publications/geologic-time-age-earth.
13. https://www.merriam-webster.com/dictionary/replenish
14. https://en.wikipedia.org/wiki/Kalambo_structure#:~:text=The%20Kalambo%20structure%20is%20a,old%20and%20predating%20Homo%20sapiens.
15. https://www.history.com/articles/gobekli-tepe.
16. https://answersingenesis.org/genesis/gap-theory/mind-the-gap/?srsltid=AfmBOor34VnFJV01hUyQSrgQAM6Zz77Jfm9GYIqilaeqmPF4WRcJBDm4.
17. https://www.dakebibleboard.com/viewtopic.php?t=5930.

Chapter Three

1. https://www.gotquestions.org/young-earth-creationism.html.
2. https://www.blueletterbible.org/lexicon/h3117/nkjv/wlc/0-1/.
3. https://www.gotquestions.org/pre-Adamic-race.html.
4. https://www.vocabulary.com/dictionary/cunning.
5. https://www.pseudepigrapha.com/jubilees/3.htm.
6. http://qbible.com/enoch/7.html#:~:text=1And%20all%20the%20others%20together,flesh%2C%20and%20drink%20the%20blood.
7. https://www.pseudepigrapha.com/jubilees/5.htm.
8. https://www.pseudepigrapha.com/jubilees/5.htm.

Chapter Four

1. chrome-extension://efaidnbmnnnibpcajpcglclefindmkaj/https://wnlnetwork.com/wp-content/uploads/2020/10/The-IVP-Bible-Background-Commentary_-New-Testament-2nd-edition-PDFDrive.com-.pdf.
2. Finis Dake Commentary on Ephesians 1:10.
3. https://biblehub.com/greek/165.htm.

Chapter Five

1. https://biblehub.com/commentaries/genesis/13-13.htm#:~:text=The%20Targum%20of%20Jonathan%20reckons,the%20Lord%3B%20see%20Isaiah%203%3A9.
2. https://zaksjerusalemgifts.com/articles/herod-agrippa-coin-i.

Chapter Six

1. *IVP Bible Background Commentary,* Isa 45:1. Cyrus's accomplishments. Cyrus of Persia was one of the greatest conquerors in world history. He inherited the throne of Persia from his father, Cambyses I, in 559. In 556 the Babylonian king Nabonidus, motivated by a dream, abandoned the treaty that his country had maintained with the Medes for over half a century and made a treaty with Cyrus. This gave Cyrus the freedom to move against the Medes (ruled by his grandfather Astyges) whom he conquered in 550. The new Medo-Persian Empire was thus formed, with control over the entirety of Iran. By 546 he defeated the Anatolian kingdom of Lydia and Ionia. For the next five years he consolidated his control over the tribes in northeastern Iran. All of this success paved the way for his crowning achievement, the conquest of Babylon in 539 B.C.

The whole of the Near East (excluding Egypt) was under the control of the Persians when Cyrus was killed in battle in 530.

2. *IVP Bible Background Commentary* on Isaiah 45:2: *Isa 45:2. gates of bronze, bars of iron.* The Greek historian Herodotus described Babylon as having "one hundred gates in the circuit of the wall, all of bronze with bronze uprights and lintels." Large bronze gates have been excavated at the Assyrian period site of Balawat, giving a glimpse of what the Babylonian walls may have been like. Gates were locked by means of a bar slid across the gateway, and iron would obviously be the most difficult to break.
3. *Book of Daniel Handbook* compiled by Chuck Missler, Session 5 Daniel Chapter 5 (Koinonia House, 2022), 61.
4. Josephus, Antiq. XI, I.2

CHAPTER SEVEN

1. https://en.wikipedia.org/wiki/Lucifer#:~:text=Luciferianism%20is%20a%20belief%20structure,star%2C%20intellectualism%2C%20and%20enlightenment.
2. https://biblehub.com/greek/3154.htm.
3. *IVP Bible Background Commentary* on Luke 11:34-36.

CHAPTER NINE

1. Spiros Zodhiates, *The Complete Word Study Dictionary* on Galatians 1:9.
2. *IVP Bible Background Commentary* on Galatians 1:8,9
3. Warren W. Wiersbe, *The Wiersbe Bible Commentary* on Galatians 1:8,9

CHAPTER TEN

1. https://en.wikipedia.org/wiki/Zealots.

2. https://www.persecution.com/stories/stories-of-christian-martyrs-telemachus/.
3. Rick Renner, *A Light in Darkness, Seven Messages to the Seven Churches, Volume One* (Harrison House, 2017), 41.

Chapter Eleven

1. https://biblehub.com/greek/4105.htm.
2. Rick Renner, *The Rapture, the Antichrist, and the Tribulation* (Harrison House Publishers, 2025), 128-135.
3. https://biblehub.com/greek/726.htm.
4. Alan Didio, *They Lied to You About the Rapture* (Destiny Image Publishers, 2025), 159-163.
5. Henry Bettenson, Chris Maunder, *Documents of the Christian Church* (Oxford University Press, 2011), 90-13.

Chapter Twelve

1. chrome-extension://efaidnbmnnnibpcajpcglclefindmkaj/https://alexantal777.org/Sermons/ChuckMissler/all/Revelation/Revelation_Notes.pdf.
2. https://notes.subsplash.com/fill-in/view?page=SJomBSJda.
3. https://www.britannica.com/topic/humanism.
4. https://www.gotquestions.org/144000.html; *IVP Bible Background Commentary* on Revelation 7.

Chapter Thirteen

1. https://www.gotquestions.org/day-of-the-Lord.html.

CHAPTER FIFTEEN

1. https://www.gotquestions.org/Feast-of-Tabernacles.html.

CHAPTER SIXTEEN

1. https://youtu.be/SWVgUwMTHEU?si=fiMoEMtIn03F9IQv.

ABOUT JOSEPH Z

Joseph Z is a Bible teacher, author, broadcaster, and international prophetic voice. Before the age of nine, he began encountering the Voice of God through dreams and visions. This resulted in a journey that has led him to dedicate his life to preaching the gospel and teaching the Bible, often followed by prophetic ministry.

For nearly three decades, Joseph planted churches, founded Bible schools, preached stadium events, and held schools of the prophets around the world. Joseph and his wife, Heather, ministered together for 15 years and decided in 2012 to start Z Ministries, a media- and conference-based ministry. During this time, they traveled across the United States, taking a studio team with them and broadcasting live from a new location several times a week.

A season came when Heather became very ill due to hereditary kidney failure. After three years of dialysis and several miracles, she received a miracle kidney transplant. Joseph and Heather decided to stop everything; they laid everything down and ministered to their family for nearly three years.

In 2017, Joseph had an encounter with the Lord and received the word to "go live every weekday morning"—Monday through Friday. What started with him, Heather, and a small group of viewers has turned into a large and faithful online broadcast family. Today, his live broadcasts reach millions every month with the gospel and current events, which he has labeled "prophetic journalism." He additionally interviews some of the leading voices in the church, government, and culture.

He and Heather have two adult children who faithfully work alongside them. Joseph's favorite saying when ending letters, books, or written articles is, "For Jesus." As "For the testimony of Jesus is the spirit of prophecy" (see Revelation 19:10).

Joseph spends his time with his family, writing books, broadcasting, and training others in the Word of God.

For Further Information

If you would like prayer or further information about Joseph Z Ministries, please call our offices at (719) 257-8050 or visit JosephZ.com/contact.

Visit JosephZ.com for additional materials.